# Commitment and Community
*Communes and Utopias in Sociological Perspective*

# Commitment and Community

*Communes and Utopias in Sociological Perspective*

Rosabeth Moss Kanter

*Harvard University Press*
*Cambridge, Massachusetts, and London, England*

Library of Congress Catalog Card Number 72-76565

ISBN 0-674-14576-3 (paper)
Printed in the United Sates of America

*For S. A. K.*

# Preface

In 1964, before the commune movement had taken new hold in America, I wrote my first paper on utopian communities, and that initial interest in alternatives to established society has changed my life. It focused my thought, research, teaching, and leisure time on the possibilities for social and personal reconstruction, as well as on exploring new models for human relations and social institutions.

In this book I consider the ideas and values underlying utopian communities and communal living, present extensive research on the forms of organization that built commitment in the long-lived communes of the nineteenth century, and deal with some of the dilemmas faced by communities of the past. I draw many links to the present commune movement, consider two kinds of contemporary communes in detail, and explore some of the moral and social issues raised by the commune movement today. The focus throughout is on how groups are built and maintained. In the process I hope to demonstrate to those who feel that communes are impractical, impossible, or unrealizable that in the past a number of utopian communities have in fact been successes. I also hope to indicate to those with the opposite viewpoint, who think that forming a commune is easy, that there are important organizational considerations to be taken into account in building a viable community.

In addition to providing a historical and sociological perspective on the contemporary commune movement, the study of utopian communities in America can also contribute to the understanding of social life in general. Communal orders represent major social experiments in which new or radical theories of human behavior, motivation, and interpersonal relations are put to the test. Social science has rarely had "laboratories" of the scale and scope of utopian communities. Contemporary social systems, from schools to families to businesses, are founded on many assumptions about human needs and the requirements of social life, which communes challenge. Confronting the "givens" of American life with data from communal orders poses interesting questions. For example, can commitment and collective feeling replace individual, material rewards as a source of motivation? Is the nuclear family in its present, isolated form a necessary ingredient for emotional satisfaction? Could productive work be reorganized, perhaps in terms of rotating shared jobs rather than individual careers? Should ritual and symbols return to communities? What pressing contemporary social problems could be solved by creating communal enclaves within larger political structures? How can commitment — an important but under-researched concept — be built and maintained? What are the real possibilities for new social institutions, from new towns to consumer cooperatives to community development corporations? As America's problems grow, so does the need for conceiving of new ways of being and doing, and hence for a return of the utopian imagination.

Although most groups today refer to themselves as communes rather than utopian communities, I have retained the word "utopian," for I think that communal ventures represent not only alternatives to life in the dominant culture but also attempts to realize unique ideals, dreams, and aspirations. For the current communal movement to succeed, it needs thinkers as well as doers, intellectuals as well as activists, who will discover and report what is known, provide new ideas, warn of dangers, and suggest alternative directions. I hope the findings in this book can contribute toward that end.

This book is the result of several research projects and a variety of personal experiences over the past five years, helped along by many people. The material on nineteenth-century utopian communities comes primarily from research conducted for my doctoral dissertation. I received valuable advice from William

Gamson, Leon Mayhew, John Lofland, Daniel Katz, and John Higham; as well as research assistance from David Berson, Joanne Brannon, Sylvia Daudt, Mark Fivenson, Earl Hamilton, Mary Kelley, Sharon Lucas, Clifford Olson, and Bruce Stevens. Funds were provided both by a National Institute of Mental Health Predoctoral Research Fellowship, and by the Center for Research on Social Organization of the University of Michigan, directed by Albert J. Reiss, Jr. The University of Michigan supplied free computer time. To William Gamson and Leon Mayhew, especially, I owe an immeasurable intellectual and personal debt. Stuart Kanter contributed insight and intelligence, warmth and wisdom — his most precious and abundant characteristics.

Material on contemporary communes was gathered both from research and from personal experience. I began visiting communes in 1967. Numerous visits to several dozen groups and participation in such commual events as the Synanon "game" (a group encounter) have provided first-hand observations. I thank many commune friends for their cooperation and assistance. In 1969 I sent a questionnaire based on the nineteenth century research to fifty communes, and received replies, often of great length, from twenty. During the summer of 1969 I joined and lived at Cumbres, a personal growth community in New Hampshire, where I first became involved with the human potential movement. The Cumbres family, and especially Cesareo Palaez, gave me a great deal both personally and intellectually that I will never forget. Beginning in the fall of 1969, I joined a project to design and build a "new city" and learned first-hand about the road blocks to creating utopian communities. In the summer of 1970 I lived in an intense training community in Bethel, Maine. My own involvement with new social arrangements and with the personal growth movement has deepened in both a personal and a professional sense.

I am also grateful to the following friends and colleagues for their criticism, suggestions, encouragement, and support: Mimi Athos, Tony Athos, Louis ("By") Barnes, Bennett Berger, Lewis Coser, Harvey Cox, Elinor Gadon, Herman Gadon, Zelda Gamson, Naphtali Golomb, Marilyn Halter, Charles Hampden-Turner, Judson Jerome, Gary Marx, Phyllis Marx, Jane O'Reilly,

Rick Paine, Menachem Rosner, Carol Rubin, Zick Rubin, Charlotte Schwartz, Morris Schwartz, Robert Sklar, Dori Slater, Philip Slater, Philip Stone, Roland Warren, Kurt Wolff, and very especially, Barry Stein.

Some of the material in Chapter 4 appeared first in my article "Commitment and Social Organization: A Study of Commitment Mechanisms in Utopian Communities," *American Sociological Review*, 33 (August 1968), 499–517. Several of the ideas discussed in Chapters 7 and 8 were originally advanced in my article "Communes," *Psychology Today*, 4 (July 1970), 56–70.

RMK

Lincoln, Massachusetts
January 1972

# Contents

*Part One*    The Utopian Faith

*Nothing short of everything will really do.*
—Aldous Huxley, *Island*
*O God . . . our refuge and our hope.*
—*Union Prayer Book*

# 1   A Refuge and a Hope

Utopia is the imaginary society in which humankind's deepest
yearnings, noblest dreams, and highest aspirations come to
fulfillment, where all physical, social, and spiritual forces work
together, in harmony, to permit the attainment of everything
people find necessary and desirable. In the imagined utopia,
people work and live together closely and cooperatively, in a
social order that is self-created and self-chosen rather than exter-
nally imposed, yet one that also operates according to a higher
order of natural and spiritual laws. Utopia is held together by
commitment rather than coercion, for in utopia what people
want to do is the same as what they have to do; the interests of
the individuals are congruent with the interests of the group; and
personal growth and freedom entail responsibility for others.
Underlying the vision of utopia is the assumption that harmony,
cooperation, and mutuality of interests are natural to human
existence, rather than conflict, competition, and exploitation,
which arise only in imperfect societies. By providing material
and psychological safety and security, the utopian social order
eliminates the need for divisive competition or self-serving
actions which elevate some people to the disadvantage of others;
it ensures instead the flowering of mutual responsibility and
trust, to the advantage of all.

Utopia, then, represents an ideal of the good, to contrast with
the evils and ills of existing societies. The idea of utopia suggests
a refuge from the troubles of this world as well as a hope for
a better one. Utopian plans are partly an escape, as critics
maintain, and partly a new creation, partly a flight *from* and

1

partly a seeking *for*; they criticize, challenge, and reject the established order, then depart from it to seek the perfect human existence.

At a number of times in history, groups of people have decided that the ideal can become reality, and they have banded together in communities to bring about the fulfillment of their own utopian aspirations. Generally the idea of utopia has involved a way of life shared with others — and shared in such a way that the benefit of all is ensured. For the most part, the vision of utopia has been a vision of community, as captured in an old Hebrew song: "How good it is for brethren to dwell together in unity."

The ideal of social unity has led to the formation of numerous communes and utopian communities. These are voluntary, value-based, communal social orders. Because members choose to join and choose to remain, conformity within the community is based on commitment — on the individual's own desire to obey its rules — rather than on force or coercion. Members are controlled by the entire membership or by individuals they respect within the community rather than by outside agents or political forces. A commune seeks self-determination, often making its own laws and refusing to obey some of those set by the larger society. It is identifiable as an entity, having both physical and social boundaries, for it has a physical location and a way of distinguishing between members and nonmembers. It intentionally implements a set of values, having been planned in order to bring about the attainment of certain ideals, and its operating decisions are made in terms of those values. Its primary end is an existence that matches the ideals. All other goals are secondary and related to ends involving harmony, brotherhood, mutual support, and value expression. These ideals give rise to the key communal arrangement, the sharing of resources and finances.

The utopian community may also be a centralized, coordinating organization, often combining all of life's functions under one roof. Economic, political, social, and family life may all occur within the community and be coordinated by it. The community may be at the same time a domestic unit (large, extended family), a production unit (farm or business), a political

order (village or town), and a religious institution. Unlike
the larger society, all these functions are concentrated in one
visible entity. And unlike monastic orders, which may serve the
interests of a wider church community, or businesses, which are
concerned with the interests of the market or of absentee
owners such as stockholders, the commune operates to serve
first and foremost its own members; any benefits it provides for
the outside are generally secondary and based on the need to
support its own. Finally, relations among members of the
community are more important than are relations of members
or the community to the outside world. For example, in the
typical nonutopian, noncommunal organization, such as a
business, the nature of the work may determine who becomes a
member, whereas in the utopian community the nature of the
people who are already members may determine what kind of
work is performed. Maintaining the sense of group solidarity is
as important as meeting specific goals.

From this definition it appears that a utopian community may
have something in common with a family or primary group,
with an organization, with a geographically-defined community,
and with a complete society, even though it differs from all
of these. It can be as small as a family of six or seven members,
like many contemporary communes, or as large as a village of a
thousand or more, like some utopian communities of the past.

## Origins of American Utopias and Communes

The United States, in particular, has been the site for the
founding of hundreds — possibly thousands — of utopian communities, from religious sects that retreated to the wilderness as
early as 1680, to the vast numbers of communes today.[1]
Historically, three kinds of critiques of society have provided
the initial impulse for the utopian search: religious, politico-
economic, and psychosocial. The earliest American community-
builders began with religious ideals. Their utopian vision
involved the creation of a purified, spiritual society based on
fundamental Biblical truths, where they could live out their
shared ideals in harmony, cooperation, and close association
with fellow believers. The origins of many of these American

utopians were in Europe separatist and pietist sects seeking
a refuge from persecution by the dominant churches and a place
where they could establish their own communities according
to their own principles.[2] Such pietist groups sought closer
contact with God, with fundamental truths, and with each
other. They wished to return, for example, to a literal interpretation of the Bible, and took as their model the communism
of the early Christian church, with its emphasis on a community
of believers possessing all things in common. They emphasized
their own separateness, rejecting the dogmas and hierarchies
of the established churches. As William Keil, the founder of the
Bethel and Aurora communities (1844–1880), taught, all
existing church regulations were the work of the human hand
and unessential to the moral teachings of Christianity; he
preferred "no title but Christian" and "no rules but the Bible."[3]

The religious utopians criticized the evil and immorality of the
surrounding society, which placed barriers between man and
God, holding that a perfect society, in close touch with fundamental truths was immediately possible for believers. The
Zoar Community (1817–1898), for example, called itself "a
refuge from the evils of this world, as the Biblical Zoar had been
from the wickedness of Sodom."[4] A major theme was the
possibility of human perfection through conversion to the more
spiritual life offered by the utopia. John Humphrey Noyes
began a group in Putney, Vermont, in the late 1830s dedicated
to Perfectionist ideals, which were to be implemented through
complete sharing of beliefs, property, and sexual life; this group
grew into the Oneida Community (1848–1881). He believed
that the individual soul could come into direct contact with God
and that through conversion it could free itself from the sins
of the existing world.

For such groups their spiritual ideals were preeminent. Communism was adopted at times only through economic necessity,
to permit the community to retreat to its own territory to live
and practice together. Often these groups coalesced around
a single charismatic figure who represented direct contact with
the diety; the route to perfection was given living embodiment
in his presence. Out of the religious utopian tradition came the
Shaker communities (1787 – ), led from England by Mother

Ann Lee; the Harmony Society (1804-1904); Amana or the
Society of True Inspiration (1843-1933); and Zoar — all
originally groups of German Separatists — and Oneida, an
American Perfectionist community. Brook Farm (1841-1847),
the community of intellectuals that Hawthorne memorialized in
*The Blithedale Romance*, also had religious utopian origins,
both in its theory of transcendentalism positing direct human
contact with the spiritual and natural worlds, and in its rejection
of the traditional church, as represented by the teachings of
George Ripley, the Unitarian minister who founded the farm.
Today, the Hutterian Brethren (founded about 1530 and in the
United States since 1873), composed of about 150 communities
and 17,000 people, and the Bruderhof or Society of Brothers
(founded about 1920 and in the United States since 1953),
encompassing three communities and about 800 members, are
modern representatives of utopias of religious origin. Other
presentday communes have their roots in spiritualism or Eastern
mysticism as well as Christianity, and often they invest their
leaders with supernatural powers.

The second major utopian critique of established institutions
is politico-economic. It began to emerge with the increasing
dislocation, mechanization, overcrowding, and poverty that
developed in the wake of the Industrial Revolution. It sought in
the small socialist community a refuge from the evils of the
factory system, characterized by dehumanizing competition and
the excessive labor of many for the benefit of a few. In the
socialist utopia all would cooperate to ensure the benefit of all,
and in time, with proper education, men of higher moral
character would emerge. Like the religious utopians, the
politico-economic utopians believed in the perfectibility of
human society. The social creed of Horace Greeley, whose ideas
influenced many utopian experiments in the 1840s, captures
many of the beliefs of these utopians: "There should be no
paupers and no surplus labor; unemployment indicates sheer
lack of brains, and inefficiency in production and waste in
consumption of the product of a national industry that has
never worked to half its capacity have resulted in social anarchy;
isolation is the curse of laboring classes, and only in unity
can a solution be found for the problems of labor; therefore,

education is the great desideratum, and in association the
future may be assured."[5]

Unlike most of the religious utopias, which grew out of
ongoing groups coalescing around the presence of a charismatic
leader, many of the first utopias whose initial impetus was
politico-economic were brought together by ideas, notably those
of Robert Owen, Charles Fourier, and Etienne Cabet. Again,
the original ideas were imported from abroad and were planted
in an American soil rich for experimentation: Owen was English,
Fourier and Cabet were French. Owen's cooperative ideas
provided the impulse behind New Harmony (1825–1827) as
well as a number of other Owenite experiments, dedicated to
improving contemporary conditions of life:

In the present system of human concerns . . . strife and conten-
tion are unavoidable. The man who does not prefer his own
interests falls necessarily into poverty. In the round of trade and
commerce all are exposed to the danger of either gaining too
great an advantage or of falling short of securing their own. In
this state of the world it is impossible to establish the love of
good will which are necessary to the comfort and happiness of
the human race. Hence, we have evidence that some other
and different course is imperiously called for and must be
adopted.[6]

Fourier's doctrines of association, which attempted to substitute for coercive, enslaving institutions those that would be
"naturally attractive," were translated in the United States by
Albert Brisbane and Horace Greeley, and led to the formation
of over forty utopian communities in the 1840s. The best
known of these were the North American Phalanx (1843–1856)
and the Wisconsin Phalanx (1844–1850); Brook Farm later
became a phalanx also. From Cabet's novel *Voyage en Icarie*
sprang five Icarian communities, with a total life span from
1848 to 1898. Josiah Warren, an American anarchist who proposed to restructure economic life by replacing money with
"equitable commerce" via a system of labor notes, was instrumental in the formation of several communities, including
Modern Times (1851–1866) and one actually called Utopia
(1847–1851). Among later socialist groups were the Llano

Colony (1914–1939) and a small number of utopian communities springing more directly from Marxist origins. Today there are also communitarian experiments, whose original *raison d'être* was their desire to restructure economic life and to create communities in which the means of production are jointly owned and political control is in the hands of the whole community.

Historically, the greatest wave of community-building in America occurred in the 1840s; another such wave is occurring now, in the late 1960s and early 1970s. Although a number of today's communal experiments began with religious or politico-economic critiques of society, the majority are based on a third, psychosocial critique. This critique revolves around alienation and loneliness, both social isolation and inner fragmentation. It holds that modern society has put people out of touch with others and with their own fundamental nature. It rejects established society's emphasis on achievement and instead adopts as its credo "self-actualization" or "personal growth." These utopian visions revolve around creating liberating situations that are conducive to intimacy and psychological health, enabling people to "grow" or to "do their own thing." Society is seen as pushing people apart and forcing them into narrow roles that do not express their total selves nor allow them to explore their deepest and fullest human potential. In one way or another, modern institutions are considered "sick"; they are felt to be instrumental in promoting the neurotic behavior at the root of our most pressing social problems.

Several different viewpoints are represented, from the "turn on, tune in, drop out" critique of Timothy Leary to the humanistic psychology of Abraham Maslow to the theories of B. F. Skinner. Hippie communes reject the establishment and its confining, stifling, isolating institutions without providing a clear substitute vision. Walden Two groups, a few of which are beginning to appear, modeled after Skinner's utopian novel of the same name, are attempting to create close-knit communal ventures based on principles of positive reinforcement. Synanon, originally begun in 1958 as a self-help group for former drug addicts and now a full-fledged utopia of about eight communities replete with new town plans and visions of the future, draws on a number of psychological critiques, including Maslow's, and offers itself as a "healthier" society. The vast numbers of small, extended-family communes springing up in urban and rural locations are attempts to promote both greater intimacy and fuller human development. Encounter groups and the communities or personal growth centers surrounding them also grew out of this tradition.

Thus, the initial impetus for the building of American communes has tended to stem from one of three major themes: a desire to live according to religious and spiritual values, rejecting the sinfulness of the established order; a desire to reform society by curing its economic and political ills, rejecting the injustice and inhumanity of the establishment; or a desire to promote the psychosocial growth of the individual by putting him into closer touch with his fellows, rejecting the isolation and alienation of the surrounding society. These three threads vaguely correspond to the three historical waves of American utopian communities: the first lasted from early days to about 1845, when religious themes were prominent; the second, stressing economic and political issues, ran from 1820 to 1930, flourishing especially in the 1840s; and the third, psychosocial period emerged after World War Two and became especially important in the 1960s. Nevertheless there are many groups today growing out of all three traditions.

Regardless of the rhetoric, however, the three themes have much in common. They reject the established order as sinful, unjust, or unhealthy. They stress the possibility of perfection through restructuring social institutions. They seek the recreation of a lost unity — between man and God, between man and man, or between man and himself. They stress immediacy, the opportunity to achieve such harmonies now. They frequently seek a return to the land as the pathway to perfection. And they often lead to a single development: the utopian community or commune. Despite the diversity of origins of such communities, they share many similar features in both their underlying concepts and their resulting life-styles. A prime illustration is the case of Oneida, a nineteenth century community that is sparking much interest today. Oneida's origins were religious, but to some extent it represents a merger of all three utopian critiques.

Oneida, Community of the Past

To members of the Oneida Community, their way of life was not an experiment; rather, it was the norm, the shining example of the Kingdom of Heaven on earth. "We believed we were living under a system which the whole world would sooner or later adopt," wrote Pierrepont Noyes, son of founder John Humphrey Noyes. The elder Noyes was an activist and a realist, stressing faith in the realism of the spirit. To him, Heaven was "a present, existing state, one that ought to be admitted into this world."[7]

John Noyes's vision of utopia was embodied in a community of about two hundred people, four miles from Oneida, New York, with branches in Wallingford, Connecticut, and Brooklyn, New York. The community grew out of a Bible class that Noyes, a radical graduate of Yale Theological Seminary, ran in his home in Putney, Vermont. After losing his license to preach there because of his radical teachings, he proclaimed that "Christ demanded and promised perfection here on earth," and founded the group called Perfectionists. In 1848 he moved to Oneida with a number of his followers, and the Oneida Community was officially organized around the principles of the primitive Christian church: "the believers possessed one heart and one soul and had all things in common."[8] In the words of an Oneida song:

> We have built us a dome
> On our beautiful plantation,
> And we all have one home,
> And one family relation.[9]

The pattern of community life translated these principles into practice, its most distinctive aspects being economic communism, communal living, "complex marriage" or free love, communal child-rearing, and government by mutual criticism. The community was considered one large family, sharing both the material and the spiritual life. Members had only a minimum of private property, for all recruits signed a document transferring money and major possessions to the community. The community in turn provided education and sustenance in exchange for members' labor. Even clothes were the common property of all, with the wearer merely allowed the use of them: "going-away clothes" were shared by all. No accounts were kept by members, but it was the duty of each to keep his expenses as light as possible. If women, for example, were thought to spend too much of their annual appropriation from the community for personal adornment, they might be asked to give up brooches until they had conquered the "dress spirit."[10]

Communism also informed the community work arrangements. Oneidans first supported themselves by farming, but financial difficulties indicated to members the need for industrial enterprise. Their first endeavor was canning crops for sale to grocers, then in 1852 they began the manufacture of steel traps, which became the standard brand in the United States and Canada. Other industries included a foundry and the manufacture of traveling bags, silk, and later, silverware. A carpenter's shop, joiner's shop, sawmill, tin shop, tailor shop, shoe shop, harness shop, printing press, and dental office were among the enterprises conducted for the benefit of the community. Industries were regulated by a business board, composed of heads of individual industrial departments and other interested members, which met weekly. All members were free to participate in its deliberations. Each spring there was a special session of the board to make general plans. Previous to the meeting every member was invited to hand in a note stating which industrial department he wished to work in. At this annual meeting an organization committee was appointed which selected foremen and apportioned the labor, abiding by the expressed wishes of members as far as possible.[11]

In this way, members were centrally assigned to their jobs, and jobs were rotated from year to year. In the eyes of the community, all classes of work were equally honorable. As far as possible, especially in the early years, men and women shared all kinds of work equally. As a result, women wore short skirts, pantalettes, and short hair, to make it easier to do men's work (as well as to discourage feminine vanity), and men in turn invented labor-saving devices for household chores. Two of the leading businesses were superintended by the women; women kept the community accounts; and according to the community handbook of 1867, "the sexes mingle freely in many departments of industry," side by side in the field and in the factories.[12] Sharing of work extended even to the children, who worked at least one hour and as many as three hours a day, six days a week, making chains for the trap industry. A minimum quality and quantity of work were expected before they could play.

The community worked as a group whenever the nature of the job permitted, organizing the effort into "bees." In particular, jobs that would be tedious for a few but less so when shared were handled in this way. Cleaning the buildings after the departure of visitors was one prevalent occasion for a "bee." The building of the central house, the Mansion House, was accomplished completely by members (except the plastering), and the community was continually making alterations in its buildings to accommodate new members and new needs. At the same time that participation was enhanced through "bees," nearly every member had a chance to take part in directing some aspect of community life through serving on a committee. According to one member, this "active sense of participation" led to "success and harmony."[13]

The group focus informed all aspects of life. All members of the community lived in the Mansion House, slept in small rooms, with the exception of small children ate in one large dining hall at many tables, and performed most daily tasks in a public place.[14] The Mansion House had several large halls, a visitor's room, a library, two recreation rooms, a dining hall, and the printing office of the newspaper, as well as bedrooms. While older members had separate bedrooms, the younger usually shared rooms.

The whole community convened in a separate meetinghouse for daily evening meetings, consisting of prayer and discussion of community affairs. In leisure time the events most enjoyed were those that brought "their entire family together," encompassing the whole community, such as plays, operettas, concerts by the community orchestra, as well as dancing and singing. Six to seven P.M. every evening was the children's hour, when all the children congregated in one room for games, plays, and songs, and all the adults gathered to watch them. Community spirit was instilled in the children, too, for group games were especially encouraged, including card games.

Although economic communism and communal living were

themselves unusual and unconventional practices for America, it
was Oneida's controversial practice of complex marriage that
confirmed its deviance in the eyes of outside society. The roots
of the institution were in the teachings of John Humphrey
Noyes, who in 1850 wrote a pamphlet called *Slavery and
Marriage*: "Marriage is not an institution of the Kingdom of
Heaven, and must give place to Communism . . . The abolish-
ment of exclusiveness is involved in the love-relation required
between all believers in Christ." To this end the community
instituted complex marriage. Under this system every member
had sexual access to every other with his or her consent. A wide
selection in cohabitation was encouraged, but always under
"strict regulation and governed by spiritual considerations."[15]
Intercourse was supervised by Oneida's leaders and ultimately
by Noyes. A man interested in a liaison had to approach a
woman through a third party, generally an older woman, and
his choice had the right to refuse his attentions. As there was a
general feeling that the young should learn from the older,
more spiritual members, who had reached a higher level of
"fellowship," sexual contacts usually proceeded along these
lines. Boys, for example, first had intercourse with women at
menopause. To prevent breeding, a form of contraception
called "male continence" was introduced by Noyes, a practice
requiring a great deal of self-control on the part of the man.
    While a wide range of sexual contact was encouraged, special
relationships were discouraged. Couples might be broken up or
one member sent to a branch. Community members accepted
this restriction and put it into practice. One man wrote of
a sexual relationship with a woman: "Naturally our relations
became more intimate, but I avoided any avowal of special
love that, if reciprocated, would estrange her from the central
love in the community." Though love was free and monogamous
marriage unknown, outright promiscuity was also discouraged.
One reporter notes that there was enforced secession of some
people who were too amorously inclined. In fact, kissing and
handshaking were not as prevalent as in outside society, because
the community wanted these things to have meaning, and they
avoided shows of affection in public because of the public's
attitude toward them as "free lovers." The ceremonial leave-

taking and welcome for traveling members, however, did
include caresses.[16]

Although its sexual practices were attacked in the press and
from the pulpit on the outside, the community denied that it
practiced "free love." In the face of wild tales and gossip
about its orgiastic practices, it claimed to be a private family.
According to the community handbook, "free love" in the
Oneida sense did not make love between all the members any
less binding or responsible than in marriage.

The Perfectionists refrained from having any children from
1849 to 1869. For purposes of child-rearing, a kind of selective
breeding, called "stirpiculture," was adopted in 1869. All
females were encouraged to breed, and all males were allowed
to have one child, but only preferred males ("stirps") could
have more than one. Fifty-three women signed a statement that
they considered themselves to belong first to God and second
to John Humphrey Noyes, and that they would accept Noyes'
choice of candidates for mating with them. A corresponding
resolution was signed by thirty-eight men. In order to mate for
propagation purposes, couples made application to the central
committee, which passed on the fitness of the combination and,
if it was disapproved, found another combination. Of fifty-one
applications, forty-two were approved and nine vetoed on
grounds of "unfitness." Fifty-eight stirpiculture children were
born to the community, nine of them fathered by Noyes himself.[17]

Once children were born, they were raised communally. Soon
after weaning, mothers sent their offspring to the Children's
House, a wing of the Mansion House. This was divided into three
departments: a nursery to age four, a kindergarten to age six,
and the "South Room" to age twelve or fourteen. Usually
after weaning, women took their turn in the children's department as assistants. Within the Children's House, as within the
community as a whole, the emphasis was on group activity and
love for all, rather than on selfishness or exclusive love. According to Pierrepont Noyes, who grew up there, the "physical set-
up of the house — the ubiquity of sitting rooms and the
smallness of bedrooms — helped discourage personal isolation
and exclusiveness." The heads of the children's department, not

parents, raised the children, and department heads were called
"papa" and "mother." In fact, the younger Noyes reports, many
parent-child relationships existed between unrelated children
and adults with or without children of their own. Children
did visit their own parents individually once or twice a week but
accepted the " 'family life' of the group as a whole . . . as the
focus of their existence, and in their own immediate generation
they developed a sense of solidarity . . . that they carried with
them into later life." An excess of parental affection was
frowned on because it was a kind of "special love" or exclusive
love, just as special love between couples was discouraged by
complex marriage. Children were reprimanded for any "stickiness" or special love for anyone, especially for parents, but
including friends. Because of "stickiness," one boy, for example,
was forbidden to see his mother for a week. Pierrepont Noyes
recalled that his own weekly visits to his mother in her quarters
were a privilege that could be taken away at any time.[18] The
community also censured friendships that excluded others;
children convicted of being partial might be temporarily separated.

Children had their own daily routine. At age twelve, for
example, they worked in an industry for three hours, studied for
three hours, received one hour of religious education, and had
the remaining time to play. In connection with the children's
hour, children held their own evening meeting, presided over by
the head of the Children's House, who lectured about the
dangers of Satan, the plans of God for the universe, and general
moral and spiritual topics. According to Pierrepont Noyes, the
children believed him unquestioningly.[19] Children were generally disciplined by nonforceful means, including verbal rather
than physical punishments. One man working in the Children's
House invented the Order of the O and F (obedient and faith-
ful) for children, with badges to signify their membership
in good standing. Misbehaving children were deprived of their
O and F badges as a sign that they had temporarily lost some
freedom of action.

For children as well as for adults, Oneida distinguished
between "improvement" and "education." Improvement
involved spiritual enhancement and was one of the primary

goals of the community. Children, for example, were taught
that reporting each other's misbehavior was a virtue, because it
was desirable that "sinners" be corrected as soon as possible.
This dictate was embodied in one of the Perfectionists' major
forms of government and social control: mutual criticism. In
addition to the daily evening meetings where general or individual problems were discussed, members submitted themselves
periodically for criticism by a committee of six to twelve
judges; in a few cases of extreme seriousness, the entire community was present. The subject was expected to receive the
criticism in silence and confess to it in writing. Judgment was
made as to his good and bad points and how he might improve.
Members believed the experience to be very effective. As
Walter Edmonds reported:

*mutual criticism*

> The Committees mixed praise with fault-finding. The essence of
> the system was frankness; its amelioration friendliness and
> affection. Yet it was always an ordeal. Without doubt the
> human temptation to vent personal dislikes on a victim was not
> resisted by everyone; but I have heard members say that the
> baring of secret faults by impartial criticizers called for more
> grace — as they used to say — than the occasional spiteful jab of
> an enemy. The same witnesses have testified that they were
> always happier and healthier after one of these spiritual baths;
> also that just because members had a chance to criticize one
> another openly, community life was singularly free from
> backbiting and scandal-mongering.[20]

Mutual criticism was used to ensure physical health as well as
conformity to community standards. Evidently with some
success, the committee exhorted those suffering from certain
physical ailments to *act* like well men. Sick members might send
for a criticizing committee, with the usual result that the ailing
party was brought into a sweat by the ordeal, breaking the
disease. As stated by one Oneidan: "If you are sick, seek for
some one . . . to find out your weakest spot in character and
conduct; let them put their finger on the very sore that you
would best like to keep hid. Depend upon it, there is the
avenue through which disease gets access to you."[21] Even for
children this remedy sometimes applied. On one occasion when

there was a bad epidemic of colds, the housemother attributed them to the presence of an evil spirit, a criticism was started, and the ill children were counseled to confess Christ.

Probably the most important aim of mutual criticism was to imbue members with "public spirit" or "community spirit," and to fight egoism and selfishness. The community's ban on exclusive possessions extended beyond material goods and other persons to encompass even the self. Excessive introspection, for example, was considered a sin. There was no matter too private for mutual criticism. The Oneida handbook reported that "intercourse between the sexes" was often under discussion at meetings and the subject of criticisms. The community even published a pamphlet of criticisms of members, such as the following: "If R would turn round and instead of trying to interest others in his personal affairs, interest himself in universal truth, he would have no difficulty about fellowship. He would find himself in the very element of social freedom. If he would take up some study, entirely forget himself, and apply his mind to abstract truth, with perseverance, for a long season, he would be a much better judge of his own experience than he is now." In criticisms, members were often censured for their lack of "we-spirit." As one historian reported: "The odor of crushed selfishness was said to pervade the air of the communal dwelling."[22] One member gave this account of his first criticism, conducted by John Humphrey Noyes:

Every trait of my character that I took any pride or comfort in seemed to be cruelly discounted, and after, as it were, being turned inside out and thoroughly inspected, I was, metaphorically, stood upon my head and allowed to drain till all the self-righteousness had dripped out of me . . . I felt like pouring out my soul in tears, but there was too much pride left in me yet to make an exhibition of myself. The work had only been begun. For days and weeks after I found myself recalling and reviewing them in a new light, the more I pondered, the more convinced I became of the justice of what at first my spirit had so violently rebelled against. Today I feel that I would gladly give many years of my life if I could have just one more criticism from John Humphrey Noyes.[23]

Some Oneida Perfectionists called themselves "living sacrifices

to God and true communism." What the Oneidan sacrificed
was not only tobacco, alcohol, and meat; nor merely individual
rights over property, spouses, children, and the self; but also
respectability. For Oneida's religious, economic, sexual, and
familial deviance brought it into conflict with arbiters of morality in the larger society. Though the community had some good
relations with immediate neighbors, often hiring them as well-
paid laborers, and was well-regarded by many utopian sympathi-
zers, free thinkers, and admirers of its industrial expertise,
numerous forms of hostility were experienced. On one occasion,
for example, the community boys visiting the trapshop in
the village a mile away were chased, jeered, and dared to fight
by the village boys. They were called "Christ boys" and
"bastards" on the outside, and bastards they in fact were. Nearby Hamilton College and the clergy objected especially to
Oneida. In 1873 the Association of New York Methodist Ministers denounced the ethics at Oneida as "free love and licensed
indulgence" and "harlotry." Complaints about the community's
"unmoralities" were registered with magistrates of two counties,
and a Grand Jury investigation was prompted, although the
complaint was later dropped. Even their mutual criticism was
ridiculed and condemned. The New York *Times* claimed that
this practice attracted members to Oneida because it embodied
and legitimated scandal. Other newspapers scorned and mocked
the short hair and slender figures of Oneida women. Visitors
or outsiders sometimes assailed community members with
prying, obscene, and insulting questions. Even apparently
innocent practices were cast in a bad light by critics; one writer,
who was opposed to free love, for example, interpreted the
fact that Oneida publications were mailed free in response to
any request as being "malicious, shrewd proselytizing." A legal
threat to take action against the community was in fact partly
responsible for its eventual metamorphosis into a joint-stock
company without special social and sexual practices. In 1879
the Presbyterian Church agitated for special state legislation
against Oneida, and Noyes fled to Canada in response to a
rumor of his intended arrest. The community had anticipated
this outcome; one member said that "John Humphrey Noyes
could not expect to fare better at the hands of a scurrilous
public than did Christ and other reformers."[24]

The feeling of ill will was mutual. Oneida scorned the outside world as filthy and contaminating, though it did send several young men to Yale. Oneida children were horrified by the swearing and depravity of village boys. Children were forbidden to speak to outsiders, whether hired men or visitors, of which there were one hundred to one thousand at peak periods. After visitors had left, the community gathered for a ritual cleaning "bee," to efface every trace of an "unclean public" and of the "filthy invaders." Those members most exposed to contact with the outsiders underwent mutual criticism so as to be "freed from contamination by worldly influences." For members who traveled outside, there was a criticism before they left, to provide "sustaining power from the heart of the family" for the ordeal, and one on their return, "to relieve them of spiritual contamination."[25] The community thus viewed the outside world rather than itself as deviant, with the society of Perfectionists setting the example for a better, purer, and more moral life, which the rest of society would eventually adopt.

The future did not unfold in accordance with members' dreams. The Oneida community dissolved into the Oneida joint-stock company in 1881, giving up communistic sharing, complex marriage, and much of their joint housekeeping. Today the company continues to manufacture silverware, having recently issued its first public offering of stock, and maintains a small fraction of the old community spirit. In 1962, fifty-seven people still lived in the Mansion House, and eighty-five descendents of the original Perfectionists lived in the immediate area.[26] What was once a communal utopia is now a thriving capitalistic business.

### Twin Oaks, Community in the Making

One hundred years later, although a new generation of communes has arisen, Oneida is not forgotten. It is the name of a new, two-story building with bedrooms and office constructed at Twin Oaks, a commune near Louisa, Virginia. On the Great Leap Forward list posted in Oneida's living room, the building's completion, a special event in Twin Oaks' four-and-a-

half year history, is noted: "Today God has chosen Oneida for
our community home, because he caused a rainbow to shine on it."[27]
Twin Oaks frankly admires American utopias of the past. The
commune workshop building is named Harmony, after the
nineteenth century village in Indiana occupied first by the
Rappites and then by Robert Owens' short-lived New Harmony.
The old farmhouse containing the kitchen and eating space
is called Llano, after an early twentieth-century socialist group.
A weekly class on utopias informs members of their communal
heritage. The oldest member of Twin Oaks — and the nearest
it has to a communal philosopher, although members are quick
to deny her any special status — has studied histories of utopian
communities and been impressed with the clever ways in which
long-lived ventures of the past handled recurrent human problems.

Twin Oaks also has a peculiarly twentieth-century heritage,
since it was inspired by B. F. Skinner's *Walden Two*, a novel
published in 1948 about a utopian community based on the
principles of behaviorist psychology. Twin Oaks was started by
eight people who met at a Walden Two conference in Ann
Arbor, Michigan, in 1966. They talked together, discovered
common goals, met again in Atlanta, and with money received
from one member of the group, purchased a farm near Washington, D.C., from a retiring tobacco farmer. In June 1967 the
first eight moved onto the land, comprising 123 acres with a
river, creeks, woods, pastures, and fields. By March of 1969 the
group had grown to fifteen, despite the loss of some original
members. By the end of 1971, Twin Oaks was a community
routinely feeding and housing about forty-five people — thirty-
six members (including only two of the original eight) and about
ten visitors at any one time.

The commune has supported itself in a variety of ways. After
discovering that farming could supply food for the table but
no additional profit, the group began to hand-weave hammocks
and sell them by mail. After four years, however, Twin Oaks
was still not self-supporting. About half of the commune's
income in 1971 came from outside jobs; at any one time, eight
members held outside employment on two-month rotating
shifts, with each worker bringing in at least $50 a week. An-

other quarter of the income came from hammock sales. The remainder came from visitors (who pay up to $3.00 a day, depending on length of stay), crafts, and a contract to type addresses and stuff envelopes for a nearby corporation. A brief attempt to operate a country store near the commune proved unfeasible.

Twin Oaks combines many elements of the contemporary communal counterculture with its own distinctive values of order and organization, equality and social justice. These values can be seen in the nuances of Twin Oaks culture as well as in its work and government. Though sights and sounds of Twin Oaks life often resemble those of other contemporary communes, there are important differences. It is organized and growing; it has rules; and it does not turn its back on technology or commercial activities. Twin Oaks, like many communes, possesses wide fields, woods, a river, an old farmhouse, dilapidated barns, muddy roads, and the ubiquitous dome, constructed to house a conference. Yet there are signs of exceptional activity here, for two new long buildings have been built by the group, and ground is broken for a third. Cows and pigs are in the barn, pets underfoot, peanuts drying in a shed, large window boxes filled with thyme and sage, and organic gardening magazines around the dining room. But unlike many other communes, Twin Oaks farms only casually, relying instead on development of commune industries. The people look like those on any youth commune, being predominantly white, middle-class, and in their twenties, with long curly hair, some bearded, wearing tattered blue jeans, a few in long, flowing flower-print dresses, an occasional woman in a nightgown or a man fresh from a bath wrapped in a towel. But Twin Oaks also has a few members over forty, including a former computer scientist from a major corporation.

Inside Llano, the old farm building, is a typical communal sight: a cramped farm kitchen with out-of-date equipment, huge stained pots hanging overhead, newly constructed wooden shelves holding boxes and jars of supplies, and the smell of bread baking. Yet there are also dozens of cookbooks, ranging from *Larousse Gastronomique* to the *New York Times Cookbook*, a small steam table keeping meals warm for a few hours, and a snack table stocked with purchased jars of peanut butter and jelly. On one visit, a cat was being spayed on the porch by a visiting veterinarian while members learned to do it themselves, a characteristic communal attitude. Yet for their own health needs they set a day aside with a doctor in Richmond for everyone's annual checkup. Twin Oaks has not turned its back on modern medicine and has every intention of having babies in the hospital. The familiar sound of rock music emanates from the music room; but inside the room Twin Oaks' special penchant for order is evident, for records are neatly boxed, alphabetized, and labeled as to type. On bookshelves are the *Bhagavad-Gita* and works of Herman Hesse, but also behavioral psychology texts and histories of utopias, all neatly organized. There is a communal bathroom (one of two) decorated with forty-nine toothbrushes and four razors, but also a tube of K-mart toothpaste in a holder that doles out measured amounts. As on many youth communes, members roll their own cigarettes from cans of tobacco, but unlike most groups, Twin Oaks permits no drugs. The characteristic countercultural revulsion against American capitalist society is expressed, as in the statement, "The U.S. is a crummy place but I don't have to go there very often"; but requests for people to speak at conferences are posted. The language of the counterculture is used ("good vibes," "groovy"), but so is a language peculiar to Twin Oaks ("manager," "planner," "labor credits").

The commune is decorated with a typical array of arts and crafts, including pottery, woodwork, old musical instruments, crocheting, and macramé wall hangings. Even more obvious, however, are the bulletin boards in almost every common room, which include papers written by members, opinion surveys on controversial issues (such as playing music in the hammock shop), architectural plans for Twin Oaks' future development, and signs reminding people to wipe their feet or turn off lights. Signs are everywhere: a sign on a tattered towel in the laundry room points out what happens when bleach is undiluted; a bent record demonstrates the consequences of leaving records on top of the heater. There is a place for everything and everything is in its place. Tags with each member's name can be hung under "meat" or "vegetarian" to indicate meal preferences. In the woodshop, rows of neatly labeled boxes indicate the place for each piece of hardware, even including a box for "unsorted nails."

Even more dramatic than the physical order that pervades Twin Oaks is the commune's desire for social order. This stems in part from its interest in *Walden Two*, which stresses the application of environmental and behavioral controls to shaping a good life for all. But unlike *Walden Two*, which was pragmatic and scientific rather than moral, Twin Oaks' social order is informed by strong moral principles.

Equality and social justice are the commune's reigning values. Twin Oaks' behavioral code emphasized the following points:

We will not use titles of any kind among us. All members are "equal" in the sense that all are entitled to the same privileges, advantages, and respect. This is the reason we shun honorifics of any kind, including "Mrs.," "Dr.," "Mother," "Dad," etc. . .

All members are required to explain their work to any other member who desires to learn it . . . Observing this rule makes it impossible for any member to exert pressure on the community by having a monopoly on any certain skill. . .

Seniority is never discussed among us. This is because we wish to avoid the emergence of prestige groups of any kind. . .

We will not boast of individual accomplishments. We are trying to create a society without heroes. We are all expected to do our best, so making a big fuss over some accomplishment is out of place.[28]

Twin Oaks thus seeks to eliminate status and seniority by removing the bases for invidious distinctions between people. Not only are special titles not used, but neither are last names. Members are free to cast off the identities, roles, and constraints associated with the larger society and to experiment with new ones. Several members have changed their names and careers.

Female and male equality is also part of the commune's program. Twin Oaks makes no distinctions between women and men, the work of each sex, or their status or privileges. Men are just as likely to work in the kitchen, and women in the woodshop or the fields. Since the advent of the women's liberation movement, the community interest in eliminating sex role distinctions has risen. From a New York women's liberation group, Twin Oaks has taken the word "co" to use as a neutral pronoun for either women or men; thus, in conversation and writing, members commonly replace "he," "she," "hers," and "his" with "co."

Desire for equality and justice also informs property arrangements. Property is held communally at Twin Oaks, owned and used by all. An attempt is made to eliminate envy by ensuring that everyone has equal access to goods. The only exceptions are small items that can be kept in a member's room. The rooms themselves are inviolate, and the members' privacy is respected. All goods and services are provided by the commune, including a weekly allowance of 75¢ for snacks; paychecks from outside work go directly into the community treasury. Even clothing is owned jointly by most members, though a few keep their own clothes because of special size or personal preference. The "community clothes" are kept in a huge loft above the hammock shop, jammed with racks of hanging garments and boxes of underwear and tops labeled by item and sex. Here members come to pick up a supply of clean, ironed clothes. Community laundry is washed daily; private laundry on Sundays.

The community as a whole decides how to allocate funds for purchases. A request may be turned down because the item desired, such as a flute for one member, may not be of high priority. Members argue that some refusals are owing to the community's temporary poverty. However, when a need is strong, all the resources of the community are used to help an individual. When one member had an expensive operation entailing high medical costs and a week's hospitalization, about half the commune sold blood at $15 a pint to help pay the bills.

Communal sharing stemming from a concern with equality and fairness also informs the life and government of Twin Oaks. For every area of work at Twin Oaks a manager is ultimately responsible. There are, for example, a kitchen manager, a hammock manager, a health manager, a library manager, a membership manager, and a new industries manager. The manager does not necessarily do the work himself, but he oversees the project, handles the budget, and makes necessary decisions. Since there are well over forty tasks to be managed, Twin Oaks has more managerships than members, and many people manage several tasks. The position is voluntary; those who do not want a managership have been permitted, thus far, to avoid the added responsibility. Managerial roles have generally not been a function of age or experience, as members are quick to point out, and the responsibility often produces more problems than status. The kitchen manager, overseeing purchasing and menu planning for the forty-five people who regularly eat at Twin Oaks, is a young woman still in her teens; her assistant is a much older and more educated man. Two of Twin Oaks' major activities — hammock weaving and farming — are managed by a young man of nineteen. He volunteered because the jobs were open, he hoped to learn something, and "after all, *someone* has to do it."

Work is organized on a system of labor credits. Every week all members must earn the same number of credits, which at present is approximately forty-two, though the exact number is a function of the available people and jobs. Labor credits are calculated by multiplying the hours worked by a factor from .9 to 1.5, which reflects the desirability of the task to the member: the more desirable the job, the lower the factor. Each Sunday everyone ranks, in order of preference, a list of up to sixty-three tasks, ranging from laundry to morning milking to washing the supper pots. Jobs ranked one to three (the most preferred) have a labor credit factor of .9; jobs ranked four through ten have a factor of 1.0; eleven through eighteen, 1.1; and jobs ranked fifty or over carry the maximum factor of 1.5. Thus, a person assigned to less preferred work earns more credit for it. This system is the result of experiments with various ways of organizing and assigning work, including one in which overall community preference rather than individual taste was the basis for credit. After preference sheets have been turned in to the labor credit manager (an extra labor credit can be earned for getting the sheets in on time), an attempt is made to distribute needed work as nearly as possible according to indicated preferences. This complex task itself usually takes a couple of days, with the help of a large matrix listing members on one axis and jobs on the other. Some tasks, such as preparing meals, must also be scheduled at specific times. By Thursday members receive back their work sheets, listing both scheduled and unscheduled tasks.

This week-to-week labor system is flexible, equitable, and easy. Members can choose different work every week; they can mix and match tasks according to whim, fancy, or skill; and for the most part, they get the work they prefer. No special status or great credit attaches to any jobs, unless they are particularly odious. A former member who taught at a nearby university received hourly credit for his high-paying work just as anyone else did, carried lunch in a sack, and received the same weekly allowance of 75¢. On the other hand, when the septic tank had to be cleaned, which is not a routine event, members bid for the job in terms of credits. The low bidder climbed into the tank for two credits per hour while others read poetry to her. One advantage to this communal organization of work is the increased leisure it brings. When a person has finished his assigned work, he is completely free from chores. Meals are prepared for him, clothes are washed and ironed, rooms are swept; he has no more responsibilities.

The effectiveness of Twin Oaks' work system depends on the members' willingness to abide by it. Members set their own pace and often their own hours, and record their time worked. There are, however, reports of several attempts to "beat the system." One member indicated that people can fill out preference lists so that they must be assigned low preference tasks, receive more credit for them, and therefore work fewer hours. He complained that there was no effective way to counteract this situation, except by criticizing such people to their face since it is considered inappropriate to gossip; yet these same people were the ones least likely to attend the weekly, voluntary feedback meetings. Work problems were responsible for one of the two occasions on which the commune asked a member to leave. In its early days Twin Oaks included a poet who insisted that his art was more important than were communal chores; but he, like everyone, was expected to earn his assigned credits every week. A friend intervened by filling out his work sheet for him so that they would both be assigned to the same job, like dishwashing, and then she did the work for both of them. When discovered, this was felt to violate the spirit of the commune, in which a member's contribution is the basis for receiving his share from the community. Labor credits, unlike money, are nontransferable; they belong only to the person who earns them. The poet was asked to leave, and his friend followed. The desire for equality and social justice similarly informs the decision-making processes. Since Twin Oaks lacks a charismatic figure like Oneida's Noyes to serve as spiritual guide and focus, and is in any event philosophically opposed to distinctions that confer rank and status, the commune has developed a rotating leadership structure. Taking their terminology and concept from *Walden Two*, the commune gives final responsibility for policy and over-all coordination to a trio of "planners" serving for eighteen-month terms staggered at six-month intervals. This structure, like the work system, has evolved out of experience. The original eight members experimented with anarchy, but they were dissatisfied with the general decision-making that resulted and with the lack of anyone to take ultimate responsibility. At present, the three planners are not elected but are rather chosen by their predecessors. Each planning board also includes a fourth apprentice planner, groomed to replace the next member whose term ends. The commune has the power to veto the board's choice, by a process of casting individual votes in a veto box that is available for a week; "no" votes from more than half of the members constitute a veto. One planner candidate was vetoed because he was not well liked, even though the planners felt he had the requisite skills. "This taught us an important lesson," one member commented; "popularity *is* important for a leader."

Theoretically the planner system provides for not only routine decision-making but also long-range planning. While managers can make decisions in their own areas within their budgets and prerogatives, planners coordinate the over-all activities. In actuality, this system is still developing. Few planners have completed a full eighteen-month term, most preferring to resign. The high membership turnover of Twin Oaks' first few years indicates that it has attracted few members with a long-range stake in the community. Planners have likewise tended not to be interested in laying the foundations for an unknown, distant future. And being a planner, according to one of them, is not always rewarding, for the extra time and effort required is sometimes not appreciated by others. In fact, the opposite occurs. Since planners are charged with making decisions that may upset others in the group, they are continually subject to criticism.

Interpersonal relations have not been a focus of community concern as much as have work and government, partly because *Walden Two* treats them as individual matters. Even for a community of from thirty-six to forty-five persons, a surprising amount of communication is formal and impersonal instead of face-to-face. Typical forms of communication are written opinion surveys, notes on bulletin boards, or news-of-the-day broadcasts over the commune radio. The whole group meets together rarely. At one time, complaints about other people were taken to a third person known as the generalized bastard, so that direct confrontation was avoided. Because the new steam table can keep meals warm for several hours, members eat at different times. Because the work may be scheduled individually and there is no surveillance, members can continue for a long time without seeing each other. One girl who was ill remarked that if she did not come out for meals, she could remain in her room for three days without anyone noticing her absence.

This lack of communication is slowly changing, however. Many of the young people now joining the commune want family feeling, good relationships, and personal growth; such people sometimes leave if these are not available. Borrowing from both Oneida and the human potential movement, Twin Oaks has experimented with a variety of ways to work on personal and group issues. For a time, some members tried Oneida-style mutual criticism, in which a person could request criticism from the group. Lack of complete honesty and the inability of the subject to respond made this approach difficult. Accordingly, it was given up and replaced by feedback meetings, in which members respond to each other. This is not yet mandatory, however, so there is no guarantee that particular people will attend. Other kinds of group meetings are being tried, or contemplated, including weekly awareness groups.

Sex and marriage are also individual matters. Twin Oaks' membership is largely single, but it has included both married and unmarried couples, a trio, and homosexual pairs. The commune plans to have children by 1973 or 1974, to be raised communally in a children's building, but specific procedures have not yet been decided. A few members even speculate about Oneida-style group marriage, but so far this is merely a subject for discussion.

Twin Oaks has as yet few rituals and symbols, though this too is changing. A new sweat hut built by the river is a place for nude group togetherness. Games and play, folk dancing and music, also contribute to group spirit. The commune conveys a sense of specialness through such mundane matters as sending the Twin Oaks' granola recipe to other communes, posting the Great Leap Forward List in the Oneida house living room, and even establishing its own system of time (one hour ahead, with weeks running from Friday to Thursday). One member expressed the commune's special sense of triumph in the title of a pamphlet he wrote, "The Revolution Is. Over. We Won It." Members show much warmth and affection for each other, hugging and teasing. For some people, Twin Oaks has indeed become a family. As one member wrote to the group from her outside work shift: "Sudden changes in everything in me. I need to come home. It's lonely out here."[29]

Twin Oaks is still very much a community in development, trying to combine the lessons of the past with the needs and desires behind today's upsurge of communes. It is trying to develop a model for a smooth-running, full-scale village, like Oneida or the utopias of the past, at a time when many people want intensely personal solutions. Based on modern rationality, it still lacks the sense of spiritual mission that pervaded Oneida and which even today brings many people to seek utopia.

Though still in formation, Twin Oaks draws criticisms from all sides. Those whose idea of perfection is the spontaneous, natural Garden of Eden of the hippie movement find Twin Oaks too orderly and organized, too middle class. As the oldest member expressed it: "There is a language barrier between (us) and the average commune. When we say efficiency, we mean a way of getting the work done better and faster, so that we can have more time for swimming, listening to music, making love, or doing yoga. To them, efficiency conjures up visions of grim-jawed, glittery-eyed robots that have forgotten (if they ever knew) how to live joyfully."[30] At the same time, the commune is castigated by those who consider it just another hippie commune and its members "freaks." A tree-planting crew from Twin Oaks was fired from an outside job when it was learned that they were from a commune. Another member lost his job as a hospital orderly when other staff discovered, watching him change into his uniform, that he wore no underwear. The local sheriff came by to look for runaways (finding none, he has since become a friend). The sheriff also visited because of rumors that Twin Oaks was holding a love-rock festival in the summer of 1971, when in fact the event planned by the commune was a conference on intentional communities. An enterprising member tried selling Twin Oaks products to stores for a time, but decided that his appearance (long black curly hair and full beard) was against him. Yet Twin Oaks tries hard to maintain good relations with its neighbors, and it is the impression of most visitors that they do.

Twin Oaks is not everyone's idea of utopia, and many problems remain to be solved. To some visitors the commune appears poor, run-down, and cluttered. Often the work is not intrinsically meaningful. Hammock weaving is boring, as even enthusiastic members complain. Outside jobs generally involve unexciting menial labor, for which the person's only reward is knowing he is helping to support the group. One couple on outside work was accused of living in too much luxury, to which they replied that in comparison to their life outside, the commune was luxurious. There is little or no room at present for professionals, for artists, or for the exercise of advanced skills. For this reason, Twin Oaks continues to attract primarily young people who may as yet have no investment in a work role. A forty-year-old former computer scientist, moreover, chooses not to employ his skills on outside jobs. Communal sharing works at present, at least in part, because the members have little to share. Families with children have come and gone, and as yet there are no community children. Finances are a continuing problem. After completing immediate tasks, members have little energy left for planning future businesses; some seem uncertain whether they actually want to create enterprises or are puzzled by the complexities of the task. Turnover has been high. Single people sometimes do not feel as

connected or involved as couples and have often left if unable
to find a partner. Relationships are left largely to luck or
personal choice, and there is little explicit concern with building
a group. But as members are quick to point out, by and large
the critics of Twin Oaks do not live there. The members do,
and they seem to like it.

Additional problems will come with increasing size. Growth
and expansion are key items in the commune's future plans,
including more people, more buildings, and more efficient
production enterprises. Although the complex labor credit
system can work in a small group, it may prove too cumbersome
for a larger community. Some have talked of computerizing
it, but this idea has so far been rejected. Equitable distribution
of power and responsibility is not a problem when there are
more managerships than people, but when more people join,
new forms of organization may be required. Permitting relations
to develop at random instead of providing more purposeful
mechanisms may work for a group that is small enough to
ensure considerable face-to-face contact, but larger groups may
need more conscious efforts to counteract anonymity and
develop strong social ties.

Caught between their utopian vision of a comprehensive, self-
contained, organized, and orderly communal village on the
order of Oneida, and the contemporary counterculture emphasizing spontaneity and personal indulgence, Twin Oaks has not
yet been able to attract enough people willing to make a long-
term investment. Yet the wind may be changing. At the end
of 1971, Twin Oaks was only four-and-a-half years old – still
in its infancy as compared with Oneida's long history. By the
fall of that year, turnover had slowed. Plans for the children's
house were underway, and ground was being cleared. Hammock
sales had tripled in the past year, and the "sweat hut" had been
built for communal saunas and swims. Visitors continued to
pour in, contributing useful skills and ideas. A visiting clinical
psychologist and encounter group leader spent a week working
with the commune on interpersonal issues. An architect from
Richmond is helping to plan a physical center for the commune.
Consciousness of the importance of personal relationships,
group sense, and family feeling has risen.

New members often speak the language of the personal
growth movement rather than of behaviorist psychology. Old
members see no conflict in this change. Even though Skinner
and such humanists as Carl Rogers and Abraham Maslow are
ideological enemies, they express a willingness to "take good
technology wherever we get it." As a result, Twin Oaks is
becoming less like Walden Two, behaviorism is fading into the
background, and the concept of reinforcement has become
so general as to be almost meaningless as a distinctive school of
thought. Instead, Twin Oaks is developing its own culture
and its own institutions in the only way that this can be done —
through a slow and painful process of experiment and growth.
    Twin Oaks does represent an escape from the mainstream
of American life. It is a refuge for many of the spiritual orphans
of the 1970s, the children of the affluent who dislike school
and feel that they have no place else to go. It may be only a
temporary episode for these people, a year out of their lives.
However, the commune also embodies a set of hopes channeled
constructively toward the creation of new institutions. Twin
Oaks thus shares in the utopian ideal of social reconstruction.

*The ideal that grows up in familiar association*
*may be said to be a part of human nature itself.*
*In its most general form it is that of a moral*
*whole or community wherein individual minds*
*are merged and the higher capacities of the*
*members find total and adequate expression*
—Charles Horton Cooley, *Social Organization*

## 2 Society's Maternal Bed: Idealizations of Communal Life

The beliefs underlying the development of utopian communities
stem from an idealization of social life, which holds that it is
possible for people to live together in harmony, brotherhood,
and peace. Utopian thought idealizes social unity, maintaining
that only in intimate collective life do people fully realize
their human-ness. The sociological version of this aspect of
utopian thought was expounded by Charles Horton Cooley in
his work on primary groups. Cooley defined primary groups as
being characterized by intimate face-to-face association and
fusion of personalities into a larger whole. In his view, primary
groups are fundamental to the development of human nature —
to fostering sentiments such as sympathy, love, resentment,
ambition, vanity, hero worship, and a sense of social right and
wrong. These sentiments distinguish human beings from lower
animals, and they come into existence through primary group
experiences, that is, through participation in intimate collectives:

Human nature is not something existing separately in the
individual, but a *group nature* or *primary phase of society*, a
relatively simple and general condition of the social mind . . . It
is the nature which is developed and expressed in those simple,
face-to-face groups that are somewhat alike in all societies;
groups of the family, the playground, and the neighborhood . . .
In these, everywhere, human nature comes into existence. Man
does not have it at birth; he cannot acquire it except through
fellowship, and it decays in isolation.[1]

32

Such passions as lust, greed, revenge, and the need for power over others belong to man's "animal nature," according to Cooley. The "human" self, in contrast, is realized as people work together for the attainment of collective aims: "In so far as one identifies himself with a whole, loyalty to that whole is loyalty to himself; it is self-realization . . . One is never more human, and as a rule never happier, than when he is sacrificing his narrow and merely private interest to the higher call of the congenial group." Cooley thus presented an image of the cooperative, intimate face-to-face group effecting perfect harmony of interests between the individual and the collective, bringing people to a state of social perfection, generating loving, brotherly, and always social passions. As Philip Rieff put it, Cooley imagined the self "lying peacefully in the maternal bed of society."² Such utopian idealizations of the primary group are similar to idealizations advanced in utopian communities when the members describe their own collective efforts. The ways in which members idealize their groups, and their beliefs in social unity, are important for an understanding of the kinds of social processes they seek to create. The fact that communes and communal groups have historically been labeled "utopian" is a function of their idealization and romanticization of group life.

## Perfectibility

The primary utopian idea is human perfectibility. Utopians believe that tension, conflict, and disharmony derive from the environment, from social conditions outside the individual, not from sources within him. Societies, not people, are the cause of human problems. People are basically good but have been corrupted by society. Inner conflicts are merely a reflection of environmental tensions. It would thus be possible to perfect man and to bring about a higher order of human life by establishing the right environmental conditions. This principle has led to the founding of utopian communities, which are isolated, small-scale societies where every aspect of the environment can be controlled and manipulated, and in which social life can be so structured as to create the perfect society and the perfect human being here and now. Religionists in such com-

munities conceptualize the perfect society as heaven, Eastern
mystics as a higher incarnation, and socialists or scientists
as the next step in human evolution, but they all agree that it is
possible now, and that it will give rise to a more perfect person.
The leader of a utopian group currently recruiting members in
California claimed, for example: "We have a one-year-old
baby who is being brought up as a utopian; an entirely new
breed of human being. A mutation processed by other utopian
idealists." Even religious utopians who link the existence of
the perfect society to the second coming of Christ believe that
the right conditions could create a breed of "supermen" worthy
of divine attention and deserving of the Golden Age. Utopian
socialists of the nineteenth century felt that their community
experiments would prove so beneficial to the realization of full
human potential that the rest of the world would naturally
follow their lead, recreating social environments along similar
lines without the necessity for revolutionary overthrow as a
precondition to the Marxist millenium. Belief in the possibility
of "heaven on earth," of happiness in the present, thus informs
the establishment of utopian communities. Even hippie communitarians are avowedly utopian in their vision of the better
world they are creating. A member of a California commune
explained: "This kind of community is so important . . . because
there are going to be a lot of people around in the world,
and they are going to have to live with each other . . . But it
seems like all this communal living, if you want to look for
some kind of reason for it, then that in itself is an excellent
reason. Because with all those people there could be real chaos —
and that's not what we're on this earth for, you know — we're
on this earth to make a paradise . . . To put heaven on earth.
That's what it's really all about."[3]
   Perfectibility is possible, in the utopian view, if one discovers
the natural laws by which the universe operates and establishes
societies that are in tune with those laws, which follow natural
principles. By implication, present society is seen as existing
in tension, in conflict with the natural order, and thereby
promoting disharmony. The "back to the land" thrust of many
communes is an expression of this desire to return to the natural
life.
   A variety of natural orders have been proposed by utopians

as the basis for their communities. For example, the French utopian Charles Fourier suggested a doctrine of association based on the idea that the universe is operated by passions and attraction. According to him, people have twelve passions: the five senses, four "group passions" (friendship, love, family feeling, and ambition), and three "distributive passions" (planning, change, and unity). All twelve passions can combine harmoniously, leading men to love one another and to be united in society, through the power of attraction, which is the same power that draws the universe together. But in the past, Fourier reasoned, obstacles had been placed in the path of harmony. His design for an ideal society took into account the nature of human passions, so that natural attraction and gratification of the passions would automatically ensure industry and peace. His plan called for establishing communities ("phalanxes") of four hundred to two thousand people, united in work groups according to the character of their passions. Fourier's notion of the mathematical harmony of the natural order required that he specify the design of phalanxes in great detail, even to the number and type of industries. Building a utopia of phalanxes would, according to Fourier, bring human society into harmony with the physical universe, where the planets and stars already operate by the law of attraction. Fourier's cosmology was as elaborate as his sociology. Adoption of his plan of association was expected to bring about a millenium of seventy thousand "glorious years when the lions would become the servants of man, and draw men's carriages . . . when whales would pull their vessels across the waters, and sea water would taste like a delicious beverage."[4]

Koreshanity, the philosophy underlying a utopian community established at Estero, Florida, from about 1900 to 1947, purported to explain the true astronomical and religious system by which the universe operates and by which men should live. Koreshanity had hundreds of adherents at the turn of the century. According to this theory, the earth is a hollow sphere with man living inside. His feet point outward from the center, and the horizon curves upward on all sides instead of downward. The founder of this system, also known as Cellular Cosmogony, was Cyrus R. Teed, who set out to establish a world capital based on principles as mystical as astrology and spiritualism today. The city would be "located at the point where the vitellus of the alchemico-organic cosmos specifically determines. The position of the sign marks the head of the coming dispensation and will define the location of this greatest of all cities."[5] Teed, who changed his name to Koresh, settled for Estero, Florida, because land was given to him there.

Many of today's communes also operate according to their version of "universal truth." The Brotherhood of the Spirit, a two-hundred-person rural commune established in Warwick, Massachusetts is one of these. Community members believe that man goes through seven life stages: from the materialistic, to the intellectual, to a sixth level "when karmic energy uses you like the hand on a harp," and finally to escape from "this astral plane." They believe themselves to be "the teachers of the Aquarian Age" and expect to communicate their message to the world after a number of "earth changes," such as civil strife, ecological disasters, and earthquakes, have proven that the old order is no longer viable.[6]

Other Utopian theories of the natural order are more orthodox, based on more widespread doctrines such as transcendentalism, Christian millenialism, Eastern religions, Oriental philosophy, and humanistic psychology. Today's utopians sometimes make use of explicitly "scientific" theories of the natural order of things. Though they no longer concern themselves with the universe in general, they still claim to understand the "natural" basis for harmony in society. Synanon has adopted Buckminster Fuller's radical geometry and philosophy. B. F. Skinner's behaviorist psychology, as embodied in *Walden Two*, is the basis of several current experiments. The principles of reinforcement theory, which according to Skinner control human behavior, are used by these groups to build their concept of "the perfect society."

All of these theories — speculative, religious, or scientific — purport to have discovered the natural laws that must prevail in a harmonious society. It is in the implemention of these ideas, then, that the perfect society will become possible. Both society and man can be perfected if the underlying natural order is discovered. Even hippie communitarians feel that their acceptance of Eastern primitivism is in closer harmony with the

natural order than is the artificial technological society surrounding them. A member of a San Francisco commune
responded to the question, "What's the use of human progress
if you're going to revert to primitivism?" as follows: "Oh, but
that's what we're doing. That's where it's at, man. The society
feeds us machines, technology, computers, and we answer with
primitivism; the *I Ching*, the *Tibetan Book of the Dead*,
Buddhism, Taoism. The greatest truths lie in the ancient
cultures. Modern civilization is out of balance with nature."[7]

Within the communities themselves the notion of perfectibility
is expressed in a wide variety of educational practices, since
through knowledge of the truth it is believed that man can
reach perfection. Education has been central in utopian thought
from the time of Robert Owen. Many communities place great
emphasis on their educational institutions, establishing schools
that are often of such a high quality as to attract many nonutopian children from the outside, and providing continued
opportunities for adult learning, including lectures and study
groups. Oneida for a time considered founding its own college,
and this is one aim of Synanon today. Education is a central
function of many communities, and for some, such as the
personal learning or growth centers of the 1960s and 1970s, it
is their primary work.

In a number of communities, perfectibility means constant
attempts at self-improvement, constant striving for perfection
in word and deed. "Personal growth" is one way to express this
today. Confession and self-criticism are practices common to
many utopian communities; the individual continually measures
himself against the standards of the perfect society. Since his
total life may be encapsulated by the society, this process may
go on at any moment, at work as well as in leisure. In case
the individual is not always aware of his lapse from ideal standards, many communities practice mutual criticism, a group
encounter in which the group scrutinizes carefully the behavior
of each person, providing him with an assessment of his standing
vis-à-vis their goals for human conduct. The Llano Colony, a
twentieth-century socialist utopia, had a weekly "psychology
meeting," described as a combination of a "revival, a pep
meeting, and a confessional." The leader, George Pickett,

presided, delivering inspirational messages and "working up so much enthusiasm that derelicts confessed their sins against Llano and the cooperative ideal . . . At other times Pickett used the meeting to identify his enemies or to indict the colonists for their failures. He would even confess his own mistakes, permitted great freedom in the discussions, and probably enabled many colonists to work off basic hostility."[8]

Many modern utopias practice mutual criticism in the form of T-groups (sensitivity training groups) or encounter groups in which members provide one another with an objective understanding of their behavior and its impact on others. For them such knowledge and mutual understanding is a prelude not only to growth but also to the intimacy and interpersonal harmony of the community. Open, honest, authentic relations are one goal of utopias. Mel Lyman, leader of the present-day Fort Hall commune in Roxbury, Massachusetts, for example, has recognized the need for such encounters in a utopian community. "It is always hard to tell your friend he has bad breath," he wrote, "but if you keep it to yourself you will begin to hate him and wish he would go away . . . We began to criticize each other . . . This brought us closer together. Soon a policy of open criticism developed and this created a wonderful understanding amongst us. We improved each other. Now we all know each other so well that we have become as one person."[9]

Small group interaction, or mutual criticism in its various forms, is in fact such a primary and essential part of a utopian community that for Synanon the idea of perfectibility was first embodied in mutual criticism sessions treating dope addicts, and only later did the need arise for establishing a total way of life in a community — a total set of conditions conducive to human growth. Synanon's concept of mutual criticism is remarkably like Oneida's and Llano's. At its utopian community in Tomales Bay, mutual criticism is the central activity of the community. It occurs in a continuous twenty-four-hour-a-day stream called the perpetual stew, which has a constant influx of people who enter for varying stretches, perhaps ten hours, perhaps thirty. The "stew" serves educational functions of all kinds: not only do members measure each other's behavior,

but they also give lectures, French lessons, listen to talks by
outside experts, collect items for the community newspaper, or
hear announcements by the founder. About twelve people
are under scrutiny in the stew at any one time, but there is a
gallery above the stew room where any member may come to
listen and learn. The fact that the "stew" is perpetual, ever-
changing in its composition but never-ending, symbolizes the
utopian's perpetual striving for perfection.

Order

Another utopian value is order. In contradistinction to the
larger society, which is seen as chaotic, uncoordinated, and
allowing accidental, random, or purposeless events to give rise
to conflict, waste, or needless duplication, utopian communities
are characterized by conscious planning and coordination
whereby the welfare of every member is ensured. Some of
today's communes capture this quality by referring to themselves as intentional communities. Utopia is not only an
intended but a predicted society, in which events follow a
pattern and an uncertain future is made certain. To this end,
a utopian often desires meaning and control, order and purpose,
and he seeks these ends explicitly through his community.
He is convinced that they are possible, and that they can be
expressed in daily life. Mel Lyman, the leader of the Fort Hill
Community, explained: "There is always an order in life, life
is the reflection of that order as man is the reflection of God.
In every effect there is a cause and that cause is always the effect
of a GREATER cause. It takes a long time to FIND the meaning
in our day to day activities but in reflection we will always
detect the moving finger that traced the pattern we have
followed, there IS a plan."[10]
   Meaning is obtained in the utopian community from the
knowledge that all events within the community have a purpose
in terms of the beliefs and values of the group. For the Shakers,
for example, this integration of values and everyday events
meant that even getting out of bed was an act infused with
meaning by community dictates. According to an apostate
member: "Not a single action of life, whether spiritual or

temporal, from the initiative of confession, or cleansing the habitation of Christ, to that of dressing the right side first, stepping first with the right foot as you ascend a flight of stairs, holding hands with the right-hand thumb and fingers above those of the left, kneeling and rising again with the right leg first, and harnessing first the right-hand beast — but that has a rule for its perfect and strict performance."[11] For the Shakers, as for the contemporary Ba'hai commune of Cedar Grove in New Mexico, every domestic act from baking to sweeping has spiritual meaning.

Control for the utopian community is defined by the centralized coordination of activities that bring, from the utopian's point of view, all social forces into harmony. In a utopian community, for example, production, distribution, and consumption all occur under one roof for one set of people: the man who makes the clothes, wears them; the woman who bakes the bread, eats it. Communities produce primarily for their own use and offer services primarily for their own members, so that production and consumption are perfectly coordinated, and only secondarily may some communities produce something to be sold on the outside for profit. Internal consumption, not wealth, is the community's goal. This was expressed by a member of the Amana community in Iowa (1843–1933): "The worldly man is too selfish to do what we are doing . . . We keep carefully out of our thought any desire for commercial gain. We have produced here for the purpose of supplying our necessities and have not tried to make money. If we wanted to make money, we could manage this colony so that we could acquire a great deal more wealth than we possess."[12]

Planning extends to other aspects of community affairs. All life functions — eating, sleeping, praying, loving, working, playing — may be carried on in one place with one group and be centrally coordinated by community leaders so that activities are complementary and mutually reinforcing. Many communities have central buildings in which members sleep and eat. Since planning and coordination presume central control, in many communes there is a decision-making body that effectively coordinates members' lives, informing them when and where to eat and sleep, sometimes with whom to make love, and usually what hours and tasks at which to work — all in the interests of the central plan. These decision-makers range from one man to committees of the whole group to an elected board, but the larger the community, the more decisions are made centrally.

How a member spends his time is a matter not only of community policy but also of community welfare, for every member depends on the effort of every other. Most communities, therefore, establish their own particular daily routines and assign people to jobs on the basis of community need, to ensure smooth and harmonious operation. The Brotherhood of the New Life, a nineteenth-century spiritualist community, expressed this concept by calling their colony the "Use," because each person in it was to be used as God saw fit (interpreted by the community leader), and each person was given a spiritual or "Use" name to symbolize his acceptance of community control.[13] The Shakers instituted a routine prescribed in minute-by-minute detail, with bells ringing to signify the beginning of new activities. Communities sometimes even establish their own time. Synanon, at the Tomales Bay community, established a daily plan to carry out the community's goals of work and self-improvement, based on a thirty-day cycle of what are called "cubic days." Twin Oaks has its own community time and begins the week on Friday; Cedar Grove has its own months of nineteen days.

There is little room in a community for individual irresponsibility, such as a refusal to work, for the plan requires complete cooperation and the assurance that every member is carrying out his share of the job. In many cases it is felt that the good of the community transcends personal whim, for only if the community operates smoothly and harmoniously can the individual be fulfilled. The "me" spirit is subordinated to the "we" spirit. A spokesman for a present-day California commune put it this way: "What we're looking for is like a revolution of individual responsibility. I mean, the people who can't live with us are the people who are selfish, who put *themselves* first, and who can't cooperate and make the whole family work . . . But the people who can live together . . . like the man who will help set the table or build little things for the houses or repair things . . . well, this is the right kind of feeling." Self-reliance in responsibility, an Emersonian notion, is a motif of Synanon as well as of the California commune, and it is no coincidence that Emerson is read and admired by both groups. The emphasis on community responsibility is expressed in varying ways in many utopias. For the Universal Brotherhood and Theosophical Society, active in California in the early part of this century, "Brotherhood and cooperation were vital in achieving a higher level of incarnation; therefore . . . gossip was moral murder, and the good of the community transcended personal desires."[14]

At the same time, however, leisure time, entertainment, social activities, and opportunities for artistic self-expression are planned and included in the schedule. Although some nineteenth century utopias were notably austere in this respect, communities often have their own orchestras, choruses, speakers, seminars, theatrical productions, poets, and artists. Synanon, for example, has jazz bands, artists, seminars, and a radio station; the community has even invented a dance and cut a record. Many other present-day communities are built around creative endeavor or artistic accomplishment as a means of support, including music, painting, poetry, pottery, and crafts. Although individual caprice may be discouraged in favor of responsibility and cooperation, individual creative expression may be encouraged, with time arranged for it in the community's plan of days. In fact, planning and cooperation may be so effective in enabling a community to do its work that members may have more leisure time than they would if they lived and worked on the outside. Some Twin Oaks members insist that this is true for them.

Planning also gives rise to physical order, so that many communities are laid out in neat patterns of houses and buildings. Visitors to the most successful of nineteenth century communities, such as the Shakers, Harmony, Amana, and Zoar, often remarked about the cleanliness and orderliness of their villages. Cleanliness is one of Synanon's trademarks, and in fact, the cleanliness of the rest rooms at the gas stations run by them attracts a great many customers. Synergia Ranch, a contemporary New Mexican group interested in ecology, arranged its buildings and allocated space within buildings so as to fit the group's theories of energy flow; the community's physical space expressed its philosophic order.

## Brotherhood

*People brought into harmony w/ one another*

A third utopian value is brotherhood. Just as the social world can be brought into harmony with the natural laws of the universe, according to utopian thought so can people be brought into harmony with one another. This idea is captured in the names of some utopian communities: the Harmony Society of Harmony, Pennsylvania, and New Harmony, Indiana, in the nineteenth century, and the Society of Brothers (the Bruderhof) of Connecticut today. The Bruderhof also expresses their union pictorially, in art work showing animals and people holding hands with each other. In order to bring about such harmony, utopians believe that it is necessary to remove the "artificial" barriers between people that cause competition, jealousy, conflict, and tension, and prevent "natural" relationships. Utopian communities attempt to erase these barriers by substituting for individual possession community of property, of work, of lovers, or of families.

Property, in most communes, is shared, regardless of ownership. Goods are equally distributed. Individuals cannot accumulate wealth. In some communes, private property is completely abolished, with all property automatically belonging to the community as a whole, including the land, the buildings, and even the clothing on members' backs. Other communities are structured like economic cooperatives. In all, work is a community-wide affair, with members making their contribution in the kitchen, in the fields, in the nursery for young children, in janitorial services, or in the manufacturing of goods. In many communities jobs are rotated, so that individuals do not even "own" their job, but rather spend long periods of time at a variety of tasks. In the Connecticut Bruderhof community, one person distributes "community" work such as dishwashing according to group need and posts assignments daily on the bulletin board. Job rotation ensures everyone gets a chance to do both the most attractive and the least attractive tasks, and the least attractive may sometimes get the highest reward in the form either of "credit" against goods from the community store or of increased leisure time. Regardless of specific arrangements, however, usually everyone works, pitching in wherever he can. A visitor reported the following work arrangements at the nineteenth century North American Phalanx in New Jersey:

Men who have no special training in any craft, and who cannot perform the harder work in the fields, take upon themselves such chores as waiting on table, helping in the kitchen, tidying up the rooms, making beds, etc. In farming and in running the household there a great many tasks that, with good will, can be done by those without any particular specialty, and since the North American Phalanx knows no such thing as work that demeans a man, no activity of any sort draws upon itself scorn, and none is regarded by the members as either better or worse. Thus the various tasks, whatever they be are all performed willingly by everyone in turn.[15]

At the same time, communes tend to abhor specialists — even the community doctor may have to spend some time serving as janitor, or the newspaper editor washing dishes. In a modern commune in Cambridge, Massachusetts, everyone — male and female — cooks once a week. Moreover, a person with special skills is expected to share them, teach them to others, and not to retain them as a basis for status. Twin Oaks' code explicitly states that members must teach their skills willingly. Community of work, in short, aims at erasing the distinctions that can be made between people, the things that set them apart, and instead involves them in joint endeavors. Many tasks are thus occasions for the whole community to work together, as in the harvest, construction of new buildings, and cleaning after visitors have left.

To many utopians, monogamous marriage also represents a barrier in the road to brotherhood. Marriage is seen as exclusive possession, a kind of slavery, as well as a source of jealousy and tension. Thus, community of lovers is a logical step for many utopias, taking the various forms of free love, complex marriage as practiced in Oneida, polygamy as practiced by the early Mormons, or communal sex as in some modern groups.

Here sharing involves not only material objects but also private acts. Celibacy is another solution to the problem of exclusiveness, for it eliminates sexual possession entirely. Community of families also expresses the idea of brotherhood. To achieve this end, some communes do not recognize families, and no special privileges obtain between members of the same family. Children may be raised communally, with all community children living together in one building separate from the adult quarters, as they did at Oneida; under this system, parents do not have exclusive rights over their own children, and children may address all adults in the same way. Even special friendships may be discouraged, being considered a form of exclusiveness interfering with brotherhood, as in Oneida and the Shaker communities, where the composition of work groups was changed frequently to prevent the development of exclusive, close personal relationships. A temporary ban on both sex and intimate male-female relationships at the Tomales Bay Synanon may be another expression of the desire to foster brotherhood rather than exclusive relationships.

The goal of brotherhood and love in the community, transcending selfishness, exclusiveness, and jealousy, is expressed in the words of a contemporary San Francisco hippie:

When the hippie thing came along, we saw a better way to live . . . Now in a tribe, in a commune, you're with people that relate to each other, and it's a much groovier experience. Communal living is beautiful. It's the structure of the new age. The monogamous unit is going to be absorbed in communal life . . . I believe that responsibility for kids should be that of the community. I think that two people who have produced children ought to be able to decide whether they like them or not and if they want them. If not, then they should be turned over to the community for someone else to select them. The same thing holds true for kids . . . This will be the key to changing the whole love relationship we have in our society. It will free everybody from the jealous attachments that have interfered with the whole love relationship between man and woman.[16]

Finally, members of some communities may wear the same clothing, symbolizing their joint endeavor. At Twin Oaks and several urban communes, members draw their clothes from a common closet. At Synanon in Tomales Bay, both men and women wear blue denim overalls, to express their common interest in work. At the Connecticut Bruderhof community women wear peasant skirts and blouses, and the men wear work shirts, dungarees, and work boots, all from the common store. Many of these social practices and dress styles often have the additional consequence of admitting women to brotherhood. In freeing them from marriage bonds, stereotypes, and sole responsibility for care of the family, many utopian communities provide women with an equality less common on the outside.

The emphasis on brotherhood and harmony leads also to an intensive focusing on relations within the utopian group, making intimacy a daily fact of life. In contradistinction to the loneliness, isolation, and fragmentation that appear in outside society, communes attempt to promote intimate relations and total involvement in a group. The group may be an everpresent part of the member's day, for members may be his work-mates as well as his neighbors. Public opinion and gossip thus serve as effective means of ensuring conformity, and more coercive sanctions become unnecessary. In some utopian communities, members may even eat and sleep barracks-style, surrounded by the group. Pierrepont Noyes's account of life in Oneida indicates the pervasiveness of this peer group intimacy.

In small communities the intimate group may encompass the entire community. In larger utopias, the group may be a unit to which the individual belongs: the Shakers, for example, called these units "families," and Synanon has often divided the community into "tribes." The concept of the family is a useful metaphor for describing such group involvement, and one which corresponds to the utopians' own experience. Many communities, including Oneida, thought of themselves as one large family, with the leaders often being addressed in parental terms ("Father Noyes") and the members conceptualized as children. For the Shakers, their elders were "gospel parents" and the members "children of the new creation." Members are often "brothers" and "sisters" to one another. In present-day communities, the metaphor of the family is continued and extended. A hippie commune of fifty people in California, for example, calls itself the "Lynch family." One member explains: "We call ourselves the Lynch family for a variety of reasons. One is the convenience, since we consider ourselves one family — we number about fifty all told — and rather than introducing everybody with a different name, it's easier to say we're the Lynch family. Also, considering that we *are* one family, it would seem normal to take a family name. And the person who founded this group of people, who bound us all together, so to speak, is David Lynch."[17] In the Fort Hill community there has evolved "a family structure," with "all men and women brothers and sisters" and Mel Lyman "the father at the head of this family."

Group involvement is often conveyed through rituals in which the whole unit participates, symbolically affirming the commitment to their joint endeavor. These rituals both express and reinforce jointly-held values and represent ways of coming together as a group, of feeling closer to one another. For this reason group rituals are often the most significant and important aspect of community life to members, for it is here that the higher, transcendent meaning of living in utopia is affirmed. The ritual may embody, symbolically or literally, those principles on which the utopia was based. For some communities the ritual resembles a religious service, including prayers, statements of faith, sermons, and hymns. For others, such as the Bruderhof, the group gathering is like a Quaker meeting, with any member who wishes being able to get up and speak. In some communities dance or song serves ritual functions. The nightly Shaker ritual combined all of these. For the Shakers, as for other communities, the coming together of the group via the ritual was actual as well as symbolic: during this time, for example, the celibate Shakers exchanged "gifts" of kisses and hugs. An excerpt from a Shaker journal describes the feeling of the ritual, rivaling any modern encounter group:

We sung several songs on our knees, for we have become so used to standing on our knees, that it is almost as natural for us as it is to stand on our feet . . . Then Elder Brother said, let us arise from our knees and greet each other with a kiss of charity, then we may be dismissed. So we all went to hugging and kissing, and loved a heap . . . It appeared to me that the heavens were opened and I was worshipping with the Angelic host. Some times the Brethren and Sisters were passing and repassing each other — sometimes hugging and kissing the sweetest kisses that I ever tasted, for we felt love enough to eat one another up . . . Sometimes the Brethren and Sisters would follow each other around and around, sometimes they would have hold of hands, three and four and sometimes a dozen in a ring, waving up and down."[18]

Other forms of group ritual are found in current utopian communities, such as the "expansion of consciousness" sought through group use of psychedelic drugs. "A nonverbal flow of understanding and experience between people . . . (through) mysticism and free love" is the way that another modern utopia expresses its ritual search for intimacy.

In addition to ritual expressions of brotherhood, communities often experience their togetherness with great joy and laughter, gaiety and celebration.[19] The present-day Bruderhof communities, for example, celebrate whenever they have the least occasion. A visit of mine to the Connecticut community coincided with the celebration of placing new beams in the communal dining room and a twenty-fifth wedding anniversary. The children and young people had made decorations, and at every few places on the long tables appeared candle holders painted with hearts and flowers. At one end of the room, a tree of paper hearts dangled from the ceiling. During the meal, comic entertainment was provided by a group of children prancing around the room dressed as horses, by a child's parody of a conductor leading two musicians, and by the young people's group singing "Daisy, Daisy" to the names of the anniversary couple, acted out by two boys dressed up as the couple. The sounds of laughter and song reverberated through the hall. Words to a new song were written on big sheets hung on the wall for everyone to learn, adding to the more than a thousand songs already printed in Bruderhof song books. After dinner chairs and tables were cleared away, and the young people joined hands for folk dances. As bodies moved in concert, fifty people in time to the music and in step with one another, the feeling of belonging to a group, the expression of beauty and harmony of the whole, was hard to escape. The sharing of delight, the inclusiveness of the group dance, could be a motif for many communities. Synanon, too, has a group dance – the "hoop-la." In the ballroom of the former hotel in Santa Monica that they occupy, I watched rows of Synanon dancers twist their bodies in individual ways yet express their togetherness by changing direction as a group. In Tomales Bay I saw Synanon's Labor Day celebration, highlighted by a "beauty" contest between several genuine beauties and some men parodying women. One of the men won, to the delight and laughter of the spectators.

Thus, the brotherhood of the whole, the coming together of the group, is expressed through serious rituals, through the recurring events of symbolic importance, and through events of joy and laughter, of comedy and pleasure. Synanon members, for example, see their mutual criticism sessions not only as a serious matter of education, growth, and release of hostility, but also as fun and pleasure; indeed, they call them "games" and expect every session to contain its measure of humor. Sharing symbols, song, and laughter contributes to the "we-feeling" experienced by members of utopian communities.

### Unity of Body and Mind

Harmony as a utopian value has another meaning: the merging of values, ideas, and spiritual matters with physical events, the union of mind and body, spirit and flesh. This idea is captured in the name of the school of the Universal Brotherhood and Theosophical Society – the Raja Yoga, meaning "kingly union" – which was intended to foster the perfect balance of all the faculties: physical, mental, and spiritual.[20] It is also captured in the name of the Brotherhood of the Spirit's rock band: Spirit in the Flesh. Communes implement the idea of physical and mental unity in a variety of ways. In many communities, for example, physical labor is seen as a condition of mental well-being. Brook Farm, the community of intellectuals that at one time included Nathaniel Hawthorne and Margaret Fuller, believed that manual labor was spiritually uplifting, and thus every member, even the writers and poets, spent at least a few hours a day in physical effort. The founding of many utopias on farms, with an abundance of physical tasks to be done, is in part another expression of this identification of the sweat of the flesh with the health of the spirit. John Humphrey Noyes of the Oneida Community in fact advocated a periodic return to manual labor as "the only condition of healthy life."[21]

At the same time, utopians often feel that spiritual or intellectual experiences must be expressed through bodily states. Noyes of Oneida, for instance, wished to integrate sexual love with the life of the spirit. The hugging and kissing in the Shaker ritual was another example of this kind of expression, for the spiritual manifestation of the presence of God and the sharing of God's love were believed to occur in physical and bodily acts. The Shaker dance is one more instance in which the spirit was felt to be manifested through movement of the body. A Shaker journal reports:

Meeting usually begins by singing an anthem or a hymn, then the people prepare to labor. Singers place themselves and after singing sometimes one or two songs, the singing is entirely drowned by the different exercises and the sound is like mighty thunderings. Some are stamping with all their might, and roaring out against the nasty beast and filthy whore, which has made all nations drunk with wine and her fornication. Others turning with great power and warring against the flesh, while at the same time, a number are speaking with new tongues, attended with such majestic sign and motion that it makes the powers of darkness tremble. Yea, and the good believers cry out with thankfulness to God, for the special notice of God to them. The meetings frequently continue with such like exercises for two hours without cessation, though sometimes there is a pause, long enough to partly sing a hymn, and then begin more violently than ever, so that by the time meetings close the people will be as wet with sweat as though they had been plunged in a river.[22]

In another nineteenth century community, the Brotherhood of the New Life, sexual activity was supposedly prohibited, but the community believed that one could "(breathe) the atmosphere of heaven, not only into the spiritual but also into the natural lungs." The "breathing" occurred through sexual intercourse,

defined as the physical sensation of a mystical state. This
merging of the spirit and the flesh was expressed in verse:

> *Soul-life and sex-life are one*
> *In the divine their pulses run*[23]

This sentiment could be accepted by many hippies today, and it
reflects the characteristic utopian notion that the resolution
of all polarities of human life may be achieved by uniting the
mind and the body.

## Experimentation

Utopians are also characterized by a spirit of experimentation.
Not only are utopian communities major social experiments,
in which unique forms of human relationships are explored, but
within the communities themselves new ways of doing things
that may better enable the utopia to implement its ideas are
often explored. Since the utopian style of life involves a radical
departure from the conditions and assumptions about life
prevailing on the outside, the utopian community feels free to
vary any aspect of life it might choose, from matters of convenience to matters of life and death. Since the community is
already deviant, it dares more deviance. One consequence
may be that the practices adopted are often illegal as well as
deviant in a more general sense, so that the community may
face reprisals from law-enforcement officials. Nevertheless
a large number of experimental practices have characterized
utopian communities throughout American history. Dietary
experiments are found in many communities: for example,
vegetarian diets, health foods, and Macrobiotic diets (permitting
a variety of grains, no red meats) are common among hippies.
Some communities experiment with faith healing or new forms
of medicine; others, with the mental effects of drugs. In addition
to the use of psychedelic drugs, hippies experiment with
astrology and yoga. Even the Shakers, probably the most rigid
and austere American utopians, had their period of experimentation, trying spiritualism in the 1840s, including spirit-writing.
In the nineteenth century many communities, including

*Women's Clothes,*

*Sex*

*Child-rearing*

Oneida and the North American Phalanx, tried new forms of
dress and appearance for women, such as short skirts and
short haircuts, anticipating later trends. Today hippie dress
styles have also caused a mild revolution in fashion. Further,
new forms of marriage or sexual union are common to many
utopias. Oneida even had its own form of male contraception.
New ideas about child-rearing are often sought and implemented.
Synanon is now experimenting with Buckminster Fuller's
radical geometry and plans to build paper houses incorporating
his ideas. The Oneida Community conducted a major experiment in eugenics over a period of years, using their version of
genetic principles to decide who should mate for the purposes
of bearing children, and for a time no child was born into the
group who was not planned in this way. The Religious Society
of Families in New York experiments in a similar way today.
Many communes, such as Twin Oaks, see themselves as major
social laboratories in which they are proving the value of
certain practices to a skeptical outside world that will later
adopt them.

### Coherence as a Group

Finally, utopians value their own uniqueness and coherence
as a group. Members of utopias are highly conscious of themselves as a community and of their role in history. They have a
clear sense of their own boundaries — how far their land
extends, who belongs and who does not. There may even be a
map and a list of members. Whereas people on the outside
are often only vaguely aware of their membership in social
communities, people who live in a utopian community explicitly
know that they do belong, what the community stands for,
how it is distinguished from the outside, and who else belongs.
The intentional quality of the community is important. Utopias
often have a clear legal definition as well, chartered or incorporated under the law as towns, economic organizations, educational establishments, or churches. All of this involves a strong
distinction between the inside and the outside, a distinction
recognized by the larger society as well as by members. Utopias
can establish their own membership requirements and entrance

procedures. They can develop their own criteria of status
(as in Oneida's levels of fellowship or Synanon's sole standard
of "character"), their own way of accounting age (Synanon
dates from the time people join, when they are considered
"zero years old,") or their own names for members (many
religious communities provide members with "spiritual"
names; hippie communitarians sometimes take tribal or fantasy
names, such as Bilbo or Treebeard from *Lord of the Rings*; and
fifty members of a California commune all took the name
"Lynch" after their leader). Utopians can participate in outside politics or not, as they choose — in some cases not voting,
in others casting their votes as a bloc. They can develop their
own communication channels, such as newspapers or radio
stations, rather than relying on extracommunity media. They
can act toward the outside as a unit; for example, by sending
one check to cover income taxes for all the members. In
general, they can consider that their own internal affairs are
more important, more valuable, than are the demands made on
them by the larger society. Thus, many utopias are pacifist,
like the Bruderhof, refusing to fight wars for a society of which
they do not feel a part. Their separateness and uniqueness
are paramount.

For many communities the various communal themes come
together in the one ideal of a return to the land. By carving
out a piece of land of their own and engaging in agriculture,
they fulfill a number of the impulses toward utopia. They gain
closer contact with nature and the natural order and return
to a simpler life more concerned with the fundamentals of
existence. The kinds of jobs to be done around the land often
require no special skills and provide an opportunity for everyone to work equally — even the children — rather than undermining the brotherhood with excessive specialization. The
products are visible and can be consumed by the community;
members together can truly and directly appreciate the "fruits"
of their joint labor. A number of tasks, such as the harvest,
lend themselves in particular to communal work efforts with
all members participating. The physical labor required by a land-
based way of life is vital to integrating the body and the mind.
The land also provides the community with its own means of

livelihood and direct access to its own natural resources and sustenance, reducing the community's dependence on the outside and increasing its self-sufficiency. Finally, the utopia stakes out on the land its own territory, sometimes far removed from the outside world and under its own control, which can be an important source of identity.

In general, it is important for utopians to believe that life is an expression of their ideas, that there is no separation between their values and their way of life. They object to what they view as hypocrisy on the outside. Utopian communities offer to members life's services — food and shelter, a job, education for the children, care in old age — in the context of an explicit set of shared beliefs about how people should live.

## Relation to Reality

The ideas informing the communal life-style — perfectability, order, brotherhood, merging of mind and body, experimentation, and the community's uniqueness — all represent its intentional quality, with harmony as their principal theme: harmony with nature, harmony among people, and harmony between the spirit and the flesh. Yet these notions must be recognized as idealizations, not truths. They describe the ways in which members of communes wish to conceive of communal life, rather than the realities of building a group. Some utopian ideas offer romanticized versions of social practices that may be described in quite different terms. "Mutual criticism," for example, can be viewed as "brainwashing"; brotherhood can be used to justify the sacrifice of individual needs to collective demands; and emphasis on harmony can cloak an unwillingness to deal with conflict or with the fact that individuals have discrepant desires. Other utopian values may be after-the-fact explanations for social practices that arose accidentally, from expediency alone, to fit the needs of particular individuals, or to help maintain the group. A few nineteenth century groups, such as the Harmony Society, first began to share property communally as the result of pressing economic circumstances rather than consciously to implement a set of coherent values; utopian ideals were later used to justify the practice. In fact, it could be argued that the group may at first have had every intention of returning the property to the original donors and reverting to individual ownership, and that communism was later continued simply to maintain a group whose cohesion now depended on the practice. Evidence for this view comes from the fact that a book recording the original contributions was at first kept, then later burned. Such an explanation would be more compatible with a Marxist view of social life than an idealistic one. Myths and idealizations must therefore be examined in terms of their functions for the individual and the group.

Some of the idealizations of utopians are similar to the collective myths that all groups develop under conditions of uncertainty — conditions that are heightened when people leave the established order to form their own societies. They resemble, for example, the myths that Philip Slater found developing in unstructured T-groups that had come together, like some communes, to explore intimacy and group process. These myths indicated a belief that there is a plan, a set of truths explaining and informing humankind's joint existence, if only it could be discovered; that collective life is part of an experiment controlled by mysterious, godlike figures; and that order and control of group life will lend it meaning and predictability. Myths and religious themes emerge in groups, Slater indicated, when people feel abandoned and unprotected.[24] Conversely, belief in the possibility of harmony, unity, and concord in social life provides protection, certainty, and a sense that struggle and suffering are ultimately worthwhile.

Utopian thought makes a number of assumptions that contradict other viewpoints, notably the conflict theories of Hobbes to Freud. It proposes, for example, that human relationships need not be contingent on competitive, win-or-lose assumptions, but rather that cooperation is natural and that any interpersonal tensions can be eliminated through social structural patterns or re-education. It assumes that man's internal conflicts can be resolved under the right environmental conditions, and that communities can be built in which inner motivation is congruent with outer demands — that is, what people want to do is the same as what they have to do. It assumes that people can become totally and unambivalently committed to such a community and that they can unequivocally believe what they outwardly express. Utopian thought also promises that, if one starts fresh to attain perfection, it is possible both to escape the past — societal as well as individual — and to anticipate the future, because both time periods are concentrated in an eternal now. Finally, such thought assumes that conflicts between values and practical realities need not exist; that a single, harmonious value-based way of life is practicable.

Freudian theory, in particular, stands in opposition to utopian thought. Freud himself might have viewed utopian communities not as an evolution to higher stages of human development but as a regression to more primitive ones. According to Freud, the strong group is a revival of the "primal horde," and religion is an attempt to recapture childhood dependency. Whereas Cooley proposed that a person gains full humanity only through complete identification with a primary group, Freud indicated that mature human development requires separation of egos, independence of the self from the group. Because the group is an agent of repression for the ego, in Freudian thought there is an inherent and irreconcilable conflict between the individual and society. Only weak individuals exist solely through collective impulses. In short, Freud believed that strong emotional ties, similarity of life circumstances, and absence of private property — all of which characterize the commune as well as the primal horde — produce a uniformity of individual mental acts that he deplored: "The dwindling of the conscious individual personality, the focusing of thoughts and feelings into a common direction, the predominance of the affective side of the mind and of unconscious psychical life, the tendency to the immediate carrying out of intentions as they emerge — all this corresponds to a state of regression to a primitive mental activity."[25]

If utopian theories were fully tenable, then many more viable and longer-lasting utopian communities would be found than has been the case in the United States. Only a few dozen American communes have survived more than two or three years. The experiences of the few successful ones indicate the kinds of social organization that are important to implementing a utopian dream, as well as the limitations to utopian theory inherent in these very practices. For example, interpersonal harmony is in many communities often purchased at the price of limits on personal choice and on creative dissension. Full commitment and unequivocal belief, central to the viability of a utopia, involve the individual in giving up some of his differentiated privileges and attributes, at the same time that he gains belonging and meaning. Even when potential inter- or intrapersonal conflicts are resolved in favor of the group, tensions often arise between two pulls in a community — for example, between maintaining the group as an expression of shared beliefs and operating an effective organization in servicing and providing for members, that is, between communal values and the practical realities of running a production organization. The dream of utopia must be compared with the realities of creating viable utopian communities.

*Part Two*     Lessons of the Past

*Men cannot play at communism. It is not*
*amateur work. It requires patience, submission;*
*self-sacrifice often in little matters where self-*
*sacrifice is peculiarly irksome . . .* "Bear ye one
another's burdens" *might well be written over*
*the gates of every commune.*
—Charles Nordhoff, *The Communistic Societies*
*of the United States*

## 3   Commitment: The Problem and the Theory

Experiments in communal living have always been part of the
American landscape; even the Puritans established a kind of
utopian community in the Massachusetts Bay Colony. Yet
despite the large numbers of communes begun, few have lasted
more than a handful of years or attracted large numbers of
adherents. The idealized view of communal life held by utopians
is difficult to implement, and American communes have met
with varying success. An examination of the problems and
practices of communes of the past, both successful and unsuccessful, can indicate what kinds of social organization are
important for viable communes.

Between the Revolutionary and Civil wars (approximately
1780–1860), almost a hundred known utopian communities
were founded, with the peak of activity and membership from
1840–1860. Some of these groups lasted well over one hundred
years (the Shakers), while others dissolved in less than a year
(Yellow Springs in Ohio). The communes established between
1780 and 1860 provide an ideal population in which to com-
pare successful and unsuccessful groups.

Communes in the Nineteenth Century

The United States in the first half of the nineteenth century
provided fertile soil for utopian aspirations. Social protest
movements and experiments of all kinds flourished. A series
of enthusiastic revivals in many locations kindled desires for
renewal that were easily channeled into communal move-

ments.[1] The frontier provided the opportunity to seek a new
way of life. Immigrant groups found that by organizing utopian
communities, they could maintain their distinctive culture
even in the New World. Many of these groups, including
Harmony, Zoar, and Amana, represented pietest, separatist
churches in Europe, for whom utopian organization was a
logical outgrowth of their values of primitive Christianity.
Some of these groups, in fact, had maintained variants of
utopian communities even before emigrating.

Political protest in this period was also funneled into attempts
at utopia. As men were becoming conscious of economic and
social inequities, the idea occurred naturally to establish small-
scale social systems to remedy these ills of the larger society.
Frances Wright, for example, created Nashoba for emancipated
slaves. The United States had been founded on the basis of
certain ideals, and in order to create a "more perfect union," its
citizens often imported socialist theories from Europe, such
as those of Owen and Fourier. The propensity for forming
voluntary associations noted by de Tocqueville provided a
medium for the rational planning of utopian communities, so
that they did not require the particular conjunction of events
involved in the spontaneous eruption of social movement.[2]
During the 1840s, in fact, a national organization existed for
the purpose of establishing utopian communities on the Fourier
model, with its headquarters for a time at Brook Farm. Forty
such groups were created.

This period also offered an essentially secular and optimistic
culture. The feeling prevailed that the perfect society could
be founded on earth and within the context of an established
political order. Even among religious groups the notion held
that God's kingdom was possible here and now. Among eco-
nomically oriented reformers, such as Josiah Warren, who
founded a commune called Utopia with a new monetary
system, it was felt that economic improvements did not require
major political upheaval. Since utopian communities had
already been founded in America and the remnants of a colonial
tradition of cooperative societies existed, religious and economic
idealists readily converged on the communal order as a better
way of life — if not for all of society, then at least for them-

selves. In one way or another, utopian communities of the 1800s participated in all major social movements of their time: revivalism, temperance, women's rights, free love, nonresistance, anarchism, and socialism of the Owenist, Fourierist, Icarian, and even Marxist varieties.[3]

Finally, the utopian communities of 1780–1860 were established under a fairly similar set of external social conditions or environment, for the U.S. at this time had yet to face the rapid social change of later decades. There was still enough wilderness for it to be possible to find an isolated location. Many communes moved to the outposts of civilization, which both minimized their contact with the outside and supported their subsistence economies. Thus, during the first period of the communities' existence, external problems were scant, and considerations of organizing a viable internal communal order were paramount.

Ninety-one distinct communal ventures from this period have left historical records. While most involved only a single commune, others consisted of many locations; the Shakers at one time had twenty-two villages. The communes of 1780–1860 similarly varied widely in longevity. Less than a dozen of the ninety-one known groups lasted more than sixteen years; for the majority, the average life-span was less than four years. Such well-known communes as New Harmony and Brook Farm were among the short-lived groups. New Harmony faced continual crises from its inception and after two years dissolved in disaster; Brook Farm ended after six years despite support from leading intellectuals of the time. Building viable utopian communities has proven to be difficult: translating the utopian dream into reality is fraught with issues that in time may even distort the original vision.

Yet the exceptions — those utopian communities that established the social basis for a long existence — are dramatic and noteworthy; much can be learned from them about the forms of social organization that make communes a living, viable, and practical arrangement. The Shakers, for example, formed their first community in 1787 and flourished for over a hundred years, at one time encompassing twenty-two villages and thousands of members; today a few believers still maintain the remnants of Shaker communities in remote parts of New England. The Amana community, or the Society of True Inspiration, maintained seven communal villages in Iowa for ninety years, and when it divided in 1933 into a church group and an industrial group, it split more than $33,000,000 worth of assets among its members. The Oneida Community flourished as a commune for over thirty-three years.

The Shakers, Amana, and Oneida, along with Harmony (1804–1904), Zoar (1817–1898), and Jerusalem (1788–1821), are among nine "successful" nineteenth century utopian communities, lasting thirty-three years or more. They can be contrasted with twenty-one "unsuccessful" groups lasting less than sixteen years, including Brook Farm, New Harmony, and other Owenite and Fourierite ventures.[4] The differences between the success of these thirty groups lie in how stongly they built commitment.

## The Problem

The primary issue with which a utopian community must cope in order to have the strength and solidarity to endure is its human organization: how people arrange to do the work that the community needs to survive as a group, and how the group in turn manages to satisfy and involve its members over a long period of time. The idealized version of communal life must be meshed with the reality of the work to be done in a community, involving difficult problems of social organization. In utopia, for instance, who takes out the garbage?

The organizational problems with which utopian communities must grapple break down into several categories:

How to get the work done, but without coercion

How to ensure that decisions are made, but to everyone's satisfaction

How to build close, fulfilling relationships, but without exclusiveness

How to choose and socialize new members

How to include a degree of autonomy, individual uniqueness, and even deviance

How to ensure agreement and shared perception around community functioning and values

These issues can be summarized as one of commitment; that is, they reflect how members become committed to the community's work, to its values, and to each other, and how much of their former independence they are willing to suspend in the interests of the group. Committed members work hard, participate actively, derive love and affection from the communal group, and believe strongly in what the group stands for.

For communes, the problem of commitment is crucial. Since the community represents an attempt to establish an ideal social order within the larger society, it must vie with the outside for the members' loyalties. It must ensure high member involvement despite external competition without sacrificing its distinctiveness or ideals. It must often contravene the earlier socialization of its members in securing obedience to new demands. It must calm internal dissension in order to present a united front to the world. The problem of securing total and complete commitment is central.

Because communes consciously separate from the established order, their needs for the concentration of members' loyalty and devotion are stronger than are those of groups operating with the support of society and leaving members free to participate in the larger system. The commitment problems of utopian communities resemble those of secret societies, as described by Georg Simmel: "The secret society claims the whole individual to a greater extent, connects its members in more of their totality, and mutually obligates them more closely than does an open society of identical content."[5] The essence of such a community is in strong connections and mutual obligations. Communal life depends on a continual flow of energy and support among members, on their depth of shared relationships, and on their continued attachment to each other and to the joint endeavor.

### Definitions

For communal relations to be maintained, what the person is willing to give to the group, behaviorally and emotionally, and what it in turn expects of him, must be coordinated and mutually reinforcing. This reciprocal relationship, in which both what is given to the group and what is received from it are seen by the person as expressing his true nature and as supporting his concept of self, is the core of commitment to a community. A person is committed to a group or to a relationship when he himself is fully invested in it, so that the maintenance of his own internal being requires behavior that supports the social order. A committed person is loyal and involved; he has a sense of belonging, a feeling that the group is an extension of himself and he is an extension of the group. Through commitment, person and group are inextricably linked.

Commitment arises as a consideration at the intersection between the organizational requisites of groups and the personal orientations and preferences of their members. On the one hand, social systems must organize to meet their systemic "needs"; on the other hand, people must orient themselves positively and negatively, emotionally and intellectually, to situations. While the system is making specific demands for participation, group relatedness, and control, the people in it are investing more or less of themselves, are deciding to stay or to leave, are concentrating varying degrees of their emotional lives in the group, and are fervently obeying or finding ways to sabotage basic principles and rules of the system. For the group to get what it needs for existence and growth at the same time that people become positively involved requires organizational solutions that are simultaneously mechanisms to ensure commitment by affecting people's orientations to the group.

Commitment thus refers to the willingness of people to do what will help maintain the group because it provides what they need. In sociological terms, commitment means the attachment of the self to the requirements of social relations that are seen as self-expressive.[6] Commitment links self-interest to social requirements. A person is committed to a relationship or to a group to the extent that he sees it as expressing or fulfilling some fundamental part of himself; he is committed to the degree that he perceives no conflict between its requirements and his own needs; he is committed to the degree that he can no longer meet his needs elsewhere. When a person is committed, what he wants to do (through internal feeling) is the same as what he has to do (according to external demands), and thus he gives to the group what it needs to maintain itself at the same time that he gets what he needs to nourish his own sense of self. To a great extent, therefore, commitment is not only important for the survival of a community, but also is part of the essence of community. It forms the connection between self-interest and group interest. It is that identification of the self with a group which Charles Horton Cooley considered essential for self-realization.

To determine the links between person and system that forge the bonds of commitment, one must first distinguish the three major aspects of a social system that involve commitment: retention of members, group cohesiveness, and social control.[7] Retention refers to people's willingness to stay in the system, to continue to staff it and carry out their roles. Group cohesiveness denotes the ability of people to "stick together," to develop the mutual attraction and collective strength to withstand threats to the group's existence. And social control involves the readiness of people to obey the demands of the system, to conform to its values and beliefs and take seriously its dictates.

Continuance, cohesion, and control are three analytically distinct problems, with potentially independent solutions. A person may be committed to continuing his membership but be continually deviant within the group, disloyal and disobedient — that is, *un*committed to its control and unwilling to carry out the norms and values that represent system policy. A rebellious child may reject parental control but be unwilling or unable to withdraw from the family system; he may subvert the values of the system yet be committed to remain within it. Furthermore, a person may be highly attracted to a group within a social system but be uncommitted to continued participation in the system because of other circumstances. An office worker, for example, may take a better job even though his best friends work in his former office. The inmate of a prison may form close ties with fellow prisoners and even with guards, yet certainly wish to leave the system at the earliest opportunity. In specific social systems, one or another of these commitment problems may be of paramount importance. A business organization may concentrate on solving problems of continuance rather than cohesion; a T-group or encounter

group may be concerned solely about cohesion; a religious
organization may stress control. In other cases the three may
be causally related, with solutions to all three problems mutually
reinforcing and multiply determined. In a utopian community,
for instance, which emphasizes all three aspects of commitment,
the more the members are attracted to one another, the more
they also wish to continue their membership, and the more
they are able to support wholeheartedly its values. Despite this
possible overlap, however, for purposes of understanding the
roots of commitment, continuance, cohesion, and control
must be separated.

At the same time, a person orients himself to a social system
instrumentally, affectively, and morally. That is, he orients
himself with respect to the rewards and costs that are involved
in participating in the system, with respect to his emotional
attachment to the people in the system, and with respect to the
moral compellingness of the norms and beliefs of the system.
In the language of social action theory, he cognizes, cathects,
and evaluates.[8] Cognitive orientations discriminate among
objects, describing their possibilities for gratification or deprivation, and distinguishing their location and characteristics.
Cathectic orientations represent an emotional state with respect
to objects, the kind and amount of feeling they generate.
Evaluative orientations refer to standards of judgment: good
or bad, right or wrong. As a person relates to the world around
him, he gives each element a "rating" on these three dimensions, and he chooses to behave toward it in accordance with
his rating, the degree of its positive or negative value for him.

People orient themselves to social systems in the same way,
and the value of a system in each of the three dimensions
defines a person's behavior toward it. The system can organize
in such a way as to ensure its positive value for the person
around each orientation, and if it does, it gains commitment
in the three areas that are essential to maintain the system.
Each of the personal orientations has the potential to support
one particular concern of the social system. Positive cognition
can support continuance, positive cathexis can support group
cohesion, and positive evaluation can support social control.

Commitment to continued participation in a system involves

primarily a person's cognitive or instrumental orientations. When profits and costs are considered, participants find that the cost of leaving the system would be greater than the cost of remaining; "profit," in a net psychic sense, compels continued participation. In a more general sense, this kind of commitment can be conceptualized as commitment to a social system role. It may be called instrumental commitment. Commitment to relationships, to group solidarity, involves primarily a person's cathectic orientations; ties of emotion bind members to each other and to the community they form, and gratifications stem from involvement with all members of the group. Solidarity should be high; infighting and jealousy low. A cohesive group has strong emotional bonds and can withstand threats to its existence; members "stick together." This quality may be called affective commitment. Commitment to uphold norms, obey the authority of the group, and support its values, involves primarily a person's evaluative orientations. When demands made by the system are evaluated as right, moral, just, or expressing one's own values, obedience to these demands becomes a normative necessity, and sanctioning by the system is regarded as appropriate.[9] This quality is here designated moral commitment. In some respects, commitment to norms and values resembles the concept of a superego, which binds the evaluative components of the self to the norms of a system through an internalized authority.

Each of the three kinds of commitment has different consequences for the system and for the individual. Ignoring for the moment all the other diverse sources of influence on group life, groups in which people have formed instrumental commitments should manage to hold their members. Groups in which people have formed affective commitments should report more mutual attraction and interpersonal satisfaction and should be able to withstand threats to their existence. Groups in which members have formed moral commitments should have less deviance, challenge to authority, or ideological controversy. Groups with all three kinds of commitment, that is, with total commitment, should be more successful in their maintenance than those without it.

At the same time, there are consequences for the person in

making these commitments. If the group is such that a person feels he can make an instrumental commitment, he becomes invested in it and finds his membership rewarding. If the group is such that he can make an affective commitment, he gains strong social ties, relatedness, and a sense of belonging. If the group is such that he can make a moral commitment, he gains purpose, direction, and meaning, a sense that his acts stem from essential values. To some extent, a person's identity is composed of his commitments.

### Commitment-Building Processes

A group has a number of ways in which to organize so as to promote and sustain the three kinds of commitment. For each commitment, it needs to set in motion processes that reduce the value of other possible commitments and increase the value of commitment to the communal group — that is, processes both detaching the person from other options and attaching him to the community. The person must give up something as well as get something in order to be committed to a community; communes, like all other social systems, have their costs of membership. The person must invest himself in the community rather than elsewhere and commit his resources and energy there, removing them from wherever else they may be invested, or from whatever alternatives exist for commitment. Commitment thus involves choice — discrimination and selection of possible courses of action. It rests on a person's awareness of excluded options, on the knowledge of the virtues of his choice over others. A person becomes increasingly committed both as more of his own internal satisfaction becomes dependent on the group, and as his chance to make other choices or pursue other options declines. This is commitment in Howard Becker's sense.[10] A course of action may involve more of a person's resources, reputation, or choices than he consciously chose to commit, with the result that the line of action simultaneously cuts him off from the chance to commit himself elsewhere. This process is similar, according to Becker, to the making of side bets, gambling on the fact that each step toward complete commitment will pay off. If the commitment is not sustained, and the line of action is not continued, the person then loses more than his original investment. Side bets, therefore, deriving from the fact that any choice may reduce the chances of ever taking up excluded choices, help to bring about commitment. These processes of giving up and getting make the group a clearly focused object for commitment. The clearer and more defined a group becomes to a person, the easier it is for him to concentrate his commitment there. This process contains the first principles of a "gestalt sociology": to develop maximum commitment in its members, a group must form a unity or a whole, coherent and sharply differentiated from its environment – a figure clearly distinguished from the ground, whether the ground is the outside society or excluded options for behavior. Commitment to social systems, concentrating the psychic energy in a group, may operate according to the same gestalt principles as object perception. According to these principles, the issue of commitment would occur primarily around the boundaries of a group. The group builds commitment to the extent that it clearly cuts off other possible objects of commitment, becomes an integrated unity tying together all aspects of life within its borders, develops its own uniqueness and specialness, and becomes capable, by itself, of continuing the person's gratification. The strength of commitment, then, depends on the extent to which groups institute processes that increase the unity, coherence, and possible gratification of the group itself, at the same time that they reduce the value of other possibilities. The six commitment-building processes proposed do just that.

Commitment to continued participation involves securing a person's positive instrumental orientations, inducing the individual to cognize participation in the organization as profitable when considered in terms of rewards and costs. Cognitive orientations are those that rationally determine the positive or negative valences of relationships, perceiving their worth in energy and resources. In a purely cognitive judgment, no notion of emotional gratification (cathexis) or of morality (evaluation) is attached to the group. For positive cognition to be acquired by a community, the system must organize so that participation is viewed as rewarding. The individual who makes

an instrumental commitment finds that what is profitable to
him is bound up with his position in the organization and is
contingent on his participating in the system; he commits himself to a role. For the person there is a "profit" associated with
continued participation and a "cost" connected with leaving.
Thus, sacrifice (detaching) and investment (attaching) are among
the components of instrumental commitments. Sacrifice involves the giving up of something considered valuable or
pleasurable in order to belong to the organization; it stresses
the importance of the role of member to the individual. Sacrifice
means that membership becomes more costly and is therefore
not lightly regarded nor likely to be given up easily. Investment
is a process whereby the individual gains a stake in the group,
commits current and future profits to it, so that he must
continue to participate if he is going to realize those profits.
Investment generally involves the giving up of control over some
of the person's resources to the community.

Community is based in part on the desire for strong relations
within a collectivity, for intense emotional feeling among all
members, for brotherhood and sharing. Utopia is the place
where a person's fundamental emotional needs can be expressed
and met through the communal group. The community seeks
to become a family in itself, replacing or subsuming all other
family loyalties. It is this kind of relating, involving commitment to group cohesion, that enables the community to
withstand threats to its existence, both as pressure from the
outside and as tension and dissent from inside.

Commitment to group cohesion and solidarity requires the
attachment of a person's entire fund of emotion and affectivity
to the group; emotional gratification stems from participation
in and identification with a collective whole. Emotional commitment becomes commitment to a set of social relationships.
The individual commits himself to the group as his primary
set of relations; his loyalty and allegiance are offered to all the
members of the group, who together comprise a community.
The group thus has tight social bonds cementing it together.
In cases where strong ingroup loyalty is present, a community
can stick together even though it is forcibly removed from
its home, loses its crop, or is threatened with a lawsuit. Such

intense family-like involvement also makes members more willing to work out whatever conflicts and tensions may arise among them. This kind of commitment is aided by renunciation (a detaching process) and communion (an attaching process). Renunciation involves giving up competing relationships outside the communal group and individualistic, exclusive attachments within. Whatever fund of emotion the individuals possess becomes concentrated in the group itself, glueing all members together, creating a cohesive unit. It is to this unit alone that members look for emotional satisfaction and to which they give their loyalty and commitment. Communion involves bringing members into meaningful contact with the collective whole, so that they experience the fact of oneness with the group and develop a "we-feeling."

The search for community is also a quest for direction and purpose in a collective anchoring of the individual life. Investment of self in a community, acceptance of its authority and willingness to support its values, is dependent in part on the extent to which group life can offer identity, personal meaning, and the opportunity to grow in terms of standards and guiding principles that the member feels are expressive of his own inner being. Commitment to community norms and values, or moral commitment, involves securing a person's positive evaluative orientations, redefining his sense of values and priorities so that he considers the system's demands right and just in terms of his self-identity and supporting the group's authority becomes a moral necessity. The person making a moral commitment to his community should see himself as carrying out the dictates of a higher system, which orders and gives meaning to his life. He internalizes community standards and values and accepts its control, because it provides him with something transcendent. This commitment requires, first, that the person reformulate and re-evaluate his identity in terms of meeting the ideals set by the community. For this to occur, the group must first provide ways for an individual to reassess his previous life, to undo those parts of himself he wishes to change, and to perceive that identity and meaning for him lie not in an individualistic, private existence but in acceptance of the stronger influence of the utopian group.

At the same time, the person must experience the greater power and meaning represented by the community, so that he will attach his sense of identity and worth to carrying out its demands and requirements. Thus, mortification (a detaching process) and transcendence (an attaching process) promote evaluative, moral commitments. Mortification involves the submission of private states to social control, the exchanging of a former identity for one defined and formulated by the community. Transcendence is a process whereby an individual attaches his decision-making prerogative to a power greater than himself, surrendering to the higher meaning contained by the group and submitting to something beyond himself. Mortification opens the person to new directions and new growth; transcendence defines those directions. Mortification causes the person to "lose himself"; transcendence permits him to find himself anew in something larger and greater.

Six processes are thus available to build commitment to communal groups. To the extent that groups develop concrete organizational strategies around these processes — commitment mechanisms — they should generate a stronger commitment than can those without such strategies. The number and kind of commitment mechanisms instituted should contribute to a community's success — its ability to endure and continue to satisfy its members.

*The healthy mixture of manual and intellectual labor, the kindly and unaffected social relations, the absence of everything like assumption or servility, the amusements, the discussions, the ideal and poetical atmosphere which gave a charm to life, all these combined to create a picture towards which the mind turns back as to something distant and beautiful, and not elsewhere met with amid the routine of this world.*

—Charles Dana, in Lindsay Swift, *Brook Farm*

# 4  Live in Love and Union: Commitment Mechanisms in Nineteenth Century Communes

In long-lived communes of the nineteenth century, group life was organized in such a way as to support the six commitment-building processes. The nine successful groups tended to have, at some time in their histories, a large number of concrete social practices that helped generate and sustain the commitment of their members. They survived crises, persecution, debt, and internal dissension that proved the undoing of unsuccessful groups. The twenty-one unsuccessful communes, by contrast, tended to have fewer such commitment mechanisms and in weakened form.

Commitment mechanisms are specific ways of ordering and defining the existence of a group. Every aspect of group life has implications for commitment, including property, work, boundaries, recruitment, intimate relationships, group contact, leadership, and ideology. These pieces of social organization can be arranged so as to promote collective unity, provide a sense of belonging and meaning, or they can have no value for commitment. The strength of a group and the commitment of its members will be a function of the specific ways the group is put together. Abstract ideals of brotherhood and harmony, of love and union, must be translated into concrete social practices.

For example, among the successful nineteenth-century communes, much more than the unsuccessful ones, their abstinence and austerity contributed to sacrifice. Their financial arrangements contributed to investment. Their insulating boundaries and weakening of exclusive relationships in couples and families supported renunciation. The social backgrounds of their members, their property and work arrangements, and the amount and nature of their contact as a group supported communion. Their practices of confession and criticism, their ways of handling deviance and according status, contributed to mortification. Their ideology and leadership patterns contributed to transcendence. An examination of these and other social arrangements in detail indicates the differences between the strength of the nine successful groups and, in comparison, the vulnerability of the twenty-one unsuccessful communities.

Sacrifice

The process of sacrifice asks members to give up something as a price of membership. Once members have agreed to make the "sacrifices," their motivation to remain participants increases. Membership becomes more valuable and meaningful. Regardless of how the group induces the original concessions or manages to recruit people willing to make them, the fact is that those groups exacting sacrifices survive longer because sacrifice is functional for their maintenance. Sacrifice operates on the basis of a simple principle from cognitive consistency theories: the more it "costs" a person to do something, the more "valuable" he will consider it, in order to justify the psychic "expense" and remain internally consistent. It has been demonstrated in a laboratory setting, for example, that when people work for very small rewards, they must justify their doing so on the basis of belief or commitment, and they come to believe strongly in what they are doing.[1] To continue to pursue their course thus justifies the sacrifice involved. In many religions, sacrifice has been conceptualized as an act of consecration, bringing one closer to and making one more worthy of the deity. A vow of poverty, for example, may aid commitment. In the eyes of the group and in the mind of the individual, sacrifice for a cause makes it sacred and inviolable. It also represents a gesture of trust in the group, indicating how important membership is. Martin Buber described the role of sacrifice in community: "Community is the inner disposition or constitution of a life in common, which knows and embraces in itself hard 'calculation,' adverse 'chance,' the sudden access of 'anxiety.' It is community of tribulation and only because of that community of spirit; community of toil and only because of that community of salvation."[2]

*Abstinence.* One kind of sacrifice that successful nineteenth-century communities often involved was abstinence from alcohol, tobacco, coffee, tea, rich foods, or meat. The parallel today is the insistence in many communities that members give up drugs in order to belong. Some of the earlier forms of abstinence were justified either on the basis of necessity or under a variety of ideological guises, but it was often clear to the community that sacrifice aided commitment. In Oneida, for example, an austere diet was "at first a necessity," but "later such limitations remained as an adjunct to spiritual improvement."[3] The most common form of oral abstinence was the prohibition of alcohol, and since many communities came under the influence of the nineteenth-century temperance movement, there was almost as high a proportion of unsuccessful as successful groups that banned alcohol. The Shakers, for example, while prohibiting certain other indulgences, permitted some alcoholic consumption during their early years and operated village distilleries until they were influenced by the temperance movement; they then confined the use of alcohol to medicinal needs.[4]

Sexual abstinence is another important sacrifice mechanism, which was required at times by many more successful than unsuccessful communities. Most successful communities, including Oneida, which later adopted a form of group marriage, were celibate for at least part of their history, in contrast to the fact that twenty of the twenty-one unsuccessful utopias examined had no such practice for any time. In addition, practically all of the successful groups encouraged or preferred celibacy even though permitting marriage at times, and for some of them celibate members acquired a more spiritual status in the community's eyes or received approbation, while married members lost status, at least for a time. In the Amana community, newly married couples were reduced to the lowest rank at the "Versammlung" or church gathering, being required to sit in the front of the assembly. With the birth of each child in the family, the parents suffered the same spiritual reduction and had to earn back their status by demonstrating deeper piety. Celibacy not only indicated the lengths to which members were willing to go to suspend their own physical indulgences in the interest of building community, but it also freed for service to the group an amount of energy that would otherwise have been committed elsewhere. Communities often ban sexual relations at times in their history when it is especially important that energy and attention be devoted to group tasks. The fact of having undergone the deprivation can enhance the value of the enterprise. Harmony's adoption of celibacy in 1807 grew out of a desire for self-discipline by the young, a "powerful revival of earnestness": "Strangely enough, the younger members took the lead in this direction. The lack of food and the miseries and hardships endured during their first two years may have been a predisposing cause."[5]

Many communities involved other kinds of abstinence. The Shakers, Oneida, Amana, Zoar, and Snowhill, of the successful communities, and Preparation, of the unsuccessful ones, forbade personal adornment, including jewelry, attractive clothing, or personal luxuries. Amana in addition prohibited photographs. Zoar forbade dancing and novels. The Shakers did not permit instrumental music, certain books, or pictures (the official rationale for the last prohibition being that they gathered dust). Behind many of these practices was a sense that personal vanity is detrimental to the community. A visitor to Amana in 1916, for example, learned from George Heinneman, leader at the time, that schoolgirls were not permitted to wear hair-ribbons; the men had no mustaches, women wore sunbonnets instead of hats; there was no modern dancing, such as the waltz or the tango, no card-playing, and no football, baseball, or other competitive sports. All these things were considered "worldly." As he was leaving, he asked his informant if he could take his picture. Heinneman replied: "No. Now you ask me to do something which is worldly. It is not wrong to you, but to me it is. It is not the spirit of Amana."[6]

*Austerity.* An austere life style, as opposed to one of relative

comfort or luxury, also serves as a sacrifice mechanism. The
vow of poverty in many religious orders functions in this way.
For most of the nineteenth-century American utopian communities, whether of long or short duration, a certain amount
of austerity, especially in their early years, was a fact of life, and
there were many things members had to do without simply
from necessity. Hard work and nonindulgence were called for
merely by the rigors of everyday existence, which often
included severe winters, grave illnesses, and food shortages. Such
joint sacrifice kept commitment strong, whereas prosperity
and affluence contributed to a lowering of commitment.
Members' struggles symbolized the importance of the shared
endeavor, for the venture was of more consequence to them
than material comfort. Some of today's communes seek a similar
feeling when they deliberately return to a struggling, subsistence
level of existence in the midst of the affluent society.

It was difficult to measure the relative austerity of successful
versus unsuccessful communities directly, but one useful
indicator was whether the community had to build its own
buildings. Not only do the struggles and austerity involved foster
commitment, but at the end of the labors the community has
physical symbols of its communal effort, structures invested
with all that the members have given up to make them possible.
All of the successful nineteenth-century utopias and most of
the unsuccessful ones built their communities from scratch, like
the Israeli kibbutzim. In Harmony alone, a descendant cited
as evidence for the existence of brotherly love and self-denial
the fact that in less than twenty-five years, without modern
technology, the commune had cleared three forests, built three
villages, and laid out and developed the town of Beaver Falls,
Pennsylvania.[7] Some of the unsuccessful groups, however,
did not engage in community-building in this literal sense.
Robert Owen purchased a fully developed community site for
New Harmony in Indiana from the Harmony Society, which
had done the building for its own use before moving back to
Pennsylvania. New Harmony, involving no shared struggle, was
a disaster.

The relationship between sacrifice and commitment was well
summed up by a nineteenth century Shaker: "Thus in the
vigor of my youth, with the bright glories of the world before

me, I was enabled to sacrifice them with all their prospects and pleasures, that I might live a pure and holy life, according to the will of God. And I can truly say, I have never looked back, with a desire to them, from that day to this: and I know that I am already rewarded a thousand fold for all I have sacrificed and suffered, which is not worthy to be named."[8] The fact that instances of sacrifice were found more often in successful than in unsuccessful communities is shown in Table 1.

Investment

The process of investment provides the individual with a stake in the fate of the community. He commits his "profit" to the group, so that leaving it would be costly. Investment can be a simple economic process involving tangible resources, or it can involve intangibles like time and energy. If a group desires a set of committed members, it should require them to devote their time and energy to the system. Utopian communities thus should not have nonresident members, who can share in

Table 1. Proportion of successful and unsuccessful nineteenth-century communes having sacrifice mechanisms at any time in their history.

| Sacrifice Mechanism | Successful Communities | | Unsuccessful Communities | |
|---|---|---|---|---|
| | n/N* | % | n/N* | % |
| *Abstinence* | | | | |
| Oral abstinence | 7/9 | 78 | 11/20 | 55 |
| Celibacy | 9/9 | 100 | 2/21 | 9 |
| Other abstinence | 5/7 | 71 | 4/14 | 28 |
| *Austerity* | | | | |
| Built own buildings | 9/9 | 100 | 18/21 | 83 |

*N represents the number of communities for which the presence or absence of the mechanism was ascertainable; n represents the number in which the mechanism was present.

organizational benefits without active participation; active involvement of time and energy should be a requirement in order to gain anything at all from belonging to the system. One is either "in" or "out." In fact, almost all of the successful nineteenth-century communities did not permit nonresident members, whereas more than half of the unsuccessful groups had nonresident members.[9]

Through investment, individuals are integrated with the system, since their time and resources have become part of its economy. They have, in effect, purchased a share in the proceeds of the community and now hold a stake in its continued good operation. Investment is made tangible by such requirements as financial donations by new members, assignment of recruits' property to the community, and transferral of any money or property received while in the community. Almost all of the successful groups had some such requirement, while more than half of the unsuccessful ones did not. And of those unsuccessful communities that did not require or encourage the signing over of property, some required no financial investment in the community at all, even such a minimal one as buying shares of stock in the organization.

*Irreversibility.* Commitment to continued participation in the community was further promoted in successful groups by emphasizing the irreversibility of investment. Some communities kept no records of a member's original investment of property, goods, or capital. In Harmony, after an initial period of record-keeping, George Rapp, the leader, to whose name members' property had been assigned, burned the book into which contributions had been entered. Successful communities also tended not to reimburse seceders or defectors either for their years of service and labor in the community or for their contributions of property or capital; a person had to continue his membership in order to reap his reward. This was both the official policy of most of the successful groups and their standard practice. In contrast, at least two of the unsuccessful communities, Hopedale and Communia, reimbursed defectors for their service to the community in every ascertainable instance. The degree to which investment mechanisms of these kinds were found more often in successful than in unsuccessful nineteenth-century communities is indicated in Table 2.

Table 2. Proportion of successful and unsuccessful nineteenth-century communes having investment mechanisms at any time in their history.

| Investment mechanism | Successful Communities | | Unsuccessful Communities | |
|---|---|---|---|---|
| | n/N* | % | n/N* | % |
| *Physical participation* | | | | |
| Nonresident members prohibited | 6/7 | 86 | 7/17 | 41 |
| *Financial investment* | | | | |
| Financial contribution for admission | 4/9 | 44 | 9/20 | 45 |
| Property signed over at admission | 9/9 | 100 | 9/20 | 45 |
| Group-assigned property received while member | 4/7 | 57 | 6/14 | 43 |
| *Irreversibility of investment* | | | | |
| No records of contributions | 4/8 | 50 | 4/14 | 28 |
| Defectors not reimbursed for property — official policy | 3/7 | 43 | 5/12 | 42 |
| Defectors not reimbursed for property — in practice | 2/6 | 33 | 0/6 | 0 |
| Defectors not reimbursed for labor — official policy | 6/7 | 86 | 7/13 | 54 |
| Defectors not reimbursed for labor — in practice | 6/7 | 86 | 3/9 | 33 |

*N represents the number of communities for which the presence or absence of the mechanism was ascertainable; n represents the number in which the mechanism was present.

## Renunciation

Renunciation involves the relinquishing of relationships that are potentially disruptive to group cohesion, thereby heightening the relationship of individual to group. Seeking renunciation, a community discourages relationships both outside the group and with internal subunits, in order to provide maximum strength to the entire system. Loyalties that might conflict with members' group obligations and block potential satisfactions are regulated by the community. According to Egon Bittner, it is functional for radical groups to require in general that all traditional extragroup ties be suspended. Lewis Coser has made a similar point with respect to sex.[10] Structural arrangements which ensure that the individual will give up relationships outside the group and with any unit less than all members of the total group concentrate not only his loyalties and allegiances but also his emotional attachments and gratifications on the whole group. His potential for satisfaction within the group increases as his options for relationships elsewhere are decreased, and he must make his peace with the group because he has, in fact, no place else to turn. Renunciation may center around relationships in three categories: with the outside world, within the couple, and with the family. Communities of all sorts regulate or take a stand on these relationships in some way.

*The Outside World.* The outside society, a changing, turbulent, seductive place, poses a particular threat to the existence of utopian communities, so that most successful communities of the past developed sets of insulating boundaries — rules and structural arrangements that minimized contact with the outside. They placed clear-cut barriers and boundaries between the member and the outside, by emphasizing differences, for example, and reduced the influence of the outside when contact became necessary. Ralph Turner and Lewis Killian proposed one additional function of insulation: to keep members away from contact with the outside's adverse evaluation of the movement.[11]

Geographical isolation is one effective means of insulation, forming part of what Arthur Stinchcombe calls the "ecological segregation of group life."[12] Four indicators of geographical isolation for the nineteenth-century American utopias were used: the community was at least five miles away from any neighbors or neighboring towns; it was not located on a waterway; it was not situated on a railroad; and few people resided in the community or in the immediate community area who were not members. These four measures were true of all unsuccessful as well as successful nineteenth century utopias studied; a certain amount of geographical isolation seems to have been a fact of life for nineteenth century groups.

"Institutional completeness," as it was labeled by Stinchcombe, also provided a measure of insulation from the outside. Groups that are institutionally complete contain within themselves the necessary organization for dealing with all aspects of members' lives, obviating the need to leave the group for any organizational services. Utopian communities of the past tended almost by definition to be institutionally complete, seeking generally to organize for residential, familial, political, economic, religious, and cultural needs. Nevertheless there are a variety of smaller human necessities that members may have to go outside the group to satisfy. Successful nineteenth-century communities tended to be, on the whole, more institutionally complete than unsuccessful ones, even to the extent of providing their own medical services.

The successful community's emphasis was governed partly by its concept of the outside. A psychic boundary was laid down in terminology that clearly distinguished the outside from the community, conceptualizing the community positively and the outside negatively. This language not only reified the boundaries but also provided members with a distinctive new identity as community members. Hence, the Shakers were called the United Society of Believers, and the Oneidans were known as the Saints. Three of the successful groups had a special name for the outside, and another consistently referred to it as "the outside." In contrast, the unsuccessful communities failed to make this distinction. There was a slight tendency for more of the successful than the unsuccessful groups to conceptualize the outside negatively. The attitude of the Shakers, for example, was the most negative, maintaining that the outside was decidedly evil and wicked. A basic tenet of Shaker ideology emphasized separation from the world and from "all worldly usages, manners, customs, loves and affections which might interpose between the individual citizen of the heavenly kingdom and his duties and privileges therein."[13] Successful groups also tended not to read outside newspapers and not to celebrate national, patriotic holidays; they tried to cut themselves off as much as possible.

A distinctive language and distinctive styles of dress can also help create insulating boundaries. More successful than unsuccessful communities tended to employ these mechanisms, whether speaking a language other than English, using slang, jargon, or esoteric terminology not in common use outside, or adopting an unusual uniform. The women of Oneida, for example, disdained the fashions of the time in favor of short skirts, pantalettes, and short hair. Shakers wore drab gray and black garments. Many of the successful groups were originally composed of German immigrants and spoke German within the community.

*controlled borders*

Successful communities also controlled movements across their boundaries, either when members went out or when outsiders entered, in such a way that they did not threaten the group's insulation or enable attachments outside the group. Ordinary members, as distinguished from leaders, of all the successful groups tended to leave the community less often than yearly; whereas ordinary members of all unsuccessful communities for which these data were ascertainable tended to leave monthly, weekly, or daily. Further, Shakers, Amanites, Harmonists, and Oneidans — members of successful groups — generally did not leave the community without special permission. In the early days of the Harmony Society, members did not leave without consultation with their leaders, and then only for things unavailable in the community, such as appointments with the dentist. The night watchman met each train and knew who was to arrive. Unsuccessful communities tended not to institute such crossboundary controls. Brook Farmers, for instance, left the community so often that they were virtually commuters to Boston. Not only were New Harmonists allowed to leave at any time, but the community supplied them with funds for travel. In some successful communes, however, even when members crossed the boundary for legitimate reasons, such as the trap salesmen sent out by Oneida, strict controls were maintained. In Oneida special criticism and confession sessions took place both on leaving and on returning.

An equally important area in which controls were exercised was the presence of outsiders or nonmembers in the community. One kind of mechanism controlling this situation was the establishment of norms or regulations covering members' interaction with visitors, restricting it in some way or informing members how to behave with visitors. Three of the successful communities — Amana, Oneida, and the Shakers — had such rules, but of the unsuccessful, only Nashoba did. In Oneida the problem of renouncing the world was complicated by the large number of outsiders visiting the community, so that various reinforcing mechanisms had to be instituted. Thus, after the daily visitors had left, those members most exposed to contact with them were required to submit to mutual criticism, so as to be "freed from contamination by worldly influences."[14] Further, the whole group joined together for a ritualistic scrubbing "bee," to "purify" the community. The Shakers had similar practices. For example, if a "world's person" offered his hand, it was to be shaken with civility, but if the person was of the opposite sex, the Shaker was required to report the contact to his elder or eldress before attending meeting. The Shakers provided rules not only for members but also for the conduct of visitors while in a Shaker village; in addition, they labeled certain events as "off-limits" to visitors. The Shakers further forbade any visiting of the community by worldly relatives, unless they were likely converts.

*The Couple.* Two-person intimacy poses a potential threat to group cohesiveness unless it is somehow controlled or regulated by the group. Groups with any degree of identity or stability face the issue of intimacy and exclusive attachments and set limits on how much and what kinds are permissible or desireable. Exclusive two-person bonds within a larger group, particularly sexual attachments, represent competition for members' emotional energy and loyalty. The cement of solidarity must extend throughout the group. It is also one tenet of community life that as little as possible should belong exclusively to any one person; instead, everything should be shared, affection as well as material possessions. Many nineteenth century utopias, in fact, anticipated the current Women's Liberation movement in declaring that a person had no right to "ownership" of another, notably that a man did not have the right to exclusive possession and domination of a wife. At the same time, an intense, private two-person relationship, where neither person is tied into the community in other strong ways, is the sort of unit that can potentially withdraw from involvement with the group. Philip Slater phrased the problem of "dyadic withdrawal" in the following manner: 'An intimate dyadic relationship always threatens to short-circuit the libidinal network of the community and drain off its source of sustenance." At the same time, the exclusive attachments of love dyads may interfere with group cohesion by generating jealousy and hostility. This was recognized by Freud: "If we do away with personal rights over material wealth, there still remains prerogative in the field of sexual relationships, which is bound to become the source of the strongest dislike and the most violent hostility among men who in other respects are on an equal footing."[15]

Stable communities, then, set policies on the issue of exclusive intimacy or institute practices designed to cope with potential dyadic withdrawal. Successful nineteenth-century groups often discouraged couples in one of two extreme and experientially opposite ways — either through free love, including group marriage, in which every member was expected to have intimate sexual relations with all others, or through celibacy, in which no member could have sexual relations with any other.[16] In both cases, private ties were structurally minimized, and cohesiveness of the total group was thereby emphasized. In other words, everyone was potentially included in every possible relationship in the community, and there were no exclusive couples. All but one of the successful nineteenth-century groups practiced either celibacy or free love at some time in their history, as opposed to only five of the twenty-one unsuccessful communities. And of those five, although four chose free love, they practiced it in such a way that couples could form if they wished. The predominant preference of the successful groups was celibacy. Given the moral tone of the nineteenth century, and the need for birth control, celibacy appeared more palatable than free love, whereas today, group marriage would be the overwhelming preference. In relatively stable communities today, however, group marriage is often practiced with the same ban on couples, as in a forty-adult Detroit commune.

Both free love and celibacy meant that the group was regulating intimacy. Both free love and celibacy also made people more available for community work since they were freed from family obligations. Though not all communities needed to establish such extreme policies in order to deal with this issue, some form of control over private intimate relations so that commitment could be concentrated in the communal group was usually present. Some groups that were celibate in the early days of their existence later returned to a form of marriage but still determined as a matter of community policy how and when sexual intimacy could occur. At those times when celibacy was not required by successful communities, it tended to be encouraged or preferred by the community, with celibate members gaining a "more spiritual" status and married members losing status. This was true, for example, in Amana and another successful community, Snowhill. The marriage ceremony at Amana included a text which read, "To be married is good, but to be unmarried is better." Engaged couples waited two years before marrying in Amana.

Furthermore, the functions of both free love and celibacy with respect to renunciation were underscored by the fact that both of these practices tended to be highly controlled in the successful communities and subject to a large number of rules, whereas in unsuccessful groups, such as Modern Times, free love was symptomatic of anarchy, of a general lack of rules and group decision about any relationships, rather than of a prohibition against couples. The free love instituted at Oneida was highly regulated, and it resembled sexual promiscuity in no respect other than its refusal to recognize marriage bonds. Oneida controlled the quantity of sexual relations and determined who could have intercourse with whom, as well as requiring a form of contraception known as male continence, involving the muscular control of ejaculation.[17] Rather than permitting indulgence and wanton pleasure, Oneida's free love thus required self-control and a certain amount of sacrifice, as well as renunciation of the exclusive right to relations with a particular person. Every member had sexual access to every other with his or her consent, while fidelity was negatively sanctioned; preference of one member for another was quickly discouraged. When two members of the community showed a marked preference for one another, they were asked to mate with two others. In the community's view, "Exclusive attachment, or the selfish possession of another, unfitted the person aspiring to perfection from practicing a cardinal social-religious ideal, loving his neighbors without discrimination."[18] What is even more striking, and at the same time supports the argument that free love and celibacy are functional alternatives, is the fact that John Humphrey Noyes, the founder of Oneida, contemplated celibacy before turning to free love. That these practices, experientially the most extreme opposites, should be equated in his mind as means to "spiritual improvement" is suggestive. In any case, Noyes regarded conventional marriage as a form of "spiritual tyranny."

At the same time that Oneida asked for self-control in the midst of free love, the Shakers faced the opposite problem: to provide outlets for male-female companionship in the midst of celibacy. Shaker villages separated men and women as much as possible, in work as well as living arrangements; they had separate governing hierarchies and were forbidden to speak to one another. But for a period of Shaker history there was a practice known as the "union meeting" which brought men and women together a few times a week for conversation. Four to ten of each sex met in a "retiring room" and sat facing each other in rows of about five feet apart. Each brother would converse freely with the sister opposite him.

Some communities extended renunciation of the couple from sexual attachments even to close friendships. The Shakers rotated members of work groups in part to limit the possibilities for strong private relationships to form between members of the same sex, and Oneida similarly taught its children not to form exclusive friendships that left out other members of the peer group. Such control of the dyad did not eliminate intimacy in successful utopian communities; rather, it spread intimacy more widely through the group instead of concentrating it only on one other. This expanded attachment must have reduced the strain born by ordinary marriage bonds, for there were few reports of divorce in utopian communities. Many other relationships were available to help fulfill individuals' needs. Members also learned that intense feelings and strong relationships were as possible with many persons as with one. In renouncing the couple, members gained the community.

*The Family.* If the dyad poses a threat to the cohesion of the communal organization by draining off emotional energy, then so does the family. It is another set of exclusive relationships

competing with community feelings, another set of separate ties
not shared by everyone. Slater noted that familial withdrawal
is as great a threat to a social group as dyadic withdrawal.[19]
This potential source of conflict includes family ties both inside
and outside the community, since the community itself is to
be the members' new family. One of the most vitriolic of Shaker
hymns, for example, is directed against the old biological family:

> *Of all the relations that ever I see*
> *My old fleshly kindred are furthest from me*
> *So bad and so ugly, so hateful they feel*
> *To see them and hate them increases my zeal*
> *O how ugly they look!*
> *How ugly they look!*
> *How nasty they feel!*

The purpose of this renunciation of the family was to increase
communal cohesiveness, which is indicated elsewhere in the
same hymn:

> *My* gospel relations *are dearer to me*
> *Than all the flesh kindred that ever I see . . .*
> *O how pretty they look! . . .* [20]

In a higher proportion of successful than unsuccessful nineteenth century communities families did not share a dwelling
unit (rooms, apartment, or house), and children were separated
from parents, sometimes to be raised in a separate children's
residence by community members assigned to that function, as
in Oneida. It was exclusive attachments that Oneida wished to
soft-pedal in favor of ties to the whole group as a family. If
a woman appeared too attached to her child alone, exhibiting
too much exclusive "mother spirit," she might be subjected
to criticism and denied visiting privileges for two weeks. At
the same time, there were reports of many parent-child-like relations between children and adults who had no children of their
own. As in many communities, all were to regard one another as
brothers and sisters.

For those communities that did preserve the nuclear, biological family as a living unit, its importance was still reduced by

a diffusion of intimacy, emotion, and family functions throughout the community. Many functions performed by families on the outside were instead performed by the communal group, including purchasing, consumption, and child-care. In otherwise successful groups where the family was not renounced as the primary or sole unit for loyalty and affection, there were instances of family rivalries disruptive to the community. A woman raised in Amana, for example, reported that family prejudices sometimes caused difficulties in marriage (which was permitted, though with disfavor), as in cases when one family felt superior to another.

Renunciation of the family often required special household arrangements. Whereas Harmony permitted the nuclear, biological family to continue in a dwelling of its own, even though its functions were drastically reduced (absence of sex, for example), other groups developed their own kinds of living arrangements. The Shakers had separate male and female households, with two to six people in a sleeping room. During its period of celibacy (1822–1830) the Zoar community was composed of twenty households of three to fifteen members, some all male or all female, and some mixed. These were identified by numbers, not by the names of the families living in them. Each house was a unit in the distribution of supplies, the preparation of food, and the care of vegetable gardens. Children were placed in the community nursery at age three.[21]

The organization of households in successful communes is one example of the creation of new social units which do not compete with the community for emotional fulfillment. Such new arrangements contribute to renunciation of special and exclusive relationships. Successful communities of the past, much more than unsuccessful ones, promoted this renunciation, discouraging ties with the outside world and weakening two-person intimacy and family loyalties. The comparison is shown in Table 3.

Communion

Communion and community derive from the same roots, and the one is basic to commitment to the other. People renounce

Table 3. Proportion of successful and unsuccessful nineteenth-century communes having renunciation mechanisms at any time in their history.

| Renunciation mechanism | Successful Communities | | Unsuccessful Communities | |
|---|---|---|---|---|
| | n/N* | % | n/N* | % |
| *Insulation* | | | | |
| Ecological separation | 9/9 | 100 | 21/21 | 100 |
| Institutional completeness | | | | |
| (medical services provided) | 7/7 | 100 | 10/18 | 55 |
| Special term for outside | 4/7 | 57 | 0/17 | 0 |
| Outside conceived as evil and | | | | |
| wicked | 2/7 | 28 | 0/19 | 0 |
| Uniform worn | 8/9 | 89 | 5/17 | 30 |
| Foreign language spoken | 5/9 | 56 | 3/21 | 14 |
| Slang, jargon, other special | | | | |
| terms | 2/9 | 22 | 2/19 | 11 |
| Outside newspapers ignored | 3/6 | 50 | 1/16 | 6 |
| American patriotic holidays | | | | |
| ignored | 3/4 | 75 | 4/6 | 67 |
| *Crossboundary control* | | | | |
| Average member rarely leaving | | | | |
| community | 2/2 | 100 | 0/7 | 0 |
| Rules for interaction with | | | | |
| visitors | 3/7 | 43 | 1/15 | 7 |
| *Renunciation of couple* | | | | |
| Free love or celibacy | 9/9 | 100 | 6/21 | 29 |
| Controls on free love, celibacy, | | | | |
| or sexual relations | 7/9 | 78 | 1/21 | 5 |
| *Renunciation of family* | | | | |
| Parent-child separation | 3/8 | 48 | 3/20 | 15 |
| Families not sharing a | | | | |
| dwelling unit | 3/9 | 33 | 1/20 | 5 |

*N represents the number of communities for which the presence or absence of the mechanism was ascertainable; n represents the number in which the mechanism was present.

separate attachments in order to find collective unity. Connect-edness, belonging, participation in a whole, mingling of the self in the group, equal opportunity to contribute and to benefit — all are part of communion. The principle is "from each according to his abilities, to each according to his needs." The communitarians believe: We are all brothers under the skin — one family. This sentiment is expressed in an Oneida song, "We all have one home and one family relation." The Shakers were explicit in calling such togetherness communion, as in this Shaker song:

> Come dance and sing around the ring,
> Live in love and union,
> Dance and sing around the ring,
> Live in sweet communion.[22]

The feelings of brotherhood and comradeship encompassed by communion are essential to the determination to continue the group even in the face of obstacles and disagreements. Through communion, the group develops a strong "we-feeling." The person who has renounced his other social ties gains a powerful set of relationships in the total community. Accordingly, the emphasis of communion mechanisms is on group participation, with members treated as homogeneous, equal parts of a whole rather than as differentiated individuals. Communion mechanisms develop equality, fellowship, and group consciousness, which lead to the formation of a cohesive, emotionally involving, and affectively satisfying community.

*Homogeneity.* A certain amount of homogeneity of background facilitated communion in successful nineteenth-century communities, for members shared a fund of common experiences to ease mutual role-taking and identification with one another and the collectivity. More often in successful than in unsuccessful groups the members had a common religious background, similar social or educational status, or a common national or ethnic origin. Of the successful communities, Harmony, Amana, and Zoar were all formed from groups of German sectarians. In addition, members of every successful community had some prior acquaintance with one another before coming together to form the community. Oneida, for example, grew out of a Bible class that John Humphrey Noyes had organized in Putney, Vermont, which then moved as a group to upstate New York. Community in these cases could be built on a foundation of pre-formed relations and shared experiences. Unsuccessful groups, however, like many of today's communes, more often began with an aggregate of heterogeneous strangers coming together in response to something rather more impersonal, such as a newspaper ad or a public announcement. While a degree of heterogeneity with respect to age and even background might add richness and flavor to a community, rounding it out so that it is not merely a narrow, age-segregated peer group, some common experiences or the opportunity before entering the community to establish relationships seems important to create the degree of homogeneous identity functional for communion. Today's Synanon, for example, has successfully integrated different ages, races, and ethnic groups, but for at least the early part of its existence almost all of its members entered with a common history of drug addiction.

*Communal Sharing.* In successful nineteenth century communities economic arrangements — the organization of property and work — further facilitated communion. Shared ownership of property helped to create a we-feeling and to implement those ideals of brotherhood central to the forming of utopian communities. Whereas privately and individually owned property contributes nothing to a person's identification with a group and may even be a source of competition, friction, and invidious comparison, group ownership stresses brotherhood and sharing. A communal economy emphasizes the importance of spiritual over material matters, for when the material welfare of a person is taken care of by the group, he is left free to attend only to his spiritual growth. In addition, since all tangible things are owned by the group, their presence is a continual reminder of involvement with the community.

Eight of the nine successful communities required that private property be turned over to the community, and the ninth preferred this arrangement, but of the unsuccessful cases, only eight of the twenty for whom the data were available required it. If a member received money for any reason, such as wages, a gift, or as the result of a sale, he was generally expected to turn it over to the community rather than to keep it for private use. In successful communities, furthermore, the tendency was for the community as a whole to own the land, the buildings, the furniture, tools, and equipment, and sometimes even the clothing and personal effects. Even clothes in Oneida were the common property of all, with the wearer merely allowed temporary use of them, and "going away clothes" were shared by all. In the Harmony Society, the families lived in separate but jointly owned homes. Though they had individual allotments of milk cows and poultry, all other provisions were supplied by the community. Each family kept an account in order to guard against overindulgence, and whenever a family seemed to be particularly extravagent, the leader, Father Rapp, would get them to reduce expenses so as to treat all as strictly equal. In return for goods, all owed their labor to the group. Communal sharing of this kind requires commitment to the whole community beyond the desire for individual consumption. John Bole, for example, reported that some Harmonists complained at first, thinking they deserved more consideration because of the amount of property that they had originally contributed.[23] But this violated the principle of brotherly equality.

*Communal Work.* Communal labor emphasizes joint effort, with all members, as far as possible, performing all tasks for equal reward. The important thing for the community is not who does how much of what work but that the job gets done. Work is a communal enterprise rather than being the province of specialists. Successful nineteenth-century communities more generally established communal labor practices than did unsuccessful ones. They did not pay wages to members for their labor in the community, either in the form of money or credit, whereas many unsuccessful groups did. Ten unsuccessful communities gave credit that could be exchanged for goods or services, or paid wages for labor, and four of these further undermined communistic sharing by not rewarding jobs equally for an equal expenditure of time. Another three provided unequal rewards throughout part of their history. In fact, it was

the aim of Josiah Warren, who was instrumental in the founding
of Utopia and Modern Times, to establish a social system in
which goods and services would "cost" the amount of time
necessary to provide them, and men would exchange "labor
notes" representing amounts of time. The successful communities in contrast, generally believed that all tasks were equally
valuable for the system and that participation in the great
communal enterprise, with the necessities of life provided, was
its own reward and generated its own motivation. Consequently,
all of the successful communities for which information was
ascertainable provided all community services to members free
of any "charge" or specific obligation.

No admission requirements or preferences for special skills,
artistry, intelligence, or technical expertise were permitted
in almost all of the successful communities. Jobs were frequently rotated, so that the same people did not always do the
same things. In Oneida, jobs were often rotated, with everyone
expected to do his share of the noxious or tedious tasks. From
the point of view of the leaders, this plan not only relieved
monotony and gave everyone a chance at the pleasant tasks,
but also required everyone to perform the unpleasant jobs and
effectively prevented identification with any particular work.
The Shakers frequently rearranged work groups to prevent
particularistic ties from forming. Job rotation can be extremely
effective as a communion mechanism, for it increases the area
of the individual's responsibility to the group rather than
limiting it to one task, and it emphasizes that the member is
ready to perform any service the community may require of
him, regardless of personal preference. Job rotation eliminates
the concept of career.

The Shakers rotated work assignments not only to maintain
commitment but also to recognize native ability, promote
individual initiative, and increase the satisfaction gained from
variety in work. Men often had two or more occupations,
including such varied endeavors as weaving, editing, and preaching. Women followed a more systematic rotation of labor, taking
"tours" in housekeeping and the bakery, for instance. At the
same time, work was shared, and even the elders did some
manual labor. The communistic principle of "from each accord-

ing to his abilities, to each according to his needs" was given substance in Shaker work. Each Shaker village was divided into family units of about fifty people, with each unit independently engaged in industrial activity and operating its own store. Families traded with one another and came to each other's aid in times of financial crisis. Though every Shaker worked, age, sex, and ability were taken into account in the assignment of work: "each member does what amount of labor he considers right and proper, without any intervention on the part of his fellow laborers." "Consecration" rather than compulsion dictated how hard the Shakers worked. Given the fact that everyone worked, including the children, who performed piece-work in their own quarters, individual Shakers generally did not work as hard as outsiders have to — one advantage of community and cooperative work. Like Oneida, the Shakers also invented many labor-saving devices.[24] In fact, because of the sharing of work, members of communities generally had more time for rest and recreation than did those on the outside. One observer reported that in Harmony the work was assigned so that none was overburdened and there was ample leisure for all.[25]

Communal work efforts, in which the entire community joined together to perform general tasks such as harvesting, cleaning, or building, also built communion. The most common form these efforts took was the harvesting bee. Oneida accomplished much community work in the form of bees, such as the ritualistic scrubbing bee after visitors' departure. Other communities had corn-picking and apple-gathering bees. In Zoar the community joined together to make maple sugar in the spring and apple butter in the fall; the children gathered apples and pulled hops together. All of these activities were accompanied by singing. Such work efforts bring the whole community together and give everyone a sense of participation and involvement. They are often as much a festival as a chore. A member of the North American Phalanx described the communal feeling engendered by sharing work, particularly manual labor: "Day after day these philosphers and reformers who had never until this time performed any manual labor, worked with shovels and pickaxes from daylight till dark, hoisting in derricks the marl which was carried in carts and

spread over the land. The work which would have seemed
drudgery under other conditions was hardly felt to be so by
those earnest workers in their enthusiasm, as the spirit of
unity, the strong feature of group labor, lightened the burden."[26]
In work the spirit of community can be expressed. Even
when the work is not intrinsically satisfying, a person gains
satisfaction from working for a higher purpose, for the welfare
of the group, or for his own pleasure in contributing to the
common good. For the Shakers, the spiritual and the communal
were continually affirmed in labor, as revealed by the religious
overtones of this sweeping song:

> *Low, low! Low, low! In this pretty path I will go,*
> *For here Mother leads me and I know it is right.*
> *I will sweep as I go, I will sweep as I go,*
> *For this Mother bids me and it is my delight.*

Another instance of the integration of work and spiritual
matters is this Shaker song for preparing bread dough:

> *I want I want more love,*
> *Mother's love I want,*
> *I want Mother's love measured,*
> *Heap'd up, heap'd up,*
> *Press'd down, press'd down.*[27]

Communion thus involves sharing work, and work has meaning
in terms of community values.

   *Regularized Group Contact.* Communion is further accomplished by regularizing arrangements and activities that bring the
individual into continual contact with the group as a whole.
Arrangements for regular group contact permit information
sharing and participation in routine decisions. The relatively
small amount of time left for being alone dramatizes the fact
of oneness with the group. Communal dwelling and dining halls
may serve such a group contact function, although their use fails
to distinguish between the successful and the unsuccessful
communities. Successful communities tended on the whole to
provide slightly less opportunity or place for privacy than did
the unsuccessful ones, though because of their wide range

of practices, many of them did in fact provide some private space for members. Some privacy in the midst of strong group contact seems essential to success.

Frequent group meetings and member attendance at a large number of community events also serve a communion function simply because they bring together the entire collectivity and reinforce its existence and meaning, regardless of the purpose of the gathering. Participation in such events makes a member more involved in the group, keeps him more informed of events, gives him a greater sense of belonging, and increases his opportunity to help influence day-to-day decisions. Such meetings are a step toward "participatory democracy." Both successful and unsuccessful communities tended to have regular group meetings: about three-quarters of both groups had them throughout their history, and two other successful cases and one unsuccessful one had them for part of their history. However, the meetings held by the successful utopias tended to be more frequent than those held by the unsuccessful. Many of them were daily or almost daily, and none of them were less often than weekly. On these occasions the whole community usually came together, except that in the case of extremely large systems, like the Shakers, each "family" met nightly for prayers, song, and exercise; larger groups convened three times a week; and the whole village congregated in a public assembly on the Sabbath. For some of the successful communities, attendance at the daily meetings was compulsory, and they were considered highlights of the members' days. Oneida took particular pains to secure the individual's participation in community affairs. Meetings of the entire community were held every day in the Big Hall of the Mansion House, at which joint endeavors were examined. This system guaranteed the survival of a sense of involvement.[28] In these meetings there was public discussion of problems in the business or social life of the community, a religious talk, and public airing of general or individual problems. Regularized group contact of this sort contributes to communion.

*Ritual.* Group ritual, involving collective participation in recurring events of symbolic importance, also enhances communion. Through ritual, members affirm their oneness and pay

homage to the ties that bind them. Ritual provides symbols
by which "the group loyalty is commonly raised to the level of
the universal and abiding." This characteristic has been noted
by many writers. Herbert Blumer, for example, included
participation in formal ceremonial behavior among the mechanisms promoting esprit de corps.[29]

Roland Warren has proposed that music serves a ritual function, providing "a common affirmation of faith, supported by
rhythm and melody," regardless of the context for the songs.
He found, for example, many of the same elements in both Nazi
patriotic songs and Christian hymns.[30] Many of the successful
nineteenth century utopias had their own songs and group
singing. For the Harmony Society, music was so important that
any member of the community was given free instruction in it
as long as he did not make it a specialty. They had what might
have been the first organized town band in Indiana.[31] Shaker
songs and dances are famous to this day.

In addition, a higher proportion of successful than unsuccessful groups celebrated special community occasions or important
dates in community history. These celebrations served ritual
functions. Oneida celebrated the anniversary of John Humphrey
Noyes' enlightenment; Saint Nazianz, a successful Catholic
group, and Harmony celebrated their founding; Bethel and
Aurora honored the leader's birthday; and Amana celebrated
the Liebesmal (love-feast or communion), a deeply religious
occasion. The few remaining Shakers today still celebrate the
birthday of their founder, Mother Ann.

It is difficult to measure directly the use of ritual in nineteenth
century communities because detailed information does not
always exist. There is evidence, however, that both successful
and unsuccessful communities had rituals in group meetings.
The ritual employed by the Shakers was probably the most
extreme, both in elaboration and in the overt goal of reinforcing
group ties. One Shaker ritual, begun in 1842, was a holy "feast"
held twice a year, in May and September, at a secluded place
such as a mountaintop. The imaginary feast was preceded
by confession and silent prayer. The participating Shakers wore
"spiritual" (that is, imaginary) garments symbolizing holiness,
meekness, freedom, and peace, which they had received the

night before in another ceremony; the women's gowns were supposedly of twelve beautiful colors. On the morning of the feast, members of every family gathered at eight and marched in pairs to the site. The ritual included a lively dance, shouting, the giving of "spiritual gifts," and a ceremonial "washing" from an imaginary "fountain," described as follows:

> The Elder then placed two vessels at the head of the fountain for Brother Grove and Sister Dana to use and dippers to dip from the fountain and fill the tubs . . . Brothers Joseph Patten and Shester Hulett were directed to take a large basket of sponges and place them around the fountain for the brethren and sisters, and each one was to take one from the ground and all dip them into the respective tubs of water, which was now prepared for bathing, and give each other a good scrubbing, that is for brethren to assist brethren and sisters to assist sisters.[32]

This episode was followed by singing, the building of an imaginary altar, and the giving of more "gifts," among them some from the spirits of famous men and women such as Napoleon Bonaparte, George Washington, Queen Esther, and Queen Isabella. Such ceremonies were intended to cement the bond between families — the Shaker "families," their "parents" the elders, and their gospel parents Mother Ann Lee and Jesus Christ.

Most Shaker rituals occurred in the private, nightly family meetings. For a time in the 1830s family members upon occasion washed each other's feet and breakfasted on milk and honey. The most common ceremony was the exchange of spontaneous embraces ("gifts of love") at the end of meetings. This ceremony promoted communion and group solidarity in a number of ways. For example, while under the influence of the spirit of the ritual, members would approach each other, state how much they loved one another, apologize for being cross or disagreeable, exchange affectionate embraces, and then resolve to let their deep love prevent disagreements and friction in the future.[33]

Shaker ceremonies served unparalleled expressive functions. During the day Shakers tended to work in silence. Even meals were eaten quickly and silently, and there was a rest period or "retiring time" after the nightly meal and before the meeting. But then during the ritual, emotion, feeling, tension, and physical energy literally exploded. Singing, shouting, stomping, embracing, and dancing in a group with waving hands, all occurred as a great physical release, with members perspiring profusely in the process. As one participant reported, at the end of the ritual, "we felt love enough to eat one another up."[34] Such were the communion functions of ritual.

   *The Persecution Experience and Social Vaccination.* Persecution serves several functions for communion and cohesiveness. Facing a common enemy binds people together, such integration being one of a number of functions of social conflict. Blumer has proposed that the development of an ingroup-outgroup relation is one of the mechanisms creating an esprit de corps in social movements, and that persecution clarifies this relation. Freud also noted that outgroup hostility aids ingroup cohesion. According to Turner and Killian, persecution "heightens the symbolic intensity of a group's values."[35]

   One further function of persecution is to operate as a kind of "social vaccination." In medicine a vaccination is an injection of a mild form of a disease so that the body can build defenses against it and thus cope with more extreme and dangerous forms. Such a "vaccination" is also useful for groups: through the experience of persecution and conflict, defenses are built up and strengthened, so that the group is made immune to (prepared for) future and more extreme attacks on it. Since group cohesiveness has been defined as the ability to withstand threats to existence, social vaccination in the form of persecution should help to build up group defenses. If a group has experienced persecution, then it should be able to withstand other kinds of threats to existence, such as natural disasters, famines, and epidemics. In addition, persecution gives the ends of group existence more meaning and importance, because they hold enough threat for the outgroup to lead it to take steps against the organization. The group's increased self-esteem thus strengthens it in the face of disaster.

   Three forms of persecution of nineteenth century communities were measured: economic discrimination; public denouncement in newspapers, books, or elsewhere; and physical persecution, mob violence, or the use of force. A slightly higher proportion of successful than unsuccessful nineteenth-century groups suffered through these experiences. In fact, all communion mechanisms, including communal sharing and labor, regularized group contact, ritual, and persecution experiences, were found in a higher proportion of successful than unsuccessful nineteenth-century communities, as shown in Table 4.

### Mortification

Mortification processes provide a new identity for the person that is based on the power and meaningfulness of group membership; they reduce his sense of a separate, private, unconnected ego. Self-esteem comes to depend on commitment to the norms of the group and evaluation of its demands as just and morally necessary. These processes convince the person that true meaning and worth derive from opening his self-concept to direction by the group. Mortification processes provide a new set of criteria for evaluating the self; they reduce all people to a common denominator and transmit the message that the self is adequate, whole, and fulfilled only when it lives up to the model offered by the community. In extreme forms these kinds of processes take place in religious communities and in total institutions in general. One intended consequence of mortification processes in these settings has been to strip away aspects of an individual's previous identity, to make him dependent on authority for direction, and to place him in a position of uncertainty with respect to his role behavior until he learns and comes to accept the norms of the group. Erving Goffman called this process "mortification of the self," which operates by removing the individual's sense of self-determination and making him acutely aware of the presence of others.[36]

In less extreme and coercive forms of mortification, religious groups often attempt to erase the "sin of pride," the fault of being too independent or self-sufficient, substituting instead a self that identifies with the influence of the collectivity. Eric Hoffer called this process "the effacement of individual separateness."[37] In noncoercive groups, such as sensitivity training

Table 4. Proportion of successful and unsuccessful nineteenth-century communes having communion mechanisms at any time in their history.

| Communion mechanism | Successful Communities | | Unsuccessful Communities | |
|---|---|---|---|---|
| | n/N* | % | n/N* | % |
| **Homogeneity** | | | | |
| Common religious background | 8/9 | 89 | 10/20 | 50 |
| Similar economic and educational status | 7/8 | 88 | 10/16 | 63 |
| Common ethnic background | 6/9 | 67 | 3/20 | 15 |
| Prior acquaintance of members | 8/8 | 100 | 17/20 | 85 |
| **Communal sharing** | | | | |
| Property signed-over at admission | 9/9 | 100 | 9/20 | 45 |
| Group assigned property received while member | 4/7 | 57 | 6/14 | 43 |
| Land owned by community | 8/9 | 89 | 16/21 | 76 |
| Buildings owned by community | 8/9 | 89 | 15/21 | 71 |
| Furniture, tools, equipment owned by community | 8/8 | 100 | 15/19 | 79 |
| Clothing and personal effects owned by community | 6/9 | 67 | 5/18 | 28 |
| Legal title in name of community (not individuals) | 7/8 | 88 | 18/21 | 83 |
| **Communal labor** | | | | |
| No compensation for labor | 8/8 | 100 | 7/17 | 41 |
| No charge for community services | 7/7 | 100 | 9/19 | 47 |
| No skills required for admission | 7/8 | 88 | 13/17 | 77 |
| Job rotation | 3/6 | 50 | 8/18 | 44 |
| Communal work efforts | 7/7 | 100 | 7/14 | 50 |
| **Regularized group contact** | | | | |
| Communal dwellings | 3/9 | 33 | 14/21 | 67 |
| Communal dining halls | 5/9 | 56 | 15/19 | 79 |
| Little opportunity or place for privacy | 2/9 | 22 | 2/16 | 13 |
| More than two-thirds of typical day spent with other members | 5/8 | 63 | 3/13 | 23 |
| Regular group meetings | 9/9 | 100 | 13/16 | 81 |
| Daily group meetings | 5/9 | 56 | 1/16 | 6 |

Table 4 continued

| | Successful Communities | | Unsuccessful Communities | |
|---|---|---|---|---|
| Communion mechanism | n/N* | % | n/N* | % |
| *Ritual* | | | | |
| Songs about community | 5/8 | 63 | 2/14 | 14 |
| Group singing | 7/7 | 100 | 8/11 | 73 |
| Special community celebrations | 5/6 | 83 | 5/10 | 50 |
| *Persecution experience* | | | | |
| Violence or economic discrimination | 5/8 | 63 | 10/20 | 50 |

*N represents the number of communities for which the presence or absence of the mechanism was ascertainable; n represents the number in which the mechanism was present.

groups, mortification can be a sign of trust in the group, a willingness to share weaknesses, failings, doubts, problems, and one's innermost secrets with others. People often come to such groups or join communes deliberately seeking the identity change involved in mortification; they may call it "personal growth" instead.

In communities, unlike coercive systems such as total institutions, the use of mortification is a sign that the group cares about the individual, about his thoughts and feelings, about the content of his inner world. The group cares enough to pay great attention to the person's behavior, and to promise him warmth, intimacy, and love, as well as power and responsibility, if he indicates that he can accept these gifts without abuse. Mortification thus facilitates a moral commitment on the part of the person to accept the control of the group, binding his inner feelings and evaluations to the group's norms and beliefs: it operates through the community's invasion of phenomenological privacy. Mortification processes induce what today's encounter group culture calls "openness," "trust," and "regaining one's sense of basic humanity." The road to renewed selfhood first passes through humility. The concept and functions of mortification are captured in lines from several Shaker songs — "That great big I, I'll mortify," "I will bow and be simple" — and in this Shaker verse:

*Whoever wants to be the highest*
*Must first come down to be the lowest,*
*And then ascend to be the highest*
*By keeping down, to be the lcwest.*[38]

*Confession and Mutual Criticism.* Systems of confession, self-criticism, and mutual criticism are one means to promote mortification. In such sessions in successful nineteenth-century communities the individual "bared his soul" to social control, admitting weaknesses, failings, and imperfections. The individual humbled himself before the group (which was present either actually or symbolically). No part of his life was left unexamined and uncriticized, since all belonged to the system. The group might probe and pry into the most intimate matters, indicating its right to be a significant presence in the internal life of the individual. These mortification practices thus indicated to members that even their innermost "selves" were being "watched" by others, that the group cared about their thought and character, and that the community provided standards for growth.

Successful communities more often than unsuccessful ones, also tended to require "confession" of previous misconduct when joining the community; regular "confession" of ongoing difficulties, failings, or weaknesses; or "mutual criticisms," in which members revealed to each other their strengths and weaknesses or areas that needed improvement. Furthermore, for Amana and Oneida the confession or criticism was often public, taking place before the entire community. At the same time, in Harmony, Amana, and Oneida the criticism was constructive as well as destructive, and members were told of their good points as well as their bad. In none of the unsuccessful communities was there a public confession or criticism. The system of mutual criticism carried out by Oneida was especially elaborate, even including publication of a pamphlet in which the experiences of members were recounted, and where they attested to the purifying and cleansing nature of the revelation. Mutual criticism in Oneida was carried out both in face-to-face confrontations between individual members and in meetings before boards or panels of leaders. Oneidans were required to submit to this criticism in silence, as well as to "confess" to the board's criticism by acquiescing to it in writing. In Bethel and Aurora, confession was deliberately employed by the leader, William Keil, to ensure the humility of members.[39]

In only two communities, both of them extremely disciplined, was confession or criticism also supported by some kind of surveillance over the activities and behavior of members. Both Harmony and the Shaker villages achieved this goal through practices resembling "honor systems." A Shaker transgressor, for example, was required to report his error to his elder, and any witness was likewise duty-bound to report. Some Shaker villages also had towers from which elders could observe the activities of members. George Rapp of Harmony, its founder, used a series of underground tunnels to appear suddenly and mysteriously before members.

*Sanctions.* Another mortification mechanism is the use of particular kinds of sanctions against deviance, which embarrass the member before the community and indicate to him that his membership status in the organization is always in question. The punished deviant also serves as an example to the rest of the community and shows them that retaining their privileged status as members is always problematic. Mortification functions can be served by public denouncement, as by calling the deviant to the attention of the whole community on a public occasion (as Keil of Bethel/Aurora used to do); by removal of the privilege of membership for a period of time; or by not allowing the deviant to participate in some community activity. In general, to be effective, deviants should be punished within the community rather than expelled from it, so that the sanctioning process and product are visible. In the nineteenth-century utopian communities, public denouncement was used frequently as a sanction in four of the nine successful communities and occasionally in another two, whereas it was used occasionally in only three of the sixteen unsuccessful communities. Removal of the privilege of membership was used frequently in two of eight successful communities, but it was used frequently in only one of sixteen unsuccessful ones and occasionally in one other case. Not allowing a deviant to participate in a community activity was used frequently or occasionally in three of eight successful communities but in only two of fifteen unsuccessful ones. Finally, deviants were more often punished within the community than expelled from it in four of six successful cases but in only two of five unsuccessful ones. These results are not conclusive, however, because for many communities in the sample there were no or few recorded instances of deviance, so that particular sanctions appeared to be infrequently used.

One kind of mortifying sanction practiced by the Shakers was the ritual known as the "warring gift," engaged in when a member was thought to be losing his commitment or violating community norms. A number of Shakers would approach the deviant, point at him, and shout "Woe! Woe!" or invectives in gibberish while shaking, whirling, and trembling, supposedly under divine inspiration. The purpose was to elicit a confession before the elders.[40] The Shakers were also known to pursue couples who had "fleshed off" into the world (eloped) and attempt to reason them out of their mistake. Both confessed deviants and returned couples were not only humbled before the community but also served as a lesson and an example to the rest. In Synanon today sanctions are sometimes made visible, as when punished deviants have their heads shaved and wear signs.

*Spiritual Differentiation.* In successful nineteenth-century groups, mortification was also aided by a type of stratification system known as "spiritual" differentiation, which distinguished members on the basis of their achievement in living up to group standards and taking on the community identity. This stratification tended to reward complete mortification and thus make it desirable in the eyes of the less committed and hence lower-status members. Members were distinguished on spiritual or moral grounds, according to how well they exemplified ideal traits of membership or how thoroughly they were committed to the community, with the more spiritual, moral, committed, or zealous members receiving greater deference. This kind of spiritual differentiation was found in over half of the successful communities (five of nine), but in only 15 percent of the unsuccessful ones (three of twenty). In addition, the deference was formally structured in three of the successful communities, rather than occurring informally. Oneida, for example, was stratified on a scale of "fellowship" indicating where people stood in relation to each other. The more "spiritual" or committed members had "descending fellowship" with the less spiritual; the less spiritual members' relation to the more spiritual was known as "ascending." Noyes, the leader, had descending fellowship with the rest of the community; he was "horizontal" only with the Patriarchs and Jesus Christ. The kind of fellowship a member had helped determine other social relations: young Oneidans, for instance, were initiated into sex by older, more spiritual members with whom they had "ascending fellowship." The Shakers divided their communities into three "families" representing class distinctions: novitiate, junior, and senior families. Special privileges obtained to the senior or "church" family.

The Amana community rather deliberately used spiritual differentiation to reward commitment to community ideals by making this differentiation visible to the group. There was a strict order of seating in the church based on degree of piety, with the less pious in front and the more pious in back. Further, the community was divided into three Versammlungs or church gatherings, which met in different rooms. Elders could either promote or demote members by moving them to the front or back of the room or to a higher or lower group. Once a year there was a spiritual examination at which all members except the elders, who were in a class by themselves, were judged and placed in appropriate rank, generally with the older in higher classes. According to a woman who grew up in Amana, "seating position was such an important social index that it provided the only punishment, spiritual or civil, that was needed in these colonies."[41]

At the same time, there were no other distinctions among members of Oneida that would allow them to take pride in anything but their fulfillment of the conditions for ideal membership. There was no other kind of status, as in Synanon today, where "character is the only status." Successful nineteenth-century utopian communities did not distinguish among members on the basis of skill, intelligence, or expertise, although two of the unsuccessful groups did.

Spiritual differentiation could further aid mortification by means of the community's socialization process. For instance, in some cases new members were given instruction in the community's doctrines, whereby the new terms and criteria for their behavior and identity were set forth and the recruit's ignorance before an esoteric body of knowledge was made clear. New members were given lists of rules to learn, books or pamphlets to study. New members were also segregated from old members, so that the disparity between their present, "unworthy" condition and that of people deemed worthy of full membership was made graphic. Some communities had a formal probationary period, during which a new member was allowed to participate to a limited extent without the rights of full membership. The probationary period not only underscored the distance the person had to travel before he was acceptable to the organization, but it also provided a time in which to effect an identity change gradually. None of these practices clearly distinguished between successful and unsuccessful communities, although a slightly higher percentage of successful groups tended to employ these aspects of socialization.

*De-individuating Mechanisms.* Though successful communities tended to differentiate members on spiritual or moral grounds, they tried not to differentiate them on any other basis. One of the important aims of communal living is to erase distinctions between people, to eliminate the loneliness of individual separateness. A part of the process of commitment is to find a common denominator with other people, to substitute a group-based identity for one based on individual differences. De-individuating mechanisms are strategies for removing the individual's sense of isolation, privacy, and uniqueness. They change his identity so as to anchor it in things that are communal rather than personal.

A uniform style of dress is one kind of de-differentiating

mechanism. Two of the successful nineteenth-century groups, the Shakers and Harmony, required a uniform for members, but none of the unsuccessful communities did. Amana refused to differentiate among people at burial: all coffins were of the same style and quality. As one observer reported, "there was no discrimination in Amana even in death."[42] Requiring that members live and eat together, with little opportunity for privacy, was another kind of de-individuating arrangement. Though the use of communal dwellings and dining halls fails to distinguish between successful and unsuccessful communities, because it was a minimum requirement for establishing most communities, the successful groups tended to provide less time for privacy. In Oneida, as in other communities, "excessive introspection" was considered a sin.

An inability to promote mortification was cited by members of the Yellow Springs community as a reason for the collapse of the commune after only a few months. A contemporary observer wrote:

Notwithstanding the apparent heartiness and cordiality of [the commune's] auspicious opening, it was in the social atmosphere of the Community that the first cloud arose. Self-love was a spirit which would not be exorcised . . . It reminded the favorites of former society of their lost superiority; and in spite of all rules, tinctured their words and actions with the love of self . . . *Individual* happiness was the law of nature, and it could not be obliterated; and before a single year had passed, this law had scattered the members of that society, which had come together so earnestly and under such favorable circumstances, back into the selfish world from which they came.[43]

Successful communities, in contrast, included mortification. The greater frequency of mortification processes, including confession and mutual criticism, sanctions, spiritual differentiation, and de-individuation, in successful nineteenth-century utopian communities is shown in Table 5.

Transcendence

Martin Buber indicated that transcendence is a universal human need, even though it is often suppressed. He defined it

Table 5. Proportion of successful and unsuccessful nineteenth-century communes having mortification mechanisms at any time in their history.

| Mortification mechanism | Successful Communities | | Unsuccessful Communities | |
|---|---|---|---|---|
| | n/N* | % | n/N* | % |
| *Confession and mutual criticism* | | | | |
| Regular confession | 4/9 | 44 | 0/20 | 0 |
| Confession upon joining | 4/8 | 50 | 0/19 | 0 |
| Mutual criticism or group confession | 4/9 | 44 | 3/19 | 26 |
| Mutual surveillance | 2/7 | 29 | 0/17 | 0 |
| Surveillance by leaders | 3/7 | 43 | 1/17 | 6 |
| *Sanctions* | | | | |
| Public denouncement of deviants | 6/9 | 67 | 3/16 | 19 |
| Removal of a privilege of membership | 2/8 | 25 | 2/16 | 12 |
| Participation in a community function prohibited | 3/8 | 38 | 2/15 | 14 |
| Deviants punished within community more often than expelled from it | 4/6 | 67 | 2/5 | 40 |
| *Spiritual differentiation* | | | | |
| Members distinguished on moral grounds | 5/9 | 56 | 3/20 | 15 |
| Formally structured deference to those of higher moral status | 4/9 | 44 | 1/20 | 5 |
| No skill or intelligence distinctions | 9/9 | 100 | 15/17 | 88 |
| Instruction in community doctrines | 3/8 | 38 | 2/11 | 18 |
| Learning of rules and dictates required | 2/8 | 25 | 2/11 | 18 |
| New members segregated from old | 2/7 | 28 | 0/17 | 0 |
| Formal probationary period with limited privileges for new members | 5/8 | 63 | 8/15 | 53 |
| *Deindividuation* | | | | |
| Uniform worn | 8/9 | 89 | 5/17 | 30 |
| Communal dwellings | 3/9 | 33 | 14/21 | 67 |
| Communal dining halls | 5/9 | 56 | 15/19 | 79 |
| Same meals eaten by all | 3/7 | 43 | 4/10 | 40 |

*N represents the number of communities for which the presence or absence of the mechanism was ascertainable; n represents the number in which the mechanism was present.

as "the need of man to feel his own house as a room in some greater, all-embracing structure in which he is at home, to feel that the other inhabitants of it with whom he lives and works are all acknowledging and confirming his individual existence." To Buber, the utopian impulse itself involved transcendence: "What is at work here is a longing for that *rightness*, which, in religious or philosophical vision, is experienced as revelation or idea, and which of its very nature cannot be realized in the individual, but only in human community."[44]

Transcendence requires, first, the experience of great power and meaning residing in the community. Max Weber proposed that this experience is transmitted through a quality called "charisma," a felt connection with a central and meaningful feature of existence, which is generally connected with the presence of charismatic leaders. Utopian communities have often been established around the figures of charismatic leaders: Ann Lee of the Shakers, George Rapp of Harmony, Joseph Bimeler of Zoar, William Keil of Bethel and Aurora, Jemima Wilkinson of Jerusalem, John Humphrey Noyes of Oneida, Adin Ballou of Hopedale, Eric Janson of Bishop Hill. But for permanent commitments to result, persisting over long periods of time and independent of the presence or existence of any one person, charisma throughout the corporate group is required. Charisma in this form may be called "institutionalized awe." It is an extension of charisma from its original source into the organization of authority and the operations of the group, but not necessarily attached to a particular office (status) or hereditary line. The group itself is charismatic. Edward Shils also reformulated the meaning of charisma in this way, calling it the "awe-arousing centrality" of a social system: "[Charismatic qualities] may also become resident, in varying degrees of intensity, in institutions — in the qualities, norms, and beliefs to which members are expected to adhere or are expected to possess". Shils called this "institutional charisma."[45]

Institutional awe, then, is a means by which surrender to the greater power of a social system can be effected. Institutionalized awe first requires an ideological and structural system that orders and gives meaning to the individual's life, and which attaches this order and meaning to the organization. According to Shils, "the attribution of charismatic qualities occurs in the presence of order-creating, order-disposing, order-discovering power as such; it is a response to a great ordering power."[46] Such systems with great ordering power not only satisfy the individual's need for meaning, but they also provide a sense of rightness, certainty, and conviction that promotes transcendence and surrender to the source of power.

*Institutionalized Awe through Ideology.* Successful communities need shared beliefs. A sense of order and meaning was provided in the nineteenth century groups by particular kinds of ideology, which also served to legitimate the individual's surrender to the system. Explanations of human nature, of the essential character of humanity, were included in the communities' ideologies. All but one of the nine successful communities had a comprehensive ideology, which provided explanations and dictums for many areas of life. The one exception, Bethel/ Aurora, confined its ideology to a simple but very general principle concerning brotherhood and love. In contrast, five out of fifteen unsuccessful communities did not have elaborate, comprehensive ideologies; these groups generally confined their ideology to a limited sphere of existence, such as economic organization, and had no shared principles regarding other matters.

The ideology in successful communities tended to provide for the investing of power in persons with particularly awe-inspiring qualities, such as wisdom, experience, spiritualness, inspiration, creativity, or age. Seventy-eight percent of the successful communities (seven of nine) had this kind of ideology, as contrasted with only 10 percent of the unsuccessful ones for their entire history and another 10 percent for part of their history. In the Amana community, a highly successful group, the particular quality that the ideology defined as necessary for power was inspiration, the ability to receive divine messages and guidance; Amana was officially called the Society of True Inspiration. The person through whom God spoke to them, they believed, was an "inspired instrument" and acted as the spiritual head of the community. Before receiving inspirations, the instrument was generally greatly agitated, sometimes shaking and trembling for an hour. The message of the instrument varied, though it was usually an exhortation to holier life. Sometimes it called for a major change in the community, such as a move to another place; sometimes it reproved individuals for their faults. When the community was founded, there were two instruments, Christian Metz and Barbara Heinemânn; in 1867 Heinemann became the sole instrument. When William Alfred Hinds visited the community in 1876 and asked about a successor to her, he was told, "The Lord has always given us an inspired leader, and we can trust him for the future."[47]

The ideology in successful groups, as well as in half of the unsuccessful ones, legitimated demands made on members by reference to a higher principle, which gave meaning to the demands, such as justice, the will of the people, the will of nature, or the will of God. Shils proposed that a charismatic social order must seem to be connected with a transcendent moral order. Some of the successful groups also built institutionalized awe by imputing special or magical powers to members of the organization. Merely by virtue of their participation in the system, members could partake of its special fund of qualities. In a sense, this is a charisma of belonging, for all members gained a measure of charisma just by being members, and the degree of awe surrounding the system was correspondingly enhanced by virtue of the fact that only a great and powerful system could distribute some of its magic to ordinary members. Among the properties that could be imputed to members solely because they were members included insight, wisdom, the gift of prophecy, or the ability to apprehend things that other people — nonmembers — could not. This kind of belief was found much more often in successful than unsuccessful communities: eight of nine successful groups had it for at least a part of their history (six for all), as opposed to only three of twenty unsuccessful groups. The Shakers, for example, had a spiritualist phase in which many members claimed special powers or revelations, such as spirit-writing and "speaking in tongues," or receiving messages in gibberish. One such revelation came to Brother Philomen Stewart of the Mount Lebanon Village, who had a space cleared and fenced in at the top of a hill near each village, named it a Holy Mount, and claimed that in this space was a fountain of life, which only believers could see. Surrounding the fountain was an ornate city

of angels, spirits, and prophets, which again only believing
Shakers could see. This instance was an extreme example of a
more common occurrence in successful communities, where
members in good standing were felt to possess special wisdom,
insight, or magical powers. Their beliefs sanctioned the feeling
that community members were a special, more spiritual brand of
human being.

In successful groups the ideology tended to tie the system
to figures of historical importance, relating it to great men and
events of the past, and by implication conferring their approval
on the system. The most prominent among past heroes to
which communities related themselves was Jesus Christ, though
he did not always have a solely religious meaning. Often the
brotherhood and communism exemplified by this figure was
what related him to the utopia. The Shakers even believed
they could convert the dead, and at their gatherings of spirits
they often reported many great men in attendance, including
Napoleon, Queen Isabella, and George Washington. In successful
communities, moreover, their ideologies were a potent part of
the life of the group, influencing decisions and everyday
operations, as in Shaker hymns for sweeping. But for many of
the unsuccessful communities, the ultimate justification for
decisions was generally expediency or practicality.

*Institutionalized Awe: through Power and Leadership.* Institutionalized awe, symbolized by an order- and meaning-creating
power underlying the group, was structurally reinforced in
several ways that maximize transcendence. One means was to
increase the distance of the ultimate decision-making process
from ordinary members, even though they were often highly
involved in daily decisions. Another means was to enhance
the sense of mystery surrounding the organization, so that
obedience and moral conviction were absolute. Distance and
mystery were promoted by several mechanisms: an authority
hierarchy, insulated from members; physical separation of
leaders from members; special leadership prerogatives; and an
irrational basis for ultimate, as opposed to routine, decisions.

Many communities were founded by charismatic figures who
were supposed to have access to special sources of power, who
served as the link between members and those higher sources of

wisdom and meaning, who represented for their followers
the greatest growth to which a person could aspire, who symbolized in their person community values, and who inspired
devotion, awe, and reverence in their followers. A few examples
may illustrate the quality of the felt relation to the charismatic
leader. Members of the Harmony Society described Father Rapp
to Charles Nordhoff on his visit in 1874: "He was a man before
whom no evil could stand." "When I met him in the street,
if I had a bad thought in my head, it flew away." " He knew
everything — how to do it, what was the best way." "Ah, he
was a *man*; he told us what to do, and how to be good." There
are several reports from Oneida of John Humphrey Noyes's
personal magnetism. One contemporary critic described his
charisma thus: "He has mastered the art of so controlling his
disciples that they think they are carrying out their own ideas
when they are really executing his designs . . . His will is
supreme." A member of the community felt that even the
children looked up to Father Noyes, "to whom in this parental
relation no child's trouble was too trivial, no sorrow too simple
to engage his heartiest sympathy." And William Alfred Hinds,
another community member, wrote: "To us he is a permanent
medium of Christ . . . an embodiment of a higher Christian
life." About William Keil of Bethel and Aurora, a historian
wrote: "It is vouched for that women, carried away by his
preaching and entering into a peculiar hypnotic state cried out,
'Thou are Christ.' "[48]
  Behind the charismatic leader, supporting him, providing a
source of additional spiritual guides if he should not be present,
and helping to diffuse charisma more widely through the
larger of the successful nineteenth-century communities was
an authority hierarchy. A hierarchy of leaders presumably
limited the members' access to the ultimate wielder of power
in the community and thus enhanced the sense of awe surrounding the demands and dictums of the system. In addition,
the hierarchy insulated the top leaders from violation of their
symbolic properties of infallibility and truth. Turner and
Killian suggest, for example, that one of the mechanisms
protecting the inviolability of a leader symbol is the delegation
to subordinates of the more routine tasks and "the assignment

to them of responsibility for actions which might compromise the leader symbol."[49]

A hierarchy, or various forms of joint leadership, also prevented too strong an identification of the institutional charisma with one person. A hierarchy provided alternative charismatics or subordinates groomed for the role who could step up when the charismatic figure was gone. Whereas many utopian communities, even successful ones, ended when their top leader died, others that had established a leadership hierarchy or a basis for succession persisted beyond this event. In fact, the notable success of the Shakers, lasting well into a highly industrialized age, may be partly attributed to a lack of succession crises owing to an elaborate authority hierarchy from family to village to central ministry, with dual leadership (male and female, over separate male and female families) at each level. Their elaborate hierarchy served not only an insulating function but also emphasized the remoteness of ultimate decisions. In Harmony, a hierarchy protected George Rapp's inviolability as spiritual symbol of the community during his lifetime. Economic and administrative matters were handled by subordinates, protecting the belief of many Harmonists that Father Rapp was God.

The successful communities that lacked hierarchies often concentrated ultimate guiding power tightly in the hands of one man (Keil of Bethel/Aurora, Noyes of Oneida, Jemimah Wilkinson of Jerusalem, Joseph Bimeler of Zoar.) However, these leaders at times delegated routine matters to subordinates and protected their inviolability in various ways that combined participatory democracy with centralized control. Oneida, for example, was partly governed by an elected board that handled routine matters while Noyes himself remained primarily a spiritual figure. In the unsuccessful communities that did have hierarchies, they often did not function as buffers for the top power-holders, protecting the charisma of the organization, but rather were bureaucratically designed for administrative efficiency or to implement a democratic ethic. Often there was no great power of any kind residing at the top of the organization, and routine responsibility was diffused throughout the system. This was true of the Owenite communities at Yellow Springs and Kendal, of Northampton, of Brook Farm, and of

the Wisconsin Phalanx. When unsuccessful communities lacked
hierarchies altogether, it was often not because ultimate power
was tightly concentrated at the top, or because it was distributed
democratically, but because the community did not believe
in delineating any lines of power and authority or in making any
demands on members. This was true, for example, of the
anarchist community Modern Times.

The top leaders of successful communities tended to live in a
residence separate from that of most of the community membership. Bimeler of Zoar, for example, lived in a large, impres-
sive house. Top leaders also enjoyed privileges not available
to the membership at large, as well as immunity from some
community obligations or social controls. Bimeler rode while
others walked, and he generally lived better than ordinary
members. William Keil of Bethel/Aurora was immune from
confession or manual labor. The Shaker ministry was exempt
from confession, though many elders engaged in manual labor.
John Humphrey Noyes of Oneida had increased sexual access to
members of the community and was not required to submit
to confession or mutual criticism, not only because of his
higher spiritual status, but also because of his special position
in the community: "If he is practically exempt from criticism
nowadays, it is to be considered that all the informal grumbling
falls on him, and that he takes the principal share of the criticism that comes from the world outside; which is whipping
enough to keep one man sober."[50]

In addition, leaders of successful communities tended to be
addressed by special titles, different from the forms of address
used for ordinary members and indicating the special respect
that they received. The most common name was "father,"
as in Father Noyes of Oneida, Father Rapp of Harmony, and
Father Ochswald of Saint Nazianz. This title stressed one of
the underlying beliefs of community life for these groups: that
all members together were children, brother and sister in a
family parented by leaders representing the great power of the
organization. Bethel/Aurora's Keil was known to his followers
as "doctor" (a nonprofessional title), Jerusalem's Jemimah
Wilkinson was the "universal friend," and Shaker and Amana
leaders were called "elders."

Institutionalized awe also tended to be reinforced in successful communities by a decision-making structure that was non-participative for general organizational decisions and for decisions as to the definition, structure, or character of the community — as opposed to routine, everyday decisions. At some point the group, however democratic its own everyday functioning, turned to the leader for ultimate decisions and spiritual guidance, because of his access to higher sources of wisdom inaccessible to ordinary members. The special, awe-inspiring magic of the community was thereby enhanced, as the top leaders supposedly provided guidance far from the ability of ordinary members. Control by top leaders was true only of important structural decisions about the community and issues of values, however, for nonparticipation in these matters promoted transcendence, whereas participation in routine matters promoted cohesivensss, which was another important utopian aim. Oneida, again, was highly partici-patory in its day-to-day operations, governed by committees and general meetings of the whole membership. But the shape, philosophy, and ultimate direction of the community was given by Noyes, who was the final arbiter, judge, and authority.

*Mystery.* A sense of magic and mystery pervaded successful nineteenth-century groups. Decisions were sometimes based on divine revelation or messages from the spirit world, or on intuition or inspiration. No ordinary member could marshal evidence that the command of God had not ordered a particular activity or that Brother X's "special feeling" was incorrect. These irrationally based decisions were not only generally unchallengeable but also inaccessible to any but the "instru-ments" or "chosen prophets." In some communities, such as the Shakers, the irrational base was spiritualistic. Mystery was also promoted by such devices as Harmony's tunnels, through which George Rapp was supposed to "appear" mysteri-ously.

*Guidance.* "Guidance," or the provision of a specific program of behavioral norms, reinforces the role of the organi-zation as an order-creating power and gives direction to even the most discrete behavior of its members. By providing mem-bers with minutely detailed instructions for dealing with specific situations, nineteenth century communities rendered meaningful in terms of their values even the most minute and mundane behaviors and acts. Guidance further ensured uniformity in members' execution of community demands and reinforced the official structure of the community, eliminating the need for individual variability or disruptive innovation. Every bit of daily life was infused with the group's philosophy.

All of the successful communities, but less than half of the unsuccessful ones, had a somewhat fixed daily routine throughout their history. In four successful communities, the daily routine was specified in at least some detail, accounting for hours if not minutes; but in most of the unsuccessful cases with a fixed routine, it contained no detail, just the order of daily events, leaving members free to do what they wished at several times during the day.

In general, the successful communities tended to provide programs and philosophic guides for much of the behavior of members, whereas the unsuccessful ones did not. Among the unsuccessful groups, Modern Times was conspicuous for its lack of even the most basic rules; all kinds of variability were tolerated. Blue Spring, Utopia, Oberlin, Northampton, and Brook Farm also failed to program. At Brook Farm, members prescribed their own hours for community work and in fact were proud that their system gave members the opportunity to do whatever they pleased. But that system ultimately failed.

Successful communities provided not only guides for work but also free time and recreation in line with the group's ideals. Shaker programming extended even to such minor activities as dressing: the right shoe, right glove, and right breeches leg were to be put on first – a custom derived from Biblical allusions. Men and women were assigned separate stairs, and they were not allowed to pass on a stairway or speak to each other unless a third party was present. The daily routine was minutely programmed. At the first "trump" (bell) everyone arose according to the following program: "Put your right foot out of the bed first. Place your right knee where your foot first touched the floor in kneeling to pray. Do not speak, but if absolutely necessary whisper to the room leader." Women were to walk to breakfast "on the toes, left arm folded across the stomach, right hand at the side, tips of the fingers touching the thumb."[51] And so on, throughout the day.

*Ideological Conversion.* Transcendence is supported by faith or ideological conviction, a set of beliefs that evaluate the demands of the organization as being morally necessary because of their relation to ultimate values. The organization has unquestionable power because members share a faith that gives it meaning and legitimacy. As William Hinds pointed out in reviewing the fate of nineteenth-century American utopian communities, the particular faith is not what promotes the success of a utopia, but rather the fact that all members believe in it.[52] Agreement, shared belief, and common purpose are indispensable to the creation of transcendence. A mechanism aiding transcendence, then, would be the requirement that all members undergo a conversion to the movement's ideology. Structurally, this can be implemented in various ways: insisting on ideological conversion for membership, requiring vows to change behavior on the part of recruits, instituting a formal procedure for selecting recruits, requiring a probationary period, rejecting potential members as unacceptable, and requiring some sort of "test of faith" for community children before accepting them into full adult membership. All of these practices tended to exist in successful nineteenth-century communities in higher proportion than in unsuccessful ones.

Eight of the unsuccessful communities not only failed to ask any ideological conversion or commitment, but also exhibited a general lack of selectivity in recruitment. For example, they tended to welcome individuals of all ideological persuasions and to recruit by impersonal means, such as advertising, rather than by personal contact. Some of the successful communities solved this problem altogether by never recruiting new members. The brief history of New Harmony in particular points up the problems of unselective recruitment. In the early months of 1825, Robert Owen, founder and financial backer of New Harmony, gave several speeches in Washington at which he invited the "industrious and well-disposed of all nations" to come to New Harmony. Through such blanket invitations, the community, which had taken over a set of buildings from the Harmonists, was filled to overflowing, and Owen, who also was absent during many early months, had no opportunity to select recruits. By October 1825 there were eight hundred people in the community. Owen's son, Robert Dale Owen, described the membership as a "heterogeneous collection of radicals, enthusiastic devotees to principle, honest latitudarians and lazy theorists, with a sprinkling of undisciplined sharpers thrown in."[53] Perhaps more than anything else, this lack of selectivity was responsible for New Harmony's failure. Members had no prior relationship to one another, no basis for knowing whether they could live together in community, and no necessary commitment to a set of unifying ideals. Given Owen's money and the Harmonists' buildings, they did not even need to be committed to building a community.

*Tradition.* Finally, tradition can serve as a transcendence-facilitating mechanism. Tradition, which Max Weber described as the "authority of the eternal yesterday," imbues community demands with a legitimacy they might not otherwise have. Tradition defines what is as what should be and preempts the ability of those not yet involved with the tradition to offer alternatives and suggest changes. It asks members to submit to principles that have "stood the test of time." The aura of history surrounds it. Therefore, if a utopian community is not created *de novo*, it is not started from scratch on the basis of a totally new set of norms and principles for members who have never before encountered the group, but instead, is derived from a prior organization of some duration, it can make use of tradition. It can count on a measure of members' attachment to community norms because they are continuous with earlier norms and are thus enhanced with the authority of age and familiarity, of custom and habit. Such derivation increases a utopian community's chances of success, for a higher proportion of successful than unsuccessful nineteenth-century groups derived from prior organization. For five of them, this prior group had existed at least ten years before the utopia was formed. For two, it had existed more than fifty years previously. In conclusion, as shown in Table 6, successful nineteenth century American utopias, much more often than unsuccessful ones, tended to build transcendence through institutionalized awe, mystery, programming, ideological conversion, and tradition.

Table 6. Proportion of successful and unsuccessful nineteenth-century communes having transcendence mechanisms at any time in their history.

| Transcendence mechanism | Successful Communities | | Unsuccessful Communities | |
|---|---|---|---|---|
| | n/N* | % | n/N* | % |
| *Institutionalized awe (ideology)* | | | | |
| Ideology explained essential nature of humanity | 9/9 | 100 | 16/19 | 84 |
| Ideology a complete, elaborated philosophical system | 8/9 | 89 | 15/20 | 75 |
| Power invested in persons with special, magical characteristics | 7/9 | 78 | 4/21 | 20 |
| Demands legitimated by reference to a higher principle | 9/9 | 100 | 11/19 | 58 |
| Special, magical powers imputed to members | 8/9 | 89 | 3/20 | 15 |
| Possession of special powers as evidence of good standing | 6/8 | 75 | 2/19 | 10 |
| Ideology related community to figures of historical importance | 8/9 | 89 | 5/21 | 24 |
| Values formed ultimate justification for decisions | 6/7 | 86 | 7/17 | 41 |
| *Institutionalized awe (power and authority)* | | | | |
| Authority hierarchy | 4/9 | 44 | 8/20 | 40 |
| Top leaders were founders or were named or groomed by predecessors | 9/9 | 100 | 10/20 | 50 |
| No impeachment or recall privileges | 7/8 | 88 | 7/12 | 58 |
| Special leadership prerogatives | 7/9 | 78 | 3/18 | 16 |
| Special leadership immunities | 5/8 | 63 | 3/18 | 16 |
| Separate, special residence for leaders | 6/8 | 75 | 1/15 | 7 |
| Special forms of address for leaders | 6/9 | 67 | 2/19 | 10 |
| Irrational basis for decisions | 4/7 | 57 | 3/20 | 15 |

Table 6 continued

| Transcendence mechanism | Successful Communities | | Unsuccessful Communities | |
|---|---|---|---|---|
| | n/N* | % | n/N* | % |
| *Guidance* | | | | |
| Fixed daily routine | 6/6 | 100 | 8/15 | 54 |
| Detailed specification of routine | 4/6 | 67 | 2/15 | 13 |
| Personal conduct rules (demeanor) | 5/8 | 63 | 6/19 | 31 |
| *Ideological conversion* | | | | |
| Commitment to ideology required | 5/9 | 56 | 4/21 | 19 |
| Recruits expected to take vows | 7/8 | 88 | 6/21 | 29 |
| Procedure for choosing members | 6/8 | 75 | 13/17 | 77 |
| Prospective members often rejected | 3/6 | 50 | 6/11 | 54 |
| Tests of faith for community children to receive adult membership status | 7/9 | 78 | 5/21 | 24 |
| *Tradition* | | | | |
| Community derived from prior organization or organized group | 7/9 | 78 | 13/21 | 62 |
| Prior organization in existence at least ten years before | 5/9 | 56 | 1/21 | 5 |

*N represents the number of communities for which the presence or absence of the mechanism was ascertainable; n represents the number in which the mechanism was present.

*When I get up in the morning, I'm happy. I never felt that way before. I know people love me. It's really groovy waking up and knowing that 48 people love you. It gives you all sorts of energy. You're standing alone — but you're standing with 48 people.*
—Member of a commune in Taos, New Mexico

# 5   The Comforts of Commitment: Issues in Group Life

Successful nineteenth-century communities built strong commitment through the sacrifices and investments of members on behalf of the community; through renunciation, which discouraged extragroup ties and built a strong family feeling within the community; through mortification, which offered identity changes for members; and through transcendence, which gave meaning and direction to the community by means of ideological systems and authority structures. Such communities involved people instrumentally, emotionally, and morally, thereby building commitment to continued participation, to group cohesiveness, and to social control. Specifically, long-lived communities tended to require certain sacrifices of their members as a test of faith, and full investment of money and property, in order to give participants a stake in the fate of the community. They tended to ensure the concentration of loyalty within the community by geographical separation and by prohibitions against contact with the outside. They spread affection throughout the whole community by discouraging exclusive relations based on two-person attraction or on the biological family, by encouraging either free love (in which sexual contact with all others was required) or celibacy (in which no one had sexual contact), and by separating biological families by means of communal child-rearing, so as to give everyone a more equal share in man-woman and adult-child relationships.

Family feeling was enhanced by selection of a homogeneous group of members; by full communistic sharing of property; by communistic labor in which no jobs were compensated, everyone shared equally in benefits, jobs were rotated, and some work was done by the whole community; by regular group contact through decision-making meetings; and by rituals emphasizing the communion of the whole. The processes encouraging identity change in long-lived communes tended to consist both of mutual criticism sessions in which issues of commitment to and deviance from community standards were examined and of stratification systems that accorded deference to those best living up to community norms.

Long-lived communes tended to have elaborate ideologies to provide purpose and meaning for community life and to serve as the ultimate guide and justification for decisions. They tended to have strong central figures, charismatic leaders, who symbolized the community's values, made final decisions, and set spiritual and structural guidelines. That is, while routine decisions might be made by assemblies of the whole or committees with special responsibilities, and while administrative and other work assignments might be rotated and shared, the charismatic leader, as value bearer, remained the ultimate source of authority. Long-lived communities also tended to have fixed daily work routines and personal conduct rules – all deriving from ideology and informing an individual of his responsibilities. Finally, they tended to require ideological conversion for admission and did not automatically admit all applicants.

### Longevity and Success

To create a long-lived communal order thus requires many fairly strict and demanding social practices. A number of questions remain about the cost as well as gains involved in commitment to a strong community. One central issue is whether longevity is a necessary or sufficient measure of a group's success. With respect to nineteenth-century utopian communities at least, longevity is a valid criterion of success, not only because it is easily measurable but also because for many communities in the nineteenth century their over-riding goal was simply to exist — to establish a social order embodying all their ideals and to make of it a viable, stable, and permanent organization. In addition, the long-lived communities are assumed to have been successful at generating and maintaining commitment and at providing whatever satisfactions people wanted from life in a utopia, because over a long period of time members remained loyal, loving, dedicated, and obedient. Their devotion and will to survive weathered economic crises, physical relocations, natural disasters ranging from fires to famines to disease, societal persecution, internal dissension, and even crises of leadership succession. The unsuccessful communities, however, often fell apart at the first sign of stress or difficulty. Although there are other possible ways of evaluating the "success" of a utopian community — such as the personal satisfaction of members or the degree of congruence between original ideals and actual existence — in many cases these other indicators of success contribute to longevity and thus are usually found to a greater extent in the long-lived communities than in the short-lived ones. Maintenance of the community, in fact, can in itself contribute to personal satisfaction, in that it offers safety, security, and a stable group with which to build deep, fulfilling relationships, as well as being a source of pride and self-esteem for the individual because he is part of something successful and hence important and worth-while.

In the successful nineteenth-century utopias, there were a number of ways of dealing with group relations, property, work, values, and leadership that created an enduring commitment — providing the motivation to work, the will to continue, fellow-ship, and cohesion as a group. At the same time that these practices enabled the successful communities to survive in terms of longevity, they also created strong communities in the utopian sense and fulfilled the same desires that even today impel people toward community. The successful groups asked people to give up separateness, personal pride and vanity, exclusive ownership, conflicting social ties, other value systems, and disruptive personal prerogatives, and to submit to the control of the group over even their thoughts and feelings. In return, successful groups provided for their members strong feelings of participation, involvement, and of belonging to a family group. They built a world centered around sharing — of property, work, living space, feelings, or values. They offered identity and meaning, a value-oriented life with direction and purpose. Both the giving up and the getting were perceived by members as rewarding.

Martin Buber has written about the psychic benefits of community. He indicated that only a comprehensive community, one that touches the individual in every aspect of his life, can give him a sense of complete affirmation as a person and of belonging to some greater, all-embracing structure. Only the full cooperative, amalgamating production and consumption and asking a person's total commitment, can offer such rewards.[1] It takes shared activity and a common goal to bring about the benefits of community. William Alfred Hinds, a member of the Oneida Community who traveled to other communities in the summer of 1876, asked members of Zoar what advantages they enjoyed in communal living:

The advantages are many and great. All distinctions of rich and poor are abolished. The members have no care except for their own spiritual culture. Communism provides for the sick, the weak, the unfortunate, all alike, which makes their life comparatively easy and pleasant. In case of great loss by fire or flood or other cause, the burden which would be ruinous to one is easily borne by the many. Charity and genuine love one to another, which are the foundations of true Christianity, can be more readily cultivated and practiced in Communism than in common, isolated society. Finally, a Community is the best place in which to get rid of selfishness, willfulness, and bad habits and vices generally; for we are subject to the constant surveillance and reproof of others, which, rightly taken, will go far toward preparing us for the large community above.[2]

### Commitment, Centralization, and Control

The most enduring communes were also the most centralized and the most tightly controlled. Georg Simmel in writing about secret societies pointed out an important paradox in social life: that groups which leave the established order to get away from its restrictiveness often end up duplicating that very order in their own internal structure. Simmel called this a "ubiquitous social norm": "structures which resist larger, encompassing structures through opposition and separation, nevertheless themselves repeat the forms of these structures." One reason is that separation from the society diffuses human energy, while centralization in the new group holds it together. Simmel indicated that people seek a balance between freedom and control. Groups that enjoy autonomy and separateness with respect to the larger society, therefore, need internal controls in order to maintain the proper ratio: "Man needs a certain ratio between freedom and law; and . . . when he does not receive it from *one* source, he seeks to supplement what he obtains of the one by the missing quantity of the other, no matter from what additional source, until he has the ratio he needs." Philip Slater also described the human need for creating order out of chaos that occurs in groups without societally imposed limits. Unable to face uncertainty and ambiguity, members of such groups often take refuge in collective fantasies of a planned and preordained universe in which they are acting out a prescribed role.[3]

As a result, the function of strong norms, highly developed programs for behavior, elaborate ideologies, and centralized authority is not only to promote total commitment but also to provide certainty, clarity, and security for members of groups that have rejected the established order. But the norms, programs, and authorities of communal groups are different from those of the wider society in one important respect: they are self-imposed, being voluntarily chosen by the same people who must submit to them. People enter the community of their own free will and develop the rules of their joint life themselves; the norms are subject to modification; and the authorities are immediately present and participating in the group. Job rotation may involve positions of leadership and responsibility, so that some power is shared. In relatively small groups such as the nineteenth century communes, which averaged two hundred members, people are in close enough contact to influence each other and the leaders. Perhaps this close contact and potential for influence is the difference between centralized regimes that are authoritarian and alienating and those which are not; in the latter cases, the group itself creates its own rules of law. If the group is small, it can bear centralization without losing the opportunity for all members to participate. Centralization in a small face-to-face group need not therefore be coercive, but may merely be the organizational fact that lends the group coherence and unity. Buber explained: "The real essence of community is to be found in the fact — manifest or otherwise — that it has a centre. The real beginning of a community is when its members have a common relation to the centre overriding all other relations."[4]

Yet nineteenth century groups were characterized not only by centralization but also by a high degree of participation and involvement in the everyday life of the community, resulting from the development of a democratic brotherhood. Both factors were present simultaneously: strong central leaders and a democratic membership. According to Simmel, secret societies also combine despotism or centralized authority with a brotherly equality of members.[5] This seeming paradox is in part a function of the fact that in some communes the leader was often primarily a figurehead, a symbol for the group's values, who counseled the community on spiritual and ideological matters but left members free to make decisions jointly about day-to-day operations of the commune. Though John Humphrey Noyes was crucial to Oneida, as was George Rapp to Harmony, everyday affairs at Oneida were handled by a democratically elected board and rotating committees, while Rapp's adopted son Frederick was one of several people who coordinated worldly affairs at one period of Harmony's history. Perhaps the dual existence of strong central figures with democratic participation helped to effect the balance between freedom and order needed by communities. While the group had autonomy and could allow all to participate equally, there was also an ultimate guide.

The coincidence of strong leaders and democratic brotherhood is also explained by the psychoanalytic view of group process.

him, persecuted equally by him, and fear or revere him equally.[6]
According to this view, it would not be accidental that the
nineteenth century communes called their leaders "father" and
sometimes saw themselves as children, for without a parent
there can be no brothers and sisters. It is in dealing with a
parental figure that the brotherhood — and autonomy — of
members can emerge. This has been found to be the case in
laboratory training groups, which begin to cohere as a group
only when they confront their common relation to authority.[7]
In addition, the authority figure may be important for the
reduction of differences between members, since homogeneity
or mutual identification is important for commitment. Perhaps
the common subjection of members to the guidance and
ultimate authority of the leader, overwhelming all other differences, may in part help to create the equality of brotherhood.

Just as people require a balance between order and freedom,
they may also need a balance between involvement and autonomy. It is possible that there can be a surfeit of commitment
mechanisms. That is, up to a point the greater the number of
commitment mechanisms a group uses, the stronger the commitment of its members. But past that number, commitment
mechanisms may become dysfunctional for the group: they may
be perceived as oppressive and may stifle the person's autonomy
to the extent that he becomes less rather than more committed.

Successful nineteenth-century groups used most but not
all of the commitment mechanisms outlined. Each group made
its own selection and put together a "commitment package"
out of all the possible ways to build commitment. There were
always some commitment mechanisms that certain groups
did not utilize. Amana, for example, retained the family, while
Zoar did not have a particularly elaborate ideology.

Moreover, most of the successful nineteenth-century groups
retained some private space. All of them had enough land
and buildings to provide a sense of movement around community territories; members were not tightly enclosed in a
small space. There were many options about places to be within
the community, even if these places were not always totally
private. In fact, it was the unsuccessful rather than the successful groups that more frequently developed communal house-

holds in which all members lived together in one space, this being the only instance in which a higher proportion of unsuccessful groups utilized a commitment mechanism. In the successful groups, even if members spent most of their time with other people, they often had a spot where they could retire to be alone or visit with just a few. Harmony and Amana, for example, had separate houses for each family.

At the same time, the successful communes were large enough to permit some options with respect to relationships. Although "exclusive love" was prohibited by Oneida and the Shakers, extending even to friendships, other communes emphasized the unity of the whole but placed no particular strictures on special attachments. In fact, in a community of about two hundred people, regardless of the avowed standard of loving everyone equally, there are enough possible relationships with different people to offer a sense of variety and personal choice.

Finally, none of the successful nineteenth-century communes sprung into being full-blown, with a complete program of commitment mechanisms that immediately demanded the person's complete and utter devotion. The successful groups all had long, slow periods of getting organized. They derived from previously existing groups and built on already-formed relations and traditions. They developed their communities by stages, as in the case of Oneida's growth from a Bible class to a shared household in Vermont to a comprehensive community. Members often made choices at each step of the way, as in Harmony's 1807 decision to adopt celibacy. Some commitment mechanisms arose from necessity rather than ideology. The full organization grew out of a series of smaller steps and built on existing commitment as the base for generating more commitment. This process, too, gave members a sense of options. What may have looked to later generations like an overwhelming structure was merely an agreement on the part of their parents to formalize practices that had grown up at particular phases of their existence. All of these phenomena — options about space, about relationships, and a gradual development — must have enabled the members of successful nineteenth-century communes to which tend to have limited space, a small number of people, and the desire to become a community at once, and which therefore resist the ordering of group life.

Commitment is crucial for a utopian community, but it is also necessary for any group trying to develop a sense of community. Commitment mechanisms are exaggerated versions of processes that may emerge in all groups. Simmel listed, for example, a large number of properties of secret societies that resemble the commitment-building aspects of communal groups, including hierarchy, ritual, protection of the "shared truth" from outsiders, extragroup conflict, formal initiation, seclusion, de-individualization, and "group egoism," in which "selfishness" is concentrated on the attainment of group ends.[8] In its formal self-sufficiency, the commune has much in common with the secret society.

The issues around which commitment mechanisms arise, such as ownership, intimacy, selection, socialization, and decision-making, are shared by all groups. Even new groups of limited duration, to the extent that they share communal aims and are concerned about the quality of relations among themselves, often strive to achieve a specialness of the group as an entity beyond the mere collection of individuals present. For example, as certain contemporary communes emerge as a group, though they would resist the implication that they are "building commitment," they nevertheless begin informally to develop ways of binding a person to the group and cutting him off from his past or from life outside the commune. For example, a parallel to the Shakers' vitriolic renunciation of their former, biological families is the bitterness with which some communards today condemn their parents or, more often, the life that their parents have led. The firm rejection of other ways of life, particularly those representing options that the commune members once held, helps reinforce the belief that the commune is a special, valuable, and worthwhile place. Parents also represent a set of ties that not all members of the commune share, whereas the cohesiveness of the group is dependent in part on elevating that which is shared to a higher moral and emotional plane than that which cannot be included in the group or shared by all members. "What we have together is more beautiful than what we have apart" is echoed by many communes. Also recurrent is the theme: "What we have and are *now* is more important and worthwhile than what we may have been separately." In some communes this view results in a noticeable lack of interest in members' pasts and even in resentment of discussions of life before the group. A researcher at a communal farm in Oregon reported that the ten adults there knew relatively little about each other's backgrounds, claiming instead that what mattered was how one acted after joining the commune, not before: "We accept a person for what he is, not what he was."[9]

Such reasoning contributes to the elevation of the group's present existence to a higher moral plane than the individual members' past or outside lives. Even when this elevation of the group is not voiced explicitly, and when the group claims to be content with a loose federation of individuals rather than a close-knit entity, this is still an underlying theme in contemporary communes. A woman living with her husband in an urban commune which they intended to leave after one year reported the awkwardness and uneasiness she nevertheless experienced when her parents came to visit her in the commune. They were a reminder of her noncommunal past, as well as having a share with her in something that could not be shared by other commune members. The issue of outside relations and of visits from friends is a live one for groups, which is dealt with in many ways. Some groups regard visitors as the property of the entire group, no matter whom they have come to visit, so that visitors may find themselves overwhelmed by greetings, by curious children, and by efforts to secure them a place in the life of the whole commune rather than just with those they have come to visit. In other communes the process of visiting and the role of visitor may become a matter of group policy and decision. The Drop City commune in New Mexico built a special visitors' dome, particularly for parents who wished to visit, which in a sense put them in their place.[10]

One more example from contemporary communes illustrates the ways in which commitment processes emerge as a natural part of group development, even if this is not the group's intent. Members of some communes where communal ownership is not required and where property is held individually still feel the pressure to take pride only in things that are held in common rather than those which belong to them separately. In a rural California commune I spoke with a particularly respected member of the commune who had just finished building a striking one-room, two-level redwood house with the help of some others in the group. She expressed both pride and guilt — guilt that she should have such a nice house for her own.

## Religion and Community

Historians and other observers of nineteenth-century American communities have sometimes argued that it was religion which held the successful groups together; and in fact, all of the nine successful communities that I studied began with some kind of religious base. But this was also true of a large number of the unsuccessful communities, including some of those often regarded as "secular," like Brook Farm. David Smith pointed out that Brook Farm grew out of millenarian traditions partly to bring about the "Kingdom of Heaven on earth" and to herald the "second coming of Christ."[11] Its founder was a Unitarian minister, George Ripley. Other unsuccessful groups included the Christian communities of Hopedale (which managed to survive for fifteen years) and Oberlin (lasting eight years), the Mormon Order of Enoch (three years), and the schismatic Mormon community of Preparation (two years). Moreover, of the successful communities, Oneida developed from a specifically religious group into a secular community rationally implementing political, economic, and social philosophies. In general, the differences between the successful and unsuccessful communes was much broader than religion alone, so it does not seem that the presence of a religion or of religious origins per se made the difference between success and failure.

However, there are many social practices often associated with religion that were useful in building commitment. These practices include a comprehensive value system and a transcendent moral order with many moral principles, which easily give rise to spiritual differentiation. Religious groups often require shared beliefs and conversion to those beliefs, which may include belief in inspiration, revelation, or nonscientific sources of wisdom. Religious groups sometimes have charismatic leaders invested with extraordinary properties. Membership in such groups may involve sacrifice and deliberate rejection of the material world, along with confession and mutual criticism. Finally, ritual and symbolic, expressive ceremonies, including the use of music and singing, is often characteristic of religious groups. It is these specific practices, available even to groups that resist a deliberate religious focus, which build commitment, not the presence of a formally labelled religion. Even with theology totally absent, moral principles, sacrifice, mutual criticism, ritual, and expressive ceremonies can still be an important part of a group. The contemporary Twin Oaks commune totally rejects any connection with religion but still employs several of these commitment mechanisms.

The conjunction of such social forms with religious systems probably does give religious groups an edge in terms of organizing their communities for maximum viability. But in many groups lacking an identification with the sacred or supernatural and lacking a specific religious focus, such as radical political movements or Synanon, some of the same commitment mechanisms are found, and these groups should have the same chances for success. In fact, the conceptual framework offered here is potentially useful in understanding commitment to any group of people interested in building community among themselves, establishing strong social ties, maintaining control over behavior, and in general, integrating individuals with social systems. The mechanisms and the commitment functions they serve may apply, in various forms and with suitable modifications, to small groups such as sensitivity training groups, to socialization institutions such as schools and therapeutic communities; to business organizations interested in human relations, to deviant or alternative communities such as the Black Muslims or the Hasidic Jews, to residential communities such as black ghettoes, to political parties, and to nations.

The commitment mechanisms examined here represent a pool of possible ways in which groups can organize around the areas of commitment. Even though about 120 mechanisms were found in nineteenth century communities, this is not an

exhaustive list; there may be other ways in which the same
functions can be served, and many mechanisms may serve
more than one function. Some of the specific practices reported
may also be peculiar to nineteenth century America and may
take slightly different forms in cultures with different premises,
such as today's. Moreover, for a community to succeed, it
is not necessary to do all of the things described here. Successful
groups did most but not all of them and sometimes not throughout their existence. Communities choose social practices based
on their own standards, values, needs, and historical circumstances, and for communities interested in building commitment, these will represent a selection from the pool of possible
commitment mechanisms. The more commitment mechanisms a
community institutes, however, the greater its chances for
success (at least up to the limit at which the individual tends
to be completely erased in favor of the group). It should also
be clear that every aspect of community life has implications
for commitment – recruitment, property, work, decision-
making, leadership, family relations, intimacy – and all of these
can be organized in ways that build commitment or detract
from it.

I have presented those things that worked in the past to build
commitment and hence the social base for viable utopias and
communes. Achieving these is the major battle in creating
utopia. But even the successful groups did not last forever, for
there are other dilemmas to be faced by utopian communities.

*What if there is not another bright spot in the
wide world, and what if this is a very small one?
Turn your eye toward it when you are tired of
looking into chaos, and you will catch a glimpse
of a better world.*
—John Humphrey Noyes, *History of American
Socialisms*

*The daughter of a member of a hippie com-
mune was asked, "What do you want to be
when you grow up?" She replied, "Straight."*
1971 Joke


# 6    Away from Community

Whether members were strongly committed to the communal
group made an important difference in the lives of nineteenth-
century American utopian communities. The successful ones
grew and flourished, fulfilling and satisfying their members,
while others dissolved. Though all of the communes faced a
variety of natural disasters, financial problems, and internal disagreements, the successful groups had the strength to endure
despite such hardships. Yet even the long-lived communities
eventually died. Their ends were a function not of the hardships
and inevitable problems of communal life but of dilemmas
arising from longevity itself. Many suffered a progressive
deterioration of their communal ideals by virtue of the practical
needs of existence. They had difficult problems of adaptation
to a changing environment. They experienced an erosion of
membership because of population aging and through loss of
some of the second generation. They encountered a gradual
skepticism over the possibility for realizing the ideals that had
formed the original basis for communal existence. Finally,
successful groups faced a number of pulls away from communalism stemming from the nature of social life itself.

## Disasters, Debts, and Disagreements

The breakup of unsuccessful nineteenth-century groups was
prompted by a variety of circumstances that successful communities also faced but survived. Kendal, for example, dissolved

after a summer fever epidemic, whereas Harmony survived
bouts of malaria in 1804 and fever in 1814, Bethel weathered
malaria in 1845, the Shakers overcame two epidemics in South
Union, Kentucky, in 1810, and Zoar survived a cholera epidemic in 1834 that killed one hundred people, or half the
population. Although Northampton and Brook Farm broke up
after major fires, Harmony, Saint Nazianz, and the Shakers
survived several disasters, including serious fires and a flood in
the 1800s in their Groveland, New York, village (a community
still prosperous in 1874), and a fire that destroyed a Harmony
factory in 1834 causing $60,000 worth of damage. The Inde-
pendence community, site for the Mormon Order of Enoch,
dissolved when pressure from their neighbors forced them
to leave, and Utopia broke up because land prices prevented
their expansion in Ohio; yet successful groups were able to
migrate to other locations while still maintaining the community
intact: Harmony moved twice, from Pennsylvania to Indiana
and back again to Pennsylvania; and Amana moved once, from
Ebenezer, New York, to Iowa. Nashoba, Hopedale, and Northampton all had financial difficulties that made it impossible for
them to continue, while the successful groups, at least early
in their lives, rallied through similar periods of debt and deprivation. Successful groups thus faced many of the external crises
that ended unsuccessful groups, but they had the collective
strength, the commitment, to weather the blow.
   In addition to external crises, unsuccessful nineteenth-century
utopian communities faced a variety of internal difficulties.
Communia, Skaneateles, Fruitlands, Jasper, Nashoba, Bishop
Hill, and New Harmony all experienced major schisms, dissension, or challenges to the leadership that were instrumental
in prompting their dissolution. Fruitlands, a community that
never in its brief eight-month history numbered more than
sixteen, was the scene of constant differences between its
founders, Bronson Alcott and Charles Lane. Communia was
subjected to charges of embezzlement against one leader,
the secession of some members, demands to move the group to
California, and members' demands for a forty-acre deed to
the land from another leader, Wilhelm Weitling. Skaneateles
suffered constant tension between a radical faction led by John

Collins, the founder, and a less radical subgroup, until Collins finally left the community, precipitating the breakup. Nashoba faced a major schism when George Flower, one of its original backers, withdrew after Frances Wright, the major leader, had publicly espoused radical views. The North American Phalanx suffered splits and secessions that resulted in 1853 in both the formation of another community and a major religious controversy, the year before the fire that precipitated its dissolution. New Harmony experienced disagreement and dissent from the start, including quarrels over interpretation of the constitution, secession by a religious-minded group, secession by a group of English farmers to form their own community, attacks on Robert Owen's philosophy, and the organization of three separate economic societies on community land. Preparation dissolved as the consequence of a revolt against the leader, Charles Thompson and the subsequent lawsuit. In 1855 a group of members had challenged Thompson's appropriation of the community's property and demanded its division among individual members; when they were unsuccessful, some members withdrew. In 1858 the remaining members decided to force the issue and filed a lawsuit, resulting in the community's dissolution.

Successful groups tended not to suffer major dissensions of this kind until their final days, although small numbers of people would leave from time to time to seek their fortunes elsewhere or, as in the case of celibate groups like the Shakers and Harmony, to "flesh off" into the world or elope. Harmony, however did weather one major incident, the Count Leon affair. Count Leon, whose real name was Bernard Muller, was a self-proclaimed minister of Christ who arrived in Harmony from Germany with a group of followers in 1831. His views conflicted sharply with Harmony's asceticism by encouraging Harmonists to seek marriage and a better style of dress and living. In general, he fomented dissatisfaction and discord, especially among the young, which culminated in an attempt by Leon to replace George Rapp as leader, supported by 250 members or one third of the society. The outcome was an agreement whereby Leon and his followers withdrew to a site ten miles away and relinquished all claims against Harmony property

for a settlement of $150,000. The Leon group later returned
to Harmony bent on demanding additional sums by violence,
but they were driven out and eventually retreated to Louisiana.
According to one contemporary writer, the loss of 250 people
was actually a gain, for the community was relieved of discordant members, and the harmony and brotherly love of earlier
years were recaptured.[1] Despite this incident, or perhaps even
because of the resultant cohesion among remaining members,
Harmony continued to grow and prosper — in contrast to the
fate of unsuccessful groups after similar incidents.

Thus, the successful communes survived the kinds of disasters,
debts, and disagreements that proved too much for the more
vulnerable groups. Later, however, the successful communities,
too, faced serious difficulties that led to their demise, either
in a formal dissolution or through gradual disintegration. A
number of special conditions were responsible for the ultimate
collapse of even those communities that for a generation or
more had maintained strong commitment.

A Changing Environment

Communes are subject to three long-range dynamics which,
over time, may alter the basic nature of the community, confront it with difficult problems of adaptation and survival,
or contribute to its collapse. Two of these problems are common to any human group: environments change, and people
grow old. Through inaction, a communal group can become
obsolescent or die off. In fact, the "healthy" community
may be one that can countenance its own death when it no
longer fulfills the needs of its members or when it no longer
competes favorably with the rewards offered by the larger
society. If the group wishes to continue, however, it must somehow deal with changes in the external society, from choosing
to ignore them to incorporating them. The first choice runs the
risk that the changes will intrude anyway. This was what happened when the increasing technology, improved transportation,
expanding communications, and wider availability of luxury
goods intruded on the isolation and often the asceticism of
certain nineteenth-century American utopias, like Harmony

Amana, and Zoar. Because the community had no way to cope
with the changes except by turning its back or continuing
to forbid increased consumption or contact with the more
accessible outside world, it could not cope with the discontent
and disaffection aroused. The basis for community was slowly
eroded. To the extent that the community chose instead to
incorporate the products or results of external social change, it
faced the possibility that such adaptations would in themselves
drastically alter the community – though Joseph Eaton has
shown that for the Hutterites, at least, such "controlled acculturation" helped them weather the consequences of a rapidly
changing, technologically advancing society.[2]

For several of the successful nineteenth-century communities,
coping with a changing environment, whichever way they
chose to do so, proved to undermine the communal base, and
the gradually increasing introduction of goods, life styles, and
fashions from the outside world brought with it tendencies
away from community and toward individualism and material-
ism. According to Bertha Shambaugh, a member who witnessed
the dissolution of Amana as a utopian community: "The old
integrity, the old solidarity, could not successfully resist the en-
croachments of the world and the powerful influences of the
machine age. The forefathers had drawn a circle around the
Community designed to keep the world out; but the world made
a larger circle and drew the Community within its orb . . . A
machine civilization drew Amana into its inextricable circle and
taught it all it knows." Amana nevertheless survived further
into the twentieth century than any other nineteenth-century
community except the Shakers, dissolving formally in 1932 into
two separate organizations, a church and a capitalistic business.
In its last quarter-century, many things changed owing to a
changing external environment. Radios, cameras, and bicycles
became common; pianos and organs appeared, as well as a
few privately owned automobiles. Dress regulations were
relaxed, perhaps as a consequence of cotton shortages during
World War I, which halted the dyeing and printing of Amana
calico. The outside world encroached in other ways, too.
Though the community's founders had warned the membership
to avoid contact with "worldly minded men," this rule was

gradually eroded, and by the closing days of Amana there were tens of thousands of visitors, all dressed in the new fashions and influencing Amana women and men. Along with the tourists came propagandists and cash-bearing antique hunters. Shambaugh reported that religious zeal declined as contact with the outside world increased. Members were more apt to "shirk the common burdens of the Community," and many more men were employed outside.[3] Thus, the changing, industrializing, urbanizing American society surrounding this community, like others in the nineteenth century, affected it in a number of ways: isolation was reduced, and new goods and life styles were introduced that worked to the detriment of community.

Whatever relationship a group establishes with its environment, with the world outside its borders; however well it patrols its boundaries; and no matter what it decides to accept or reject of the life of the outside — this relationship is subject to continual revision in the face of changes in that external environment. By the second half of the nineteenth century, for example, the Shaker leaders were divided into three camps based on the degree of separation from the world that they favored. Oneida was split by generations over the issue of religion versus science. However, a group may institutionalize its original relation to the world as the basis of its internal commitment and life style to the extent that it cannot easily modify policies or adapt to external changes without undermining that commitment. It becomes overdependent on set conditions. This rigidity was the rule in many of the long-lived nineteenth century communities. Early in their histories, in the first half of the century, external social change was not as rapid as later, so that the communities could settle into established policies and routines without developing methods of providing for flexibility. Today's communes, facing a rapidly changing society, tend to develop such techniques as part of their routine operation. The Israeli kibbutzim, for example, are finding means to incorporate television. Synanon, whose loose structure has lasted throughout its history, continually adds elements suitable to the latest developments on the outside, incorporates new technology and changes labels and secondary concepts, which injects dynamism into a stable structure. While the framework remains, various parts are always changing. Thus, Synanon, unlike nineteenth century communities, has established channels through which change can be introduced without undermining the basis for the community's existence. For the longer-lived nineteenth century communities, external change was corrosive. To ignore it, as the Shakers did, meant a gradual withering away of the community. To adapt to it generally meant a dissolution or transformation of the community. Several of the once-comprehensive utopian communities evolved into one or two specialized parts of themselves that could more easily manage a relationship to a changing external environment: Amana divided into a church and a business, Oneida became a business, and Zoar was transformed into a municipality.

### Aging, Recruitment, and the Second Generation

A changing environment was only one of the multiple dynamics contributing to the decline or demise of the long-lasting nineteenth century communes. A second problem faced by all groups is the elementary fact of life that people grow old and die. A group can face this fact in several ways. One is to decide that it does not wish to outlive its last two members. This course ends the group naturally at a particular point, but suffers the consequence of a steadily aging population, with its associated difficulties in maintaining community. For example, as members become too infirm to do certain community tasks, outsiders are needed to supply the necessities of life. Harmony faced the problem of an aging population (even though children had been raised in the community). By the 1870s there was only a score of old people left, and the group could no longer maintain its self-sufficiency: it had to stop manufacturing and start buying. In Oneida, by 1880 fifty percent of the members were forty or older.[4]

If a group wishes to continue beyond the life spans of the original members, it has two options: to try to recruit members from the outside, or to bear children and raise them to perpetuate the community. Both measures proved difficult for the nineteenth century utopias, although the Shakers lasted a

remarkably long time as a celibate community recruiting new
members, sometimes including whole families and orphans.
But according to many reports, most of the children raised by
the Shakers did not remain in the community when old enough
to leave. In general, the second generation is not necessarily
the most reliable source of committed adults to perpetuate the
community. Regardless of how well socialized they are, their
commitment must be different from that of their first-generation
parents. The second generation did not choose to live in the
community, like their parents; nor were they converted to
a belief in the community's ideals after weighing the alternatives;
nor did they seek the commune because of personal depriva-
tions. For the children, life in the community is a given; it is
their base-line experience. Thus, as committed as they may be
to the community, their commitment stems from different life
experiences from that of their parents. In many communities,
possibly for this reason, children are not automatically admitted
to full membership status when they reach adulthood but
must indicate a firm commitment of their own. Even so, and
even though there are a number of ways in which commitment
can be built into the second generation, in nineteenth-century
American utopias the second and subsequent generations were
less committed and left the community more often, attracted
by the lures of the changing outside world. The children often
rebelled against the commitments made for them by their
parents. In Zoar the second generation was less committed to
communal property ownership than the first, the third was
even less so.

Recruitment of outsiders poses other problems, for often
they introduce a discordant element into the community. It
was outside recruits, for example, who challenged the leadership of John Humphrey Noyes in Oneida. The recruiting effort
itself, involving travel, can conceivably require more time and
community energy than the group is willing to give. Moreover,
whatever life problems the community originated in response to
may change as the world outside changes, so that over time
the community competes less favorably with the outside
or with other newer social movements for membership. None

of the long-lived nineteenth century utopias had massive
recruiting efforts, and even for those like the Shakers that
attracted many newcomers during the spiritual revivals of the
1840s, recruitment dropped off in the second half of the
nineteenth century. Saint Nazianz in particular declined as
members got older and new people stopped joining.

Aging or dying membership, difficulties in retaining the
second generation, and problems of recruitment all contributed
to the dissolution of long-lived nineteenth century communities.
The aging dynamic had especially serious consequences for
some of these communities when connected with the death of a
charismatic founder. Some communities, however successful
in other ways, could not outlive the death of their first great
leader. For Bethel and Aurora, William Keil's death left the
people at a loss. Jerusalem declined after Jemimah Wilkinson's
death. The death of Father Ambrose Ochswald of Saint Nazianz
resulted in confusion and brought to the surface complaints
that people had not dared to express during his lifetime.[5] To
add to the confusion, communal property had been held in
his name, and although he willed it to the community, that
body could not inherit property because it was not incorporated.
The death of the charismatic founder in these three groups
led to the death of the community.

The fact that environments change and that people get older
and die are problems shared by utopian communities with
other human groups. There is a third dynamic more specifically
associated with utopian communities which, intertwined with
the other two, resulted in the dissolution of successful nineteenth-century communes. This is the tension connected with
the duality inherent in utopian communities: they are concerned
both with applying values in a new way and with functioning
in the existing world. To some extent, the social structure and
patterns associated with the second aspect are incompatible
with the factors building community. To the degree that the
successful nineteenth-century groups began to develop efficient
systems for production and management of external relations,
they also began to undermine community, weakening commitment, and making the group vulnerable to the forces that finally

dissolved it. To indicate the nature of this strain in the life histories of utopian communities requires an excursion into theory.

## Two Pulls in Social Life

Utopian communities in the nineteenth century sought both to enhance meaningful interpersonal relationships and to provide political, economic, and other services for their members. They attempted both to express values and to implement practical concerns in a single social unit. If the term utopian has come to connote impractical and impossible, it may be owing to what many have felt to be an inherent contradiction between these two sets of aims of utopian communities. Criticisms have been leveled at utopian communities to the effect that social life cannot be both "human" and "efficient," that brotherhood and economics do not mix, that it is impossible both to satisfy individual needs and to work toward the collective good, and that value expression is incompatible with pragmatism. This theme of the incompatibility of two strains in social life is also central to sociological thought in the distinction between *Gemeinschaft* and *Gesellschaft*.

Gemeinschaft relations include the nonrational, affective, emotional, traditional, and expressive components of social action, as in a family; Gesellschaft relations comprise the rational, contractual, instrumental, and task-oriented actions, as in a business corporation. In Gemeinschaft relations, actors are said to interact as whole persons; in Gesellschaft relations, as specific parts of their personalities, interacting for specific and limited purposes. Three early social theorists, Ferdinand Toennies, Max Weber, and Emile Durkheim, were responsible for first formulating elements of this dichotomy.[6]

Though Gemeinschaft and Gesellschaft refer to ideal types rather than actual social groups and are old-fashioned sociological terms, they are useful in describing the two pulls experienced by utopian communities. The Gemeinschaft aspects of a utopian community consist of those mutually expressive, supportive, value-oriented, emotion-laden, personally-directed, loving social relations often called "community." They include mutual recognition of the values, temperament, character, and human needs of group members. Their highest priority is maintenance of values and close relations, and they are based on commitment, the personal involvement of participating members. In contrast, the Gesellschaft elements in a utopian community consist of those relations that are functional for dealing with environments, whether physical, social, or supernatural; for "getting the job done"; for acquiring things the group needs from its environment; for maximizing feedback and exchange with other systems in the form of information, resources, or acceptance. They include any activity that is relevant to conducting environmental exchanges regardless of the specific people involved. Gesellschaft systems organize group relations around the demands of tasks. Since any group that forms a "community" must also produce something or manage exchanges with an environment, and since these aims may require different and possibly incompatible forms of organization, a tension is set up that can force the group to make a choice of emphasis. The predominant movement of many of the successful nineteenth-century groups was away from a heavy initial emphasis on community toward the predominance of Gesellschaft. This change meant the end of the community and its transformation into a specialized organization. Amana, for example, evolved from a highly value-oriented Gemeinschaft community, in which production was secondary and designed only to meet subsistence requirements of the group, to a business-oriented system, hoping nevertheless to maintain its now secondary spiritual and human concerns: "The new Amana [after its dissolution and reorganization] is something more than a modern business structure with emphasis on methods and efficiency and the earning power of the dollar . . . There is a manifest desire to keep intact, as far as possible, the Community consciousness born of a precious heritage — a wealth of common aspirations and memories, and of spiritual assets that cannot be weighed, nor measured, nor tabulated, nor charted."[7] The evolution of Oneida in a similar direction, ending in a joint-stock company carrying on a silverware-manufacturing business, is strikingly demonstrated by changes in the community's newspaper, *The Circular*, noted by

Maren Lockwood. In 1851, three years after the founding of
Oneida, almost all of *The Circular* was devoted to religion.
By 1861, about half dealt with religion, and by 1870, less than
a third. In 1876 *The Circular* was renamed *The American
Socialist.*[8]

This tension between the two pulls in social life was a factor in
practically all of the nineteenth century communes studied,
for the great majority of them were more than simple agricultural societies; they were to some extent concerned not only
about production of enough goods and services for the community but also about their commercial and political relations
with the larger society. Most of them had businesses of one kind
or another, sometimes servicing the community primarily but
also exchanging goods with the outside society. Zoar had both
agriculture and industry, including woolen, linen, and flour
mills, a timber planing business, and a wagon shop. Oneida in its
early years engaged in farming and silk-jobbing besides running
a flour mill, saw mill, and machine shop. It then began successful
fruit-canning, bag-manufacturing, and animal trap businesses,
and still later a successful silverware factory. Saint Nazianz sold
cheese, beer, straw hats, shoes, and wheat. Among Harmony's
items of commerce were hides, grains, furs, waxes, linen,
tobacco, and cheese. The Shakers are still known for the furniture they manufactured.

The kinds of organization that are functional for production
and business operations may often conflict with the commitment mechanisms that serve to maintain community feeling.
This issue is being faced by communal groups today. As the
Israeli kibbutzim, for example, industrialize and build modern
factories on their grounds, they are coping with the issue of
maintaining a value-oriented, communal society that at the same
time permits efficient industrial production and remains fully
a part of the modern world. So far they have avoided the several
dilemmas arising from the two pulls in social life that contributed to the weakening of commitment and the dissolution of
the successful nineteenth-century groups. These dilemmas
involved pulls toward permeability, isomorphism, value indeterminism, and perpetuation strategies that undermined community.

Permeability refers to the degree to which community boundaries are open and permit penetration of movement across them; that is, the ease with which people can pass over the group's boundaries. Such easy passage is functional for economic and political tasks for several reasons. The necessity of dealing with external systems requires an organizational structure that is not totally encapsulated. For one thing, commercial enterprises need information about the state of the environmental systems with which they must deal — about market conditions, for example. Permeability facilitates the garnering of information and the attainment of feedback, for it is relatively easy for information and feedback-bearers to pass in and out of the organization. Similarly, organizations can exchange personnel if easy passage into the system is possible and can thereby learn about external systems. Furthermore, when boundaries between the organization and its environments are not well defined or rigid, the line between what constitutes the organization's and the environment's interests may appear to be erased, so that helping the organization meet its goals may at the same time fulfill more general public interests.

Permeability can further aid dealings with the environment through the creation of boundary roles for the organization — roles such as salesman, customer relations specialist, or ambassador — which must often operate both within and outside the organization simultaneously. Many nineteenth-century groups, for example, had salesmen. In order for these roles to be effective and to facilitate exchange with the external systems with which they deal, organization boundaries must be relatively permeable. In addition, organizations must perform jobs for their members, and to this end they require resources and personnel. If necessary, these must be quickly attainable and deployable without requiring a difficult passage through a rigid boundary. If labor is required to meet immediate needs, for example, it is not altogether functional to insist that manpower wait through a six-month probationary period or that it make financial contributions. If boundaries are relatively permeable, appropriate experts, resources, and staff can be more easily imported. The most production-oriented of the successful nineteenth-century groups (Amana, Oneida, Harmony, the

Shakers, and Zoar) all opened their boundaries and waived their usual requirements in the hiring of outside labor at periods of peak demand. In Oneida in 1880 there were 200 hired workers at peak times in a community otherwise totaling only 288.[9] Finally, permeable boundaries make it possible for the organization to co-opt threatening elements from the outside, since they may be more easily incorporated into the system.

Permeability, while it may aid exchange goals, nevertheless conflicts with many commitment mechanisms that help to maintain communal relations. For example, insulation from the outside is a major renunciation mechanism, but permeable boundaries are almost diametrically opposed to insulated boundaries. The community's distinctiveness and social isolation may be lost when boundaries are relatively permeable. Permeability means almost by definition that stringent entrance requirements, such as investment and ideological conversion, which serve as commitment mechanisms, can no longer exist. Furthermore, permeable boundaries interfere with the cross-boundary control that is functional for communal relations, since the social limits of an organization and its demarcation from the environment are somewhat vague. An organization with permeable boundaries tends to become more heterogeneous, because it more readily admits diverse elements to its ranks, whereas homogeneity is the attribute that facilitates communion in utopian communities. The provision of boundary roles further tends to create people who have at least two allegiances — inside and outside the system — but what is required by utopian communities to maintain their communality are strong exclusive loyalties. Since occupants of boundary roles are not encapsulated within the organization, they need not be totally committed to it. Finally, if it is easy to import relevant experts and personnel, if people can pass in and out of the system with relatively little difficulty, the organization will tend to become staffed by a corps of "professionals," personnel who are relatively disinterested in the purposes of the organization and have little personal stake in its success or failure. Nineteenth century groups had such personnel late in their lives in the form of hired labor. Yet the required characteristics for maintaining communal relations are just the opposite:

a strong interest and involvement with the community qua community, as well as a sizable stake in its future.

Isomorphism refers to the structural similarity between the community and its environment.[10] Such parallelism facilitates cross-boundary dealings and exchanges for several reasons. In the first place, social systems that attempt to conduct relations with one another should generally share language, symbols, and media of exchange, which isomorphism implies. Second, labor and experts imported from the outside are more easily deployable in organizations that are isomorphic with respect to the environment, since these personnel need not be resocialized in order to participate in the system; roles in such a system are familiar and can be adopted by new members with less elaborate preparation than in nonisomorphic systems. Similarly, resources and information can be imported without having to transmute them. To offer a simple example, if outsiders speak the same language, communication with them does not require translation. Structural isomorphism may also aid the attainment of exchange goals, since organizations find it easier to deal with each other if they are set up in a similar fashion. If there is point to point correspondence, through similar structures and roles, it will be easier to form a relationship: for example, there will be a purchasing agent to deal with salesmen. An organization may also find itself in a more competitive position if it imitates other organizations of similar type. Finally, a certain amount of similarity to external systems is necessary for an organization to have dealings with other social systems, for being different in a cultural sense poses a threat to other systems at the most, and at the least hampers outstanding and public relations.

Isomorphism for purposes of exchanging with environments interferes to an extent with organization for the attainment of communal goals, however. For utopian communities, the sharing of symbols and media of exchange often means accepting the terms of the larger society and thereby subverting their own ideals and values. Sometimes it forces them to give up a distinctive language and dress, or to end job rotation. It creates practical problems as well. One such problem arises when utopian communities that do not use money in their internal dealings and do not reimburse their own members for labor must pay outside labor in money, becoming in this respect isomorphic with other employing organizations. Internal conflicts and value conflicts may ensue when outsiders are paid in cash and members are not, as happened in Zoar. Isomorphism owing to the pressure for favorable public relations may be similarly detrimental to communal goals and commitment mechanisms. One of several pressures for the transformation of Oneida from a group-marriage commune into a joint-stock company resembling other production organizations was unfavorable publicity and the threat of legal action concerning its practice of free love. Isomorphism also obviates the need for resocialization, since the community already parallels the outside, but in so doing it eliminates the resocialization practices that have value as mortification and surrender mechanisms. While isomorphism may aid environmental and exchange goals, therefore, it may also interfere with the maintenance of communal systems, whose purpose in existing may be their expression of unique and different values.

Value indeterminism is a third functional characteristic of production and exchange systems, one which aids organizational flexibility, especially in light of the need to deal with environments that may be continually changing. In order to ensure the ability to meet the challenge of such change, production organizations may either divorce values from actions and decisions, or adopt values of such wide scope that they encompass a large number of alternative courses of action. In either event, the organization is left free, at least in terms of its values, to make decisions and take actions with respect to external systems. This value indeterminism of organizations is similar in concept to the indeterminism of the collective conscience in modern society described by Emile Durkheim. Communal systems, however, are supported by the opposite phenomenon, value determinism, characterized by elaborate ideologies, detailed specification of rules and procedures, and the basing of decisions on values and ideals. For utopian communities, then, the requirements of communality versus those of outside relations provide a possible source of conflict. I am making no judgments about rationality or irrationality here, merely about the guiding and determining role of values.

Communes can take several paths to resolve this dilemma.
One strategy is to make values highly determinate of the personal conduct of members but relatively indeterminate of
organizational policies, that is, to make them specific with
respect to the appropriate behavior of individual members but
relatively vague with respect to appropriate organizational
behavior. This solution tended to characterize the accommodation of the Shakers.

Another solution is to have dual leadership:
one set of leaders can interpret and protect the community's
values, serving as ideological spokesmen and watchmen; the
other set can take care of the day-to-day dealings of the community, free from any otherwise desirable ideological coercion.
This arrangement was generally chacteristic of Harmony, Zoar,
Oneida, and Amana, all of which had business managers as
well as spiritual leaders. Saint Nazianz also developed a dual
leadership after its founder's death. In addition, however, all of
the successful utopias toward the end of their lives (with
the exception of Jerusalem, which dissolved much earlier) faced
environments quite different in nature from those that existed
when the utopias were founded. In order to deal with these
changes, value indeterminism became increasingly prevalent in
all of the communities. The fact that in Oneida the amount
of space devoted to spiritual matters and ideology in community
newspapers decreased over the years of the community's
existence indicated that increasing attention was paid to practical matters. Even when rules proliferated, as with the Shakers,
values tended to become obsolete. In fact, Joseph Eaton pointed
out with respect to the Hutterites that a rule proliferation
in itself represents an accommodation to a changing environment.[11]

The use of perpetuation strategies represents another way in
which social systems can be organized to facilitate cross-
boundary exchanges. Provision for leadership succession and
for recruitment are two such strategies. Not only do these
mechanisms ensure adequate personnel and leadership for the
Gesellschaft-type system to accomplish its ends in the external
relationship, but they also make the organization appear to
have a life extending into the indefinite future, which facilitates
its entering into stable and relatively permanent contracts,
obligations, and networks of ties with outside environments.

Such organizations must make provision for the continual
availability of leadership and personnel, as well as acceptance
of them by current members. In contrast, communal relations
in the abstract require no such provisions, for they need no
personnel, accomplish no tasks, and need not outlive the
community of the committed, since it was founded to satisfy
the needs of a specific group of people. If a communal system
expresses the symbolic outputs and emotional feelings of
particular people, then as a group it need not continue when
those people are no longer present. In fact, in one sense a
communal relation is by definition a relationship among particular people who are committed not only to the system
as such but also to each other as the system's participants. Commercial and political orders, however, are often required by their
systemic nature to continue even when particular leaders and
particular personnel are no longer available, for they have in
a sense contracted with their members and with the outside
world to continue to serve their needs with respect to the
environment, and to continue to bring in the appropriate resources or feedback, regardless of which particular personnel
cooperate to perform these tasks. In addition, such systems may
have entered into contractual relations with the environmental
sources of feedback and must continue to exist in order to
carry out their contracts.

For nineteenth-century utopian communities, the problem of
leadership succession was an acute one. Many, both successful
and unsuccessful in terms of number of years of existence,
fell apart when their founder and charismatic leader died.
Those that provided for continuity of leadership, however,
managed to outlive their founders. Charismatic leaders thus
may facilitate commitment and sustain communal relations,
but they are somewhat dysfunctional for the perpetuation
of other kinds of organization, such as Gesellschaft systems.

Recruitment is another general means of ensuring perpetuation, but it too may interfere with communal relations. Member
homogeneity and communion may be disturbed by the addition
of new elements into the community. New recruits may not
be moved by the same values as the original members, and
elaborate selection and processing procedures may be required.

Recruitment itself represents a relationship between an organization and an environmental system, in this case the utopia's "public," and by virtue of the decision to recruit, such communities may find themselves changing in order to be competitive in the personnel market. This phenomenon characterized many nineteenth-century utopias.

These are a few of the dilemmas faced by utopian communities of the past owing to the dual pulls in their social life between Gemeinschaft and Gesellschaft processes. Early in their histories the successful communes had concentrated on building community, on developing strong commitment, and gave only secondary importance to production and other goals with respect to their environment. As they grew, however, these secondary goals also grew in importance, and "conducting business" began to conflict with maintaining community feeling. By the end of their histories, many commitment mechanisms had disappeared, and commitment itself was eroding.

## Prosperity and Decline

One indication of the increasing attention shown to practical matters in the successful nineteenth century groups is the fact that they tended, on the whole, to become financially prosperous. Whereas in their early years they had suffered through periods of struggle and hardship, by the time they dissolved they were often wealthy, or if they had many outstanding debts, these had followed a period of prosperity. For nineteenth century communities at least, financial prosperity may be associated with the decline of community — partly because it indicated the growth of efficient Gesellschaft organization and partly because of the social consequences of prosperity, such as emphasis on individual consumption. Prosperity may lead to bureaucracy and privatism. Richard Ely wrote in 1885 that whereas poverty can knit members into a compact whole, "prosperity can be fatal." Charles Gide stated: "Perhaps the gravest [peril] of all lies in the fact that these colonies are threatened as much by success as by failure . . . If they attain prosperity they attract a crowd of members who lack the enthusiasm and faith of the eariler ones and are attracted only

by self-interest. Then there is a conflict between the older
element and the new."[12]

There is evidence that if financial prosperity is not associated
with a utopian community's failure, then at least it is unrelated
to its ability to continue in existence. A number of both
successful and unsuccessful utopias weathered periods of hardship and suffered financial losses without dissolving, but then
broke up at a time when they had accumulated great wealth and
showed a profit. Bethel, for example, began in 1844 with
$30,000 in assets and, when it dissolved in 1880, had over
$3,000,000 to distribute. Hopedale started in 1841 with under
$5,000 in property and suffered a loss the following year,
but in 1856, the year it broke up, it earned a net profit of
$7,000 for the year and had a quarter of a million dollars in
assets. The North American Phalanx increased its assets from
$8,000 to $67,000 in addition to paying dividends of about five
percent a year to stockholders, yet it dissolved after thirteen
years. The Wisconsin Phalanx not only showed profits but also
increased its assets from $1,000 to $33,000 over a six-year
lifetime. Skaneateles doubled its assets in its two-and-one-half
year history, and Communia increased its assets by more than a
third. Oneida, after many years of losses, dissolved in 1881 at
a time when profits were at an all-time high. Amana distributed
well over two million dollars when it broke up in 1933, even
though it also faced mounting debts. This evidence suggests that
at the very least one can agree with Ralph Albertson's conclusion that American utopias with few exceptions were successful in earning their living: "Few colonies, if any, failed because
they could not make their living . . . They failed to like communal housekeeping. They failed to hold their young people.
They failed to compete with growing industry and commerce
in a new, unexploited country. But they did not fail to make
an independent subsistence living — and pay off a lot of debts
and help a lot of stranded people."[13]

With prosperity came not only reinforcement of forms of
organization that were often in tension with community but
also other kinds of conflict that contributed to the death of
successful nineteenth-century groups. In particular, competition
between individuals and families increased, as did the desire
for private rather than shared ownership. In 1895 in Zoar, a few

years before its final dissolution, the newspaper, *Nugitna*, began agitating for the right to withdraw from the communal society and to acquire property. As forms of organization oriented toward production, commerce, and exchange superceded commitment mechanisms, the old zeal and devotion to communal ideals declined, the will to continue the community in its utopian, communal form decreased, and the end was in sight.

Prosperity is enough of an issue for communal groups even today that not only do many communes self-consciously choose austerity and poverty rather than affluence, but also some refuse to work at making any more money than will meet their immediate needs. The Bruderhof, for example, have a successful toy-manufacturing business and could sell as much as they produce; but they often stop production when they feel they have earned enough to meet their daily needs.

All of the factors described — environmental change, population aging, and a growing tendency away from community toward organizational efficiency — intertwined to erode the commitment that had held successful communes together in the nineteenth century. Jerusalem had grown and become wealthy, but after the death of Jemimah Wilkinson, celibacy declined and hence the community. Bethel and Aurora suffered a similar fate after thirty-six years of existence. In Harmony by the 1870s only a few dozen old people were left, so that the group had to stop running its factories and start buying. By 1892 it faced large debts and lawsuits by exmembers and would-be heirs. It dissolved formally in 1904 after one hundred years. Saint Nazianz faced confusion after Father Ambrose Ochswald's death, for he had such complete authority that there was no one to replace him. The community property had been held in his name and willed to the community, but it could not be inherited because the community was not incorporated. At the same time, the population was aging and there were few recruits, while the remaining members desired changes in the commune's financial arrangements. What resulted was a dual management structure, with temporal and spiritual leaders. Litigation over division of the property and inheritance led to the formation of a joint-stock company to be administered by a board of directors. Saint Nazianz ended in 1896 after forty-two years.

Zoar, too, faced internal dissension and a decline in the desire for communal property. There were strains over the fact that title to the land was in Joseph Bimeler's name. Hiring of outside workers led to a money economy in which outsiders were paid but Zoarites were not. Although visitors were discouraged in the early years, they were encouraged after 1850, the period of the community's decline. A general store and hotel were built in the village to cater to neighboring settlements and visitors; the tourist trade was encouraged to increase income. Families began to sell surpluses to visitors, and competition was introduced. The management of the hotel was a cause of dissension, in that there were complaints that the members associated with it had special privileges. In general, the second generation was less committed to communal ownership; the third even less so. When business propserity declined and expenses exceeded income, the membership began agitating for a division of property. Finally in 1898, after eighty-one years of existence, about $2,500 per person was distributed, and the utopian community of Zoar became the village of Zoar.

Oneida began to face difficulties in the 1870s. Attention was increasingly directed toward practical social and economic concerns, away from spiritual matters. The businesses were flourishing. There was a growing "generation gap" over the issue of science versus religion. Oneida's concern with education conflicted with commitment to the community. Youth who had been educated on the outside returned to the commune but with an undercurrent of discontent. In 1874 a newcomer named James William Towner, a lawyer, led a faction opposing John Humphrey Noyes's leadership, and Towner gained authority over business matters. In 1879 Noyes left for Canada because of the threat of legal action by local ministers with regard to the community's practice of complex marriage. In 1880 the adult members of the community signed an Agreement to Divide and Reorganize, giving up communal property and complex marriage, and in 1881, after thirty-three years as a commune, the Oneida Community became a joint-stock company, Oneida, Ltd.[14]

The commitment that had enabled the successful nineteenth-century utopian communities to withstand threats to their existence early in their history, which had provided members with the determination to continue, which had developed relationships that could weather disagreement, dissatisfaction, or defections, and which had reinforced firm belief in the community's ideals and values, had declined by the time they dissolved. They faced a set of forces that grew in magnitude as the communities progressed, and which eventually proved too much for even the strongest. Some groups died slowly (like the Shakers), others dissolved formally, and still others reorganized to perform a specialized job. But whatever the issues, problems, and concerns that first brought these utopian communities together, the world they faced at their conclusion was very different from that existing at their beginning. In today's world, a new set of communes has arisen, growing out of the issues and concerns of today, but with much still to be learned about their problems and prospects by examining the lessons of the past.

*Part Three*   Problems of Today

*The things that make up community are*
*terribly subtle; its the little things . . . Someone*
*getting his hair cut on the porch, the children*
*around sweeping up the hair, each taking a turn*
*snipping . . . Putting in a sewage system, leaving*
*trenches for the kids to build tunnels and play*
*in . . . Building the barn together, finding that*
*putting in a toilet can be an edifying experi-*
*ence . . . Left at home babysitting and someone*
*inevitably calling to ask if you need relief. That*
*awareness and caring . . . Doing craft things*
*together. We got a weaving frame and are*
*having a communal weave . . . Making dinner*
*with a crew once a week, remembering who's a*
*vegetarian and needs a special meal. Expanded*
*consciousness of others . . . Nothing big and*
*spectacular. The scenes that move me are the*
*little things about our life together.*
    —Founding member of a Vermont commune

# 7   Retreat from Utopia

Today there is a renewed search for utopia and community in
America — for alternative, group-oriented ways of life. But
overwhelmingly, the grand utopian visions of the past have been
replaced by a concern with relations in a small group. Instead of
conceptions of alternative societies, what is emerging are
conceptions of alternative families. Whereas communes of the
past were described in books about socialism, communism,
and cooperation, communes today are increasingly discussed
in books about the family. Communes of the past called themselves "societies" (the Society of Believers, the Harmony
Society), indicating their interest in comprehensiveness; today's
groups are more frequently called "families" (the Family of
the Mystic Arts, the Lyman Family).

    Some grand visions remain, but they are the exception rather
than the rule. Even the grand visions do not breed grand communities. B. F. Skinner's *Walden Two*, a fictional description of
a flourishing, comprehensive, industrialized utopian community
on its own land with one thousand people, has inspired the

formation of several communes, but one of these, Twin Oaks in Virginia, as yet consists of less than fifty people living at a subsistence level; another, the Association for Social Design in Boston, folded after several attempts to enlarge beyond a half-dozen residents; and still another, Walden Three, began in Providence with six residents, all working at outside jobs. Of the vast numbers of communes emerging today (one New York *Times* estimate in 1970 was over two thousand; in 1971 a National Institute of Health spokesman estimated three thousand), only a few are larger than thirty people.[1] The grand visions of the past have been taken over by experts, city planners, and developers. The only modern equivalent of Robert Owen, the British industrialist who funded and founded New Harmony, seems to be James Rouse, developer of the New Town of Columbia, Maryland, a community with a projected population of over one hundred thousand, but far from communal.

## Today's Commune Culture

The contemporary commune movement is characterized by a diminishing scope. By and large, contemporary communes encompass fewer visions of social reconstruction, fewer hopes for permanence, fewer people, fewer demands on those people, and fewer institutions, than did the utopian communities of the nineteenth century. Much of this change is a function of differences between American society at the height of the commune movement of 1840–1860 and American society of 1960–1970. In some respects the two periods are remarkably similar. Social movements surfaced around the same kinds of issues: women, blacks, and even temperance (alcohol then, drugs today). Religious revivalism was at its height in the 1840s and 1850s, serving many of the same expressive, emotive, and interpersonal contact functions as the encounter group movement today.[2] Similar dissatisfactions with capitalism were expressed. For every type of commune then, a similar instance can be found today. In both periods there have been anarchists resisting any kind of structure as well as spiritualists totally obedient to their messiah. Concern with life style and

nutrition as integral parts of spiritual growth were found among
the Shakers of the past as well as the macrobiotic communes
today. Large numbers of people wandered from commune to
commune then, just as others are doing today. A concern with
individual fulfillment can often be found beneath reformist
impulses in both periods. In the nineteenth century this concern
was expressed in religious rhetoric as "salvation"; in the twentieth, in psychological language as "personal growth." But the
dominance of psychological over religious or political rhetoric
among communes today is itself indicative of their diminishing
scope. "Doing your own thing" is a pervasive ethic in many
contemporary communes, which places the person's own growth
above concern for social reform, political and economic change,
or the welfare of the community. The person is free to leave
when no longer satisfied; his involvement with the group is
limited.

Related to the pervasiveness of the personal fulfillment ethic
is the rise of nonutopian communes. An outgrowth of the
hippie movement, these groups share property, close relations,
and a livelihood, but they lack ideology or programs for social
reform. They resemble an extended family more than a utopian
community — a family of brothers and sisters without parents.
They develop from friendships rather than groups welded
together by shared ideology; their basis is solidarity. Composed
primarily of seventeen- to thirty-year-olds, these communes may
be temporary ways of "making do" for a particular phase in a
person's life, rather than permanent settlements oriented toward
the future. The language of the counterculture signals this
impermanence: terms like "into," "trip," and "scene" convey
an episodic quality, a temporary contact that one dips "into,"
then quickly and easily moves "out of." In these communes,
lacking any highly developed utopian or transcendent vision,
the personal and the intuitive define the quality of life; for
example, how good are the "vibes," how many "uppers" can a
person have. For this reason, personal fulfillment rather than
strength or endurance of the group are measures of success
for these communes, even though the first is not often possible
without the latter.

In place of the weakened utopian faith of the twentieth

century, a sense of nostalgia pervades the commune movement, from youth communes to Christian homesteads. The strong belief in progress held by nineteenth century groups is considerably diminished today. Communes of the past were often looking ahead, anticipating the future, and building on their concept of history. The Shakers, for example, conceived of themselves as anticipating the next stage of human evolution. More often today, however, communes are looking behind them, toward a romanticized past, turning their backs in horror on the movement of history. Throughout the commune movement is found nostalgia for the small town, for the farm, for crafts and hand work, for natural foods, and for the dress styles, hair styles, toys, herbal medicines, and equipment of the nineteenth century. The folksy, down-on-the-farm tone of *The Mother Earth News*, which publicizes communes and back-to-the-land technology, expresses this nostalgia. Also involved is a longing to return to the more recent past, a nostalgia for the simplicity, innocence, playfulness, and lack of obligation of childhood; the flower child image of the hippie movement symbolizes this tendency. Judson Jerome characterized these phenomena as part of a movement to create "Eden" rather than "utopia."[3]

Despite the distinctive elements developed by today's commune culture, many remnants of the nineteenth-century utopian movements remain. A few strong utopian communities still exist that resemble the small, isolated societies of the nineteenth century, the best known being the more than one hundred Hutterite villages in the Great Plains and the three Bruderhof communes in the East. But such communities are rare among contemporary communes; in many ways, they belong to another era. Both are transplanted from earlier times and other places, for the Hutterites arrived in the United States in 1875 after several centuries in Europe; and the Society of Brothers, which was founded in the 1920s, established the first Bruderhof community in the United States in 1953, having earlier settled in Germany, England, and Paraguay. Neither are special adaptations of the communal idea to contemporary American circumstances; rather, they continue to live out traditions established long before. There is also some evidence that environmental conditions are causing them difficult survival problems, with their boundaries becoming increasingly vulnerable to the pressures of the society. In addition, many new communes are continuing the utopian tradition of the past. Twin Oaks in Virginia, for example, hopes eventually to become one of a network of utopian communities across the country, making the good life available to everyone. Other new communes are organized around charismatic leaders preaching a new religion, such as Messiah's World Crusade in San Francisco, coalescing around Allen Noonan; Fort Hill in Boston, following Mel Lyman; and the Brotherhood of the Spirit in rural Massachusetts, led by Michael Metelica.

But whether communes envision a utopian village embodying moral and spiritual perfection, or merely a temporary family, they face many of the same problems in establishing a group. In many ways these problems are more difficult today than they were in the past. The major difference between establishing a new community in the nineteenth and twentieth centuries is the degree of difficulty a group encounters in constructing strong boundaries and creating a coherent group. Whereas it was relatively easy for groups to develop clearcut boundaries in the nineteenth century, it is relatively difficult today. Although the strength of a commune today is still contingent on the presence of commitment mechanisms, the problems of employing these mechanisms have been exaggerated by the difficulties of developing and maintaining boundaries in an urban era of mass communication, easy mobility, and rapid social change. Strong communities today can generate and maintain commitment because of their adaptive solutions to boundary problems, while weak communes succumb to the boundary-denying forces in the society and become limited communities of narrow scope.

## Boundary Problems

Boundaries define a group, set it off from its environment, and give it a sharp focus, which facilitates commitment. Strong communities tend to have strong boundaries — physical, social, and behavioral. What goes on within the community is sharply differentiated from what goes on outside. As with the secret societies described by Georg Simmel, events inside the community may even be kept hidden from outsiders and reserved for members alone to know, witness, and perform. One kind of boundary may help to define another. Physical boundaries, as of location and territory, might define those people with whom a person may legitimately engage in a relationship. Social boundaries may define behavioral ones, as in a monogamous marriage, where the two people who have defined themselves through the relationship behave toward each other in ways that they do not exhibit toward others.

With strong boundaries, it is clear who belongs to the group and who does not. The outside may treat members as a unit for many purposes. Passing in and out of the community, both for new recruits and for old members, may be relatively difficult. The definition of a communal group as an expressive unit concerned with interchanges between its members, as a group of people interested in mutual support and a shared way of life, indicates in part the importance of boundaries, because of their value in preserving the uniqueness of interaction between the specific set of people comprising the community.

Many of the commitment mechanisms that differentiated successful from unsuccessful nineteenth-century communes revolved around erecting and maintaining strong affirmative boundaries, which distinguished the group from its environment, so that members created for themselves psychic boundaries that encompassed the community — no more and no less — as the object of commitment and fulfillment. The commitment-generating problems of some unsuccessful groups can even be pinpointed as boundary issues, such as the fact that New Harmony let anyone in, exercising no selectivity and no socialization, or the fact that members of Brook Farm practically commuted to Boston. Many of the difficulties that successful groups later encountered stemmed in part from a weakening of the boundaries: hiring outside workers, educating children on the outside, increasing numbers of visitors, adopting the fruits of outside social change, and most important, engaging in expanded commerce and trade or decreased internal production and consumption, which destroyed the kind of self-sufficiency that itself constitutes a boundary.

Communes are conscious and purposeful in their attempt to separate from the larger society and create a special group. In the nineteenth century, conditions were such that distinct boundaries could be erected with relative ease. Physical isolation was possible, as well as a relatively self-sufficient farm and light industry economy. Technological needs were low, and contact with the outside minimized, so that a group could become institutionally complete, a comprehensive community comprised of all social institutions. Communication was slow, so that it was possible for a group to remain hidden, developing and maintaining a distinctive culture. Travel was generally confined to small geographic areas. There were fewer options for life in the society — from choice of career to choice of life style — so that it was possible to find a homogeneous group of people who were willing to share beliefs, without the confusion and pressure of constant subjection to opposing views. Some commitment mechanisms even arose unintentionally: the distinctive language and dress style of such groups as Harmony and Amana were a function of the fact that they were immigrant groups with a transplanted culture, but could in the nineteenth century, experience few pressures for assimilation.

Twentieth-century American society provides a very different kind of environment, one that is constantly intruding and penetrating the borders of groups, which contributes to the fact that the boundaries of most contemporary communes are weak and constantly shifting. Four characteristics of contemporary society are primarily responsible: urbanization, advanced technology, instant communication, and a white middle-class culture that is increasingly both national (fairly uniform across the country) and pluralistic and eclectic within the range of options provided nationally. More people live in cities and want to stay in cities, which has given rise to urban communes, a new phenomenon of this century, for evidence is lacking of any urban utopias in the last century. Advanced technology makes it less possible for any group to supply all or most of its needs by itself or for a small group easily to develop an economic base as a complete production unit. Thus, many communes today do not even attempt to constitute an economic unit, concentrating rather on being a family, which typifies the diminishment of scope characterizing a large proportion of the new communes. Institutional comprehensiveness is no longer as possible as it was in the nineteenth century. Instant communication means that new ideas and new stimuli can intrude constantly, increasing the difficulty of generating and maintaining a distinctive set of beliefs. Most communes today do not develop their own ideologies, and even when they do, they often borrow and incorporate bits and pieces from other people and other groups. The problems of ideological completeness, therefore — of any one group developing a unique, comprehensive ideology — are intensified.

These three factors — urbanization, technology, and mass communication — have supported the development of a national middle class culture that is increasingly both uniform across regions and pluralistic in terms of styles available. People are more mobile — particularly the young, who are the ripest recruits for the new communes. As they move, they carry with them across the nation the counterculture of which communes are one part. In addition, people and places are increasingly interchangeable.[4] If strong utopian communities in fact resemble secret societies, then in the twentieth century most communes participate in a culture that has become too pervasive and widespread to develop such a secret, shared truth. Developing a distinctive culture, set off from that of the surrounding environment, is much more difficult today than in the nineteenth century; many contemporary communes choose not even to try, again retreating from their former scope. Rather than separating themselves from society, as did the communes of the last century, many become a link in a chain of the national counterculture, exchanging members with other communes. The fact that modern American culture is at the same time pluralistic and eclectic, surrounding the person with a much greater number of options than in the last century — with respect to careers, consumption, relationships — makes it harder for the individual both to make definitive choices (as of one group or one culture and life style within that group) and to find one set of people with whom he can share every aspect of his life, since everyone else has the same large number of options from which to extract a life style. The individual constructs his own social world out of the myriad choices confronting him, and the chance that many others will construct

theirs in exactly the same way is much more limited than in
the less diverse environment of the last century. Without a
strong set of beliefs to indicate to the person why he should
suspend his options, he generally continues to exercise them in
the new communes. And most new communes, given the
increased difficulty of placing limits on options, choose not to
do so.

The boundary problems of today's communes are exacerbated
by the fact that communes as a unique social arrangement
lack definition and legitimacy in American society. For legal
and official purposes, they must define themselves in terms of
some other form such as a nonprofit corporation, a business, a
church, an educational institution, or a family. Sunrise Hill
set itself up as a trust fund; Synanon defined itself as a charitable foundation; the Fort Hill commune is organized into
a holding corporation, "United Illuminating." Moreover,
whereas the norms of the larger society indicate the ways in
which legitimate social institutions are to be approached,
there are not yet such established guidelines for communes.[5]
There are socially delimited ways of entering a family, for
example – through marriage, birth, or legal adoption – but
no similar guidelines for joining a commune. In America as a
whole, strangers do not knock at the doors of residences asking
for a place to sleep or inquiring whether they can become a
member of that particular family, but they do approach communes with these requests. To some extent, communes are
considered fair game for anyone, and their borders are easily
penetrable.

Thus, it is more difficult today to develop strong boundaries
than it was in the nineteenth century, and territorial or spatial
limits no longer suffice to give a group coherence. Today's
communes have had to develop other kinds of group-environ-
ment relations and other means of handling their boundary
problems, for as Eric Berne pointed out, the existence of a group
is in part dependent on being able to predict who will or will not
be present and behaving in particular ways at specific events.
That is, the very definition of a group is to some extent dependent on the existence of boundaries: "constitutional, psychological or spatial distinctions between members and non-members."[6]

Boundaries transcend people, however; they also distinguish

between events that occur within a group and those that do
not. Boundary distinctions can be established on two principles,
affirmative and negative. Affirmative principles define the
group by what it accepts; negative, by what it rejects. Affirmative boundaries encompass only that which is accepted by the
group; all events or people are excluded except those specifically
included. A person is not "in" unless the group defines him
as "in." Norms are positive, specifically defining appropriate behavior and events. Negative boundaries, in contrast, encompass
everything but what the group specifically rejects; all events
or people are included except those explicitly excluded. A
person is not "out" unless the group defines him as "out."
All behavior is permitted except that defined as inappropriate.
Affirmative boundaries, then, are characteristic of secret
societies in being exclusive and strict. Negative boundaries are
characteristic of open societies in that they are inclusive and
permissive. Affirmative boundaries are more conducive to building commitment than are negative boundaries.

Today's communes can be placed in two general categories,
depending on the predominance of negative or affirmative
boundaries. One set of communes, in line with today's diminishing scope and retreat themes, has primarily negative boundaries.
I call these "retreat" communes. They tend to be small, anarchistic, and easily dissolved, predominantly rural and youth-
oriented. Some urban communes also fall into this category,
since they choose to specialize in domestic life rather than to
develop a complete set of social institutions. They limit their
goals to relationships, and like the rural retreat groups, they
tend to be permissive, inclusive, and temporary. But the rural
communes tend to be more purposeful and organized than
the urban ones, and also to have some minimal shared economy,
which urban houses generally lack. Thus, urban communes
must be considered a different phenomenon, representing
alternative forms of the family rather than new communities.

The other set of communes has affirmative boundaries. Rather
than shrinking into a small family or avoiding the issue of
boundaries altogether, these communes choose interaction
with the wider society through service. Their mission gives them
the focus around which to erect affirmative boundaries. They

are either urban or rural, tend to have a strong core group
holding the community together, and incorporate in their structure ways of coping with the mobility and turnover characteristic of today. They may also be larger and more enduring
than retreat communes. More traditional utopias, such as the
Bruderhof and Twin Oaks, and religious missionary communes
are similar to the service communes in that they, too, have
affirmative boundaries. In the twentieth century, however,
affirmation alone may not be enough to give a group strength,
and to the extent that a commune can define a special way
in which it helps or transforms the larger social environment, it
may gain added strength and ability to endure.

The distinction between retreat and service communes corresponds roughly to those made by other observers of the contemporary commune movement. Retreat groups tend to be what
Bennett Berger called "noncreedal," in that they generally lack
a shared ideology or creed; service communes more often are
"creedal." Retreat communes tend to be solidarity-based and
unintentional; service communes are generally ideology-based
and intentional. Service communes are more similar to the
utopias of the past, and many of the lessons of the past apply
to them. Retreat communes, in contrast, are part of the new
contemporary movement to regain Eden.

## Retreat Communes

One form of adaptation to the problems of establishing a new
communal order in an advanced technological society is to
retreat, in both space and time. Retreat communes seek geographical isolation, they discard technology, and they develop
pastoral visions embodying a return to a nostalgically viewed
past. They withdraw as well from facing the problems of
organization required for life in a complex society. Such communes settle on farms and in rural locations, sometimes without
the products of modernization, such as electricity and indoor
plumbing. They seek a return to a more "primitive" existence
in several senses; in terms of life-style and consumption patterns,
in terms of group organization. As a member of one retreat
commune explained: "We all wanted to live a simple, primitive

existence. We all were content to live without rules, electricity, power tools, or running water; in fact, we felt it was strongly a necessity for our emotional, spiritual, economic or political survival."[7]

On a visit in 1971 to a northern California commune, on a ranch nine miles from the nearest small town, many retreat themes were visible. Members of the commune include graduates of major urban universities and people brought up in the heart of New York City, but they felt that the cities were evil and wicked, cutting people off from nature and from each other, going against the will of God. Cities were described as breeding corruption and mistrust; and members made statements such as, "In the city you don't even know your *own* motives." Technology was similarly mistrusted. The communal house lacked indoor toilets and electricity, though in the kitchen was running water, a wood stove, and a gas refrigerator. Here members gathered to cook, bathe, and eat by candlelight and kerosene lamp. Food was organic, and eggs came fresh from the chickens. Outside, geese, dogs, and cats roamed on the grass. On a post by the vegetable garden a sign was tacked: "Love of seed nourishes." The pastoral vision of a return to nature was combined with a rejection of organized work, of schedules, and of the necessity to make money. Women in the group collected welfare payments under Aid to Dependent Children; occasional sums of money were brought in by others. Politics and events on the outside were virtually ignored. Although members sought information from visitors about happenings of particular interest, these were followed with faint interest, being part of a life left behind. Organized medicine was similarly ignored. As a woman neared the time to give birth, a special one-room house was cleaned and readied, where her child was born by natural childbirth, midwifed by other women. Finally, there was also retreat from achievement or accomplishment — collective or individual. The goal instead was internal discovery, personal growth, finding and doing one's "own thing." One concrete outgrowth of this goal was a rejection of the right of any one person or of the group to make demands of any individual.

The pastoral vision embodied in such communes is even more

prevalent today than it was in the nineteenth century. Thus, the surfacing of pastoral dreams today and the seeking of retreat can themselves be seen as adaptations to the problems of building new communities in the present, more intrusive society. In the nineteenth-century utopian communities, "communing with nature" was generally not an end in itself; agriculture was often a means of support rather than an explicit value. Technology was also employed, for practically all of the thirty communities studied engaged in light industry as well as farming. Retreat, for today's communes, however, involves rejection of all the places, behaviors, and values most characteristic of modern American society.

Thus, retreat communes are anarchistic both by conscious choice and by virtue of the act of retreat itself. This act often gives the group definition primarily by what it rejects. But negation alone is not conducive to building strong communities, for when groups separate from the larger society, they also separate from the order-giving forces of that society. Unless they substitute their own order, they cannot develop a strong, committed, and stable group. Georg Simmel pointed out that the consequences of leaving the general normative order easily are rootlessness and the absence of a stable life-feeling.[8]

Retreat as a boundary adaptation, then, is not conducive to building commitment, and retreat communes, although they provide some of the satisfactions of utopian communities, tend to be weak as groups. That is, they dissolve easily, often after little more than a year. By minimizing the importance of the collective, they often limit their ability to accomplish shared tasks; and by developing only weak ties between members, they may experience high turnover. Since commitment mechanisms do not develop, the communes lack continuous participation, group cohesion, and social control.

Among retreat communes are "Paper Farm" in California (1968–1969), Sunrise Hill in Massachusetts (1966–1967), Oz in Pennsylvania (summer of 1968, although a core of the group had previously lived together for eighteen months in California), Tolstoy Farm in Washington (1963–1968, since 1968 a cooperative farm), and Morningstar Ranch in California (1966——).[9] For some individual members, these communes have provided rich

and satisfying experiences, but as groups they have had difficulty enduring and working together. Their problems derive
from a failure to institute boundaries that permit the development of commitment mechanisms. Rather, the communes
remain anarchistic. Their boundaries are more negative than
affirmative, more inclusive than exclusive, and more permissive
than strict.

   *Definition of Boundaries: Negation.* Groups with boundaries
based on negation come together out of rebellion, to move
away from perceived ills or discomforts rather than to share a
positive vision. More time and energy is expended on ridding
the group of the evils of the environment than on developing
relations and structures within the group. The group generally
focuses more on its shared rejection than on shared ideals and
purposes; the only beliefs that members need hold in common
are their common denials.

   Communities based on negation alone tend to be held together weakly, lasting only as long as the outside "enemy"
remains a threat, or as long as they get from themselves what
they cannot or refuse to obtain from the environment. Extreme cases of groups based on negation are the communities
formed by inmates of prisons or of mental hospitals, which
stand for nothing expect expediency.

   Retreat communes come together for more than expediency,
however, and they generally have some concept of the better
life they wish to lead. Oz hoped to develop "true brotherhood"
and attain "cosmic consciousness." George Hurd, their bearded
philosopher, characterized the commune as an "extension of
a new religion."[10] But Hurd's vision was not shared by the rest
of the commune, and he did not function as a leader.

   Whereas the successful nineteenth-century communities had
not only a dominant set of values but also a number of ways of
ensuring that members accepted and lived up to them, today's
retreat communes tend to lack any kind of integrating philosophy. Many of them originated in a desire for closer personal
relationships, for group living in the most general sense, without
any specific ideas about how to implement this goal or how
to "get it all together." Often they began with a small group
that had worked together in various radical movements (Tolstoy

Farm) or had been meeting to discuss community (Sunrise Hill). One group grew out of a summer camp experience sponsored by a human relations center. A commune in Maryland centering around a school reports that their community developed simply as a "convenient way for us to live and share together."[11] Four people started this commune on a farm in the spring of 1968, and by the spring of 1969 there were ten adults and two children. The new members joined for a variety of reasons, some merely looking for any community to their liking.

Some of these communes, in fact, are virtually indistinguishable from the nameless groups of friends who spend the summer together in the country, then return to the city or school in the fall; New Mexico, Vermont, and Maine are dotted with such groups. The use of the word "retreat" here is deliberate, to convey not only withdrawal but also a place where a person goes for a renewing interlude. To the extent that some people today join communes for just such interludes, the commune may function as a kind of vacation home. Many communes have strikingly lovely settings and can provide a relatively carefree existence for a summer. I still remember the calm and beauty of an afternoon on a Vermont farm picking raspberries and cooking soup over a maple wood fire. Such interludes are indeed renewing and may serve some of the same functions for society that colleges do by housing those who have no place else to go and keeping them out of the job market. But such purposes are in themselves no basis for a community.

Retreat communes tend to define themselves by what they reject rather than what they affirm. Their solidarity depends on the existence of a wider society, and the group is delimited by what it chooses not to do rather than what it establishes for itself. Many retreat communes, for example, deplore capitalism but do not create an alternative system of communalism for themselves. Members of Oz were clear about their aversion to working for profits owing to its denial of "brotherhood," but they did not develop any system of work of their own that would affirm brotherhood. Rather, "purposeful activity . . . was a sometime thing." Men worked intermittently for neighboring farmers, being paid in kind, and a garden was planted and harvested. But in general the group depended on allowances from parents and handouts. Bennett Berger called this financial base "W and W," for "welfare and windfalls." It does not provide the commune with resources of its own, and it requires dependence on the very system that the group rejects.[12]

Retreat communes are concerned with individual freedom rather than with development of the collective. They have little common purpose except to rid themselves of the evils of the surrounding society. As a member of Tolstoy Farm pointed out, "What philosophy there is is secondary." Many of these communes therefore fail to provide answers to the questions of "who are we?" and "what are we doing?" As a member of a defunct New England commune said: "We weren't ready to define who we were; we certainly weren't prepared to define who we weren't — it was still just a matter of intuition. We had come together for various reasons — not overtly for a common idea or ideal, but primarily communitarians, or primarily farmers, or primarily political revolutionaries . . . or just plain hermits who wanted to live in the woods. All of these different people managed to work together side by side for a while, but the fact was that there really was no shared vision."[13]

The experience of Paper Farm illustrates many of the problems of negative boundaries. Paper Farm was begun in 1968 by four people on three acres at the edge of a small town in northern California. By its end in 1968, it numbered ten men, seven women, and three children. The group had come together to publish a paper distributed by the Underground Press Service. They set up a cooperative printing venture, with their own press and shop. They also had a garden and animals for food and milk, as well as small cabins, tents, and lean-to's for members. The group's major problem, according to the man who provided the land, was "too much indolence and not enough commitment." The openness of the group's boundaries, its lack of selectivity, and the fact that people joined for negative rather than positive reasons were all responsible. As the land's owner reported: "Beyond the paper staff (six or so), most people came here just to get out of the city. They had no commitment to the land — a big problem. All would take food from the land, but few would tend it . . . We were entirely open. We did not say no. We felt this would make a more dynamic group. But we got a lot of sick people."

Joining Paper Farm required no investment of money or property, and personal property remained personal property. Anyone who passed through and happened upon the commune was welcome to stay. All the materials as well as the land were supplied by one man and his wife. Some members supported themselves by working in town on construction or handyman jobs; others had enough money from parents or from previous jobs; and one or two occasionally survived without money.

"We were all more or less anarchistic," said Paper Farm's owner. The commune had no expectations or rules and no formal positions of responsibility. There were a variety of individual life styles — from conventional marriages to free love — but no agreement on what kind of life the commune members should have together. All personal decisions were made by individuals. The community met once a week on Sunday evenings to discuss group issues, but if someone refused to abide by the consensus of the group, there was no way to enforce the decision, and generally nothing happened. It ran counter to the wishes of the group to force any individual to conform or to demonstrate more commitment than he was willing to give. As a result, problems of getting the work done around the commune were never solved. The members of the commune "tried everything we would think of," including encounter groups and rotating leadership, but nothing worked. Some members left; new ones arrived.

No common purpose or binding concept existed to hold the shifting group together, to define its boundaries, and to give it meaning. The only philosophy held by the commune was a "desire to be independent and self-sufficient," to withdraw from the larger society. As the landowner said: "The system is sick and weak. To depend on it is to be also sick and weak in whatever the proporation of dependency." But even this philosophy was not shared by all members. By the winter of 1969 the owner of the land on which Paper Farm was situated had run out of money, and the commune dissolved by mutual consent. He and his wife stayed on the land, hoping to interest

other communes in the area in developing alternative institutions such as free schools. His advice to other communes,
however, was to expect much hard work.
*Across the Boundaries: Inclusion.* Many retreat communes
tend to begin with the wish to be open to all comers. Everyone
is included except those specifically excluded – and expulsion
is rare. Oz expelled a resident, but he later returned. In strong
contrast to the successful nineteenth-century communities,
which required an ideological commitment for admission or had
screening procedures for prospective members, some anarchist
communes do not even make a distinction between members
and nonmenbers; whoever happens to be staying at the commune at any time "belongs." This is particularly true of "open
land" communes such as Morningstar Ranch in California,
to which anyone is welcome to come and set up housekeeping.
And the membership is rarely the same for long. Today large
numbers of youth are roaming the country with tents and
campers, traveling from commune to commune, staying awhile
and then departing. One commune – Hog Farm – even moved
around as a group. In another commune, anyone is invited
to move in and "see if you like us and we like you."
     Sometimes this openness to all comers, regardless of their
values or their commitment, changes the nature of the commune. Tolstoy Farm, which started in 1963 as one of the first
anarchist communes, wanted to be a place where everyone
was welcome and no one could be forced to leave. But this
policy resulted in too many transients, who had no long-range
interest and little motivation to work. Originally the community
lived together in one or two buildings, but slowly the permanent people began building their own houses and working
their own gardens, and when no workers were left at the
community center, the center was dissolved, and the commune
broke into individual homesteads. The consequences of failure
to control the population of a community are sometimes
demoralizing for the group, as a resident of Morningstar Ranch
charged in 1967 with regard to Lou Gottlieb's open admission
policy: "It's not like it used to be. Too many outsiders have
been coming up here during the summer – Hell's Angels,

tourists, people who come up for the wrong reasons. I don't know if Lou's right, letting everybody in."[14] Whereas the lack of selectivity of members creates one set of problems — continual turnover in membership, resulting in feelings of instability and a lack of commitment — an open admissions policy with respect to visitors brings another set of problems. At minimum, it deflects the energy of the group from its own concerns. At Tolstoy Farm, the residents found themselves acting as "parents" to the runaway teenagers who flocked there in the summers. At worst, visitors can create serious problems for a group, in that they are not subject to whatever social controls and sanctions the community may have, and they lack even a minimum concern for the survival of the group.

Part of the pressure that finally drove Oz off its land in Pennsylvania can be traced to a problem of visitors. Controversy surrounded the decision to admit visitors, and Robert Houriet reported that the only fist fight at the commune followed one person's acceptance of beer from a visitor. Some members wanted the commune to remain isolated and self-sufficient, excluding reporters and runaway teenagers in particular, but the majority desired to keep the commune open, to develop its role as a "pilot project for the communal society." Townspeople and teenagers from hundreds of miles away came to look and stayed. Townspeople who had defended the commune against detractors turned against it when their own children began spending more and more time at Oz. On some days more than a thousand cars drove by, and as visitors increased, a few members threatened to leave the commune. Visitors began to engage in activities for which the commune was held responsible, which culminated in the arrest of several members, a raid on the commune by local police, and its dissolution. As one member described a precipitating incident: "One night . . . two teenyboppers set up what amounted to a tent of ill repute on the grounds. Naturally, many of their clients spread the word . . . Hamlets in a 50-mile radius buzzed with other rumors as well: 'All drug addicts'; 'There've been a lot of thefts around here since that group moved in' . . . The stories multiplied, fed by fears that the farm was converting . . . numbers of local youth to a radical life style."[15] Although the commune received some support, it nevertheless faced a lengthy court case and, as a result, finally agreed to leave its land. Members scattered over the country.

*Within the Boundaries: Permissiveness.* In contrast to the organization of group life, property, and work in the successful nineteenth-century communities, in the small anarchist communes of today most decisions about these matters are left to the individual. Size may make a difference here, since some of the anarchist communes have as few members as six or eight and do not grow much bigger than thirty, and they may not therefore need the elaborate systems of social organization found in the nineteenth century groups, which often numbered their members in the hundreds. Yet the consequence in today's small commune is often that jobs remain undone, conflicts never get ironed out, and "family feeling" develops only with difficulty.

In today's anarchist communes there tends to be little in the way of definable patterns, rules, or group structure. In a Maryland commune of twelve, for example, people pay nothing to join; private property remains private (although it is usually willingly shared); most members have outside jobs and contribute $30 a month for food and utilities; and members live in six separate dwellings. All work within the community is voluntary. There are no leadership positions, and decisions are made by individuals acting separately. There are no rules, other than a ban on smoking inside the buildings, and no way of defining a member in good standing. The reluctance to make formal rules is pervasive through the commune movement, and communities such as Synanon that do have a highly-developed normative structure are viewed by many other communes as autocratic. Indeed, as Judson Jerome pointed out, these communes seek Eden rather than Utopia; they strive for a spontaneous, flowing natural order rather than what they regard as a designed, programmed, and imposed social order. The needs of the animals or the pressures of the seasons dictate schedules, and impulse is sufficient to generate action. Plans seem unnecessary, while to "hang loose" is a positive value.

The unwillingness to make decisions or impose order is a

function not only of a "doing your own thing" ideology but also of a lack of trust in the group. One hip commune reported the difficulties encountered by the group when working together on construction: "Everything was a hassle, an object for discussion. Even how many hammer blows to use on a nail. Should it be 5 or 7?" On the contrary, those communes in which there is mutual trust and commitment to the group — often because of a sense of shared purpose — find that they can build an organization that enhances rather than detracts from their functioning as a group. Even members of the very anarchic hip communes sometimes indicate a longing for more order and group cohesiveness than is customary. A resident of permissive Morningstar remarked about another commune: "It's a groovy place. They don't let *everybody* in — just people who really believe in it. They've got some organization there. Everybody knows what he's supposed to be doing."[16]

Permissiveness can result in many patterns and life styles coexisting within a very small group, as each individual chooses his own. Oz's sexual practices, for example, ran the gamut from free love to marriage to celibacy. Such tolerance of any behavior almost without exception can create conflicts and tensions by posing a confusing array of choices for members. It also prevents the group from developing support structures for particular behavioral patterns, such as the elaborate supports that Oneida built into its system of free love. Finally, the failure to agree upon shared choices as a group or to set clear norms detracts from commitment in several ways. The sense of creating as a body is minimized. The sense of shared struggle and sacrifice, of belonging to a collective, is decreased. It is unclear what the group stands for except for a lack of limits, and in such a stance it is difficult to find purpose and meaning.

Not only does permissiveness foster lack of commitment, but it also may promote inefficiency. A member of Sunrise Hill reported: "As far as 'getting things done' was concerned, we were doing worse as a group than we had done as individual family units. Things which were automatic and simple for a family to accomplish became hassles for the Community to effect. Decisions that could be made in minutes by an individual took hours of conference by the Community."[17]

Sunrise Hill lasted less than a year. It was more avowedly

utopian than many retreat communes, but it could not implement its ideals. It was begun by a group meeting to discuss
intentional communities, who possessed many grand visions but
few shared ideas of how such terms as "love" and "peace"
would be defined. In July 1966 the commune, comprising
twenty people, was established on forty acres of woods and
pasture in western Massachusetts, on land owned by a middle-
aged man and wife with three children. The land was accessible
only by a dirt road, and it contained a brook, a pond, a farmhouse with modern conveniences, animal houses, and a garden.
Initially, there was excitment and enthusiasm; the members
felt themselves to be the "vanguard of the New Community
Movement." A certain amount of group consciousness developed, based on and expressed through rituals such as blessings
before meals and group nudity. The most important ritual
was group meditation, in which the whole group gathered
together in silence, broken only by statements that participants
felt would aid the group awareness. As a member reported:
"The benefits of this simple process were sometimes amazing.
Many times these meditations succeeded in soothing interpersonal tensions, developing perspective on problems, and
bringing people closer. Occasionally these meditations birthed
revelations that elevated the entire Community with their
beauty and power."[18] The group felt that religion was important, and individuals practiced their separate religions: Zen,
Quaker, and Russian Orthodox. Although it was hoped that a
group religion would spontaneously develop, none did.

Spontaneity was relied on as the organizing concept for most
of the community life. There was no specific shared philosophy,
no charismatic figures to provide vision and direction, little
agreement as to purposes, and an unwillingness to limit freedom.
The experience of freedom, in fact, overwhelmed the need to
impose order: "The whole phenomenon of the Community was
giddying to us. Here we had LAND, and land was a place to begin.
Here we could be Our Own People, the kind of people we
longed to be, and could live the sorts of lives we *desired* to live.
Here could be abolished so many of the multitude of evils
we had seen all about us on the 'outside.' "[19]

The only principle guiding the community was permissiveness;

individuals could choose their own level of involvement. Thus, some donated money and property, others held it in reserve. Outside earnings were pooled. Some wished to develop a system of free love to be called "group interlove," but the commune developed no guidelines to help them. A married man became sexually involved with another woman, and the resulting tensions caused the single woman to leave. There were no regular meetings of the community; rather, meetings were held when needed, generally by the time the conflicts had become so heated that they were difficult to resolve. At first, children were raised in a communal "nest," but eventually they were returned to their own parents because the adults could not agree on child-rearing practices. Rooms and furnishings were changed frequently as adults changed their minds about the way in which they wished to live. Several cases of interpersonal friction were dealt with by sending people on trips. One such clash involved the landowner and another man, with the community splitting over whether the way to resolve the conflict was to move west as a group. Finally the younger man left altogether.

The most serious problem stemming from the commune's permissiveness was its inability to accomplish any kind of work. Additional housing was needed, and land was excavated to build several dwellings, but then the project was abandoned. Finally, work was begun on a foundation that had previously been begun by the landowner, but the results were unfortunate:

Work was erratic; no certain schedules were established, and only rarely did all available workers actually turn out for work . . . Getting all the people, tools, and materials together at the site, and a clear plan of action before them, was no easy task. If anything was discovered to be lacking, or a problem came up, or some other involvement occurred, the work was likely to cease altogether.

This task lost focus when several members decided that they did not want to live in a central house, and those remaining workers slowed their effort. Suddenly the new building was not for all but only for some . . . It was no longer a physical meeting ground for everyone in the Community, no longer a focus

of communal energy and will . . . What a mournful note was
the sound of a solitary hammer in the early November crispness,
puttering about the remains of so joyous a beginning.[20]

Out of three buildings begun, none was completed.

Even domestic work was not organized and suffered from the
chaos. Meals were prepared hastily and late by whoever happened to volunteer; dishes were often left undone until there
were no clean ones remaining. By the end of the summer,
the community was in debt, and twelve of the original twenty
members had gone. By Christmas they had grown only to
nine. Outward shows of affection and sexual contact declined,
and group meditations became infrequent. What had been
the "happiest Fall" of one member's life turned into "drudgery,"
and he and his wife left in January. A month later, the community was dissolved by the four remaining members, belong-
ings were sorted, and the property was returned to its original
owners.

*Weaknesses.* Retreat and anarchy are clearly not viable ways
to build an enduring group. Retreat communes not only fail to
institute many commitment mechanisms, but they also establish
negative boundaries that tend to disperse whatever commitment
members initially bring to the group. There are positive elements
to these groups, and they resemble nineteenth century communes in their austerity and their desire for a close-knit family,
but the negative aspects of their boundaries outweigh the
affirmative. Without sacrifice and investment, there is a high
turnover of members. Without renunciation and communion,
there is little group cohesion. The communes investigated
dissolved or changed easily when faced by threats to their
existence that nineteenth century groups had successfully with-
stood, including debt, as in Sunrise Hill and Paper Farm; fire,
as in Tolstoy Farm; and persecution, as in Oz and Morningstar.
Finally, without mortification and transcendence, a community
lacks any social control or the ability to establish order.

It is important to realize, however, that for periods of time
these communes did provide some psychic satisfactions for
members. Though these satisfactions were generally not the kind

that stem from commitment, such as a sense of reward, belonging, and meaning, members reported feeling that they had gained individual learning, self-awareness, and interpersonal exploration. Among the benefits of his commune mentioned by the owner of Paper Farm was the satisfaction of learning more about himself while trying to live with and love many other people. But these individual satisfactions, too, are undermined and minimized when the commune fails to organize effectively. As the group begins to fall apart, the opportunity for individual fulfillment declines, as indicated by a member of a Minnesota commune that dissolved after a year and a half: "There were times at Freefolk when love bloomed, when we sang together, worked together as sisters and brothers, felt in us the power of our mother earth. There were also times when we didn't speak to each other, or care enough to reach out when someone clearly needed us . . . [By the end] eyes stopped meeting, hands stopped reaching, and we became strangers living in the same house."[21]

Some retreat communes are surviving beyond the first two or three years. These either evolve toward more affirmative boundaries and stronger commitment or consist of small groups with intense family feeling, the communal version of the family farm. New Buffalo, born in the open land hippie era, reluctantly but firmly closed its doors a few years ago in order to ensure its survival as a group. The Family, a group marriage from the Taos period of anarchistic communes (1967–1969), gradually developed a structure, rules, criteria for membership (including no drugs), and a strong leader, and in 1970 moved collectively to Detroit.

Though retreat communes may not be viable for long periods of time, often their members do not intend them to be, and they may instead represent temporary way-stations in an increasingly mobile society, as implied in George Hurd's vision of a chain of communes strung across the country like Howard Johnson's.[22] Small, dissolvable, structureless communes of five to thirty people may meet the needs of its members for a temporary home and family until they move on to other ties and other places. They may provide welcome interludes from the

pressures of society. Such groups may be increasing in importance as the modern version of the extended family. Members
may also leave not to return to the established society but
to join other communes. The retreat commune is nevertheless a
problematic way of creating community in contemporary
America.

*There is a place where people come together to*
*find in themselves more than they ever knew.*
—Brochure from Cumbres, a New Hampshire
growth community

*Come up to Utopia* . . .

*Flee to a gentle, natural society where money is*
*useless paper.*
—Advertisments for two resorts

# 8  They Also Serve:
## Communes with Missions

Another kind of communal group has grown up today which
deals with the social environment in a very different way
from retreat communes. The orientation of this group of communes is toward service to a special population; they have a
mission. Since it is impossible to separate completely from
contemporary American society, these groups define themselves
instead as "serving" the society. Where the retreat communes
seek withdrawal from the society, these communes seek engage-
ment and involvement, often settling in cities. Where retreat
communes fail to erect effective boundaries that permit them
to cohere and endure as groups, these communes produce
strong boundaries and strong commitment. Where the retreat
communes minimize the collective, these groups maximize it.
Where the retreat communes dissolve easily, many of these
communities have already demonstrated their longevity. Where
the retreat communes can be accused of fostering anarchy,
these groups are sometimes attacked for too much order, too
much organization, and for stifling the individual through a
strong group.

Service communes define themselves as "helpers" to the
society. They choose a constituency, then concentrate their
energies on reforming it. Their interactions with this constituency renew the sense of mission and zeal that binds the
commune. The service adaptation makes it possible for a

community to interact with the environment not out of weakness but out of strength, for the commune has something valuable to offer society. It is not dependent on the environment, but rather it develops an exchange relationship. All types of tools and techniques and behaviors from the society can be incorporated instead of rejected by the commune, since they are used against the current established order of the society in some way, in order to change it. This adaptation represents a kind of co-optation of elements from a threatening, intrusive environment. Philip Selznick defined co—optation as the incorporation of potentially threatening elements into a system's leadership structure, but the concept is also applicable here.[1] Defining the group's mission as one of service also promotes a certain elitism or sense of superiority, which enhances in-group feeling and reduces external threats; occupying the "helper" role places the helper in a dominant position with respect to the helped. Even when the service is performed with humility, it still promotes a sense of moral superiority. Even when outsiders refuse to accept the service or persecute the helpers, this adaptation builds cohesiveness within the commune. Doing a service for society also permits the commune to seek support on the outside without creating undue dependency, as by acquiring financial aid through charitable contributions or purchase of the group's product, or securing legal and emotional support from outsiders who respect the group's mission.

Service communes, therefore, tend to be stronger than retreat communes. Many have lasted over ten years. The service chosen varies. Koinonia, an interracial community, was founded in 1942 on a farm near Americus, Georgia, by Clarence Jordan, a theologian-farmer. Its purpose was to bear witness for Christian ideals of community and sharing and to assist local farmers by introducing scientific farming methods. Its goals were the extension of Christianity, an end to segregation, and rural development. Its constituency was the rural poor. Although it encountered hostility from the immediate area, in the form of shootings, beatings, bombings, burnings, and an economic boycott, Koinonia received financial and moral support from friends throughout the world. The commune still exists today, having reorganized in 1968. It has several businesses, from pecans to records. Reba Place Fellowship, another service commune, grew out of a gathering at Goshen College Biblical Seminary in Indiana. The group moved to Evanston, Illinois, in 1957, with the aim of providing an alternative to the corporate structure of established churches and of performing services for the city, such as day care. In 1969 it numbered thirty-six adults and over fifty-five children. The orthodox missionary activity of other religious communes, such as the Brotherhood of the Spirit, can also be interpreted as "service," in the sense of helping those who are unenlightened to see the light.[2]

Growth and Learning Communities

The vast majority of service communes are engaged in education or re-education. The connections between community and learning have always been strong. Institutions such as Oberlin and Antioch, for instance, were involved with utopian communities in the last century. Today this combination is increasingly important. Many communes have either organized as free schools or contain free schools in their midst. Many learning communities include those that have grown out of the contemporary human potential movement and spiritual revival. Of over one hundred "growth centers" or human relations centers that have formed in the last decade, some are decidedly communal in form and spirit, from the modified Zen monasteries in Hawaii, California, and Vermont, to Lama in New Mexico and Cumbres in New Hampshire. In many cities macrobiotic houses teach the Zen macrobiotic life style and diet. There are also communities centered around caring for the mentally handicapped, such as Camp Hill Village, or rehabilitating drug addicts, like Synanon and numerous urban houses. Such communities not only offer a mission around which to organize but also have found a way to legitimize the drift and mobility characteristic of the commune movement today. They tend to be composed of two sets of people — a core group that makes a permanent commitment and takes responsibility for the commune's learning functions, and a transient group with a more limited involvement and an expectation that they will move in and out of the group. At Lama the core group remains at the commune through the rugged New Mexican winter, while transients tend to come in April and leave in October.

To be organized as a school, therapeutic center, or learning community also makes it possible for the group both to generate and elaborate its own ideology and to ensure that members know these beliefs deeply and intimately. On a visit to four New Mexican communes, I was struck by how completely each of them built its community around four very different sets of ideas, growing out of the centrality of the group's educational mission. At Cedar Grove, a Ba'hai religious group with a newly organized free school, the school was the center and focus of life. Schoolrooms doubled as central dining and living rooms, their blackboards filled with diagrams of the Tree of Life, spiritual and practical messages, and quotations from scriptures. Thus, learning occurred while eating as well as in formal classes. The philosophy of the group infused its daily life in a way reminiscent of the Shakers. For instance, they compiled a household book of domestic guides from religious texts as varied as the Koran, the Bhagavad-Gita, and the Torah, and a message on the board extolled the "joy of sweeping."

Similarly, at Synergia Ranch, a joint venture including ecological experiments, a theater workshop, and craft enterprises, the scientific and ecological focus informed daily life. Written on the wall in the dining room were eight "laws of the universe," from $E=mc^2$ to $PV=NRT$. At Lama the focus was Eastern spiritualism; and at the fourth group, personal growth and humanistic psychology formed the basis for an alternative school. All of these groups had constituted themselves as schools or laboratories dedicated to their particular mission. This plan provided both a focus for daily life and a basis for internal order that made the groups viable. Cedar Grove, for example, is already over twelve years old; Synergia is four.

One of the strongest — and most controversial — of the communities in this group is Synanon, which sees itself as a "social movement of immense significance." Founded in 1958 by Charles Dederich, a former alcoholic with a $33 unemployment check, Synanon by 1968 had over twelve hundred resident members, urban communities from California to New York to Puerto Rico, and over $6,000,000 in property. Beginning as a kind of group therapy for drug addicts, it evolved into an intentional community that runs its own schools and businesses, including gas stations and an imprint advertising firm. It is now consciously utopian in its concept of the "Synanon life-style," a style that the community thinks may gradually sweep the world. The children especially hold this view. In 1968 a nine-year-old Synanon boy wrote: "I think sometimes the whole world is going to be Synanon . . . If the whole world does become Synanon, and that might happen someday, not so many people would be getting killed and they wouldn't be having so many fights because they get their [bad feelings] out in a stew or a game . . . and there wouldn't be any separation of the whites and the Negroes . . . and the whole world would be happy."[3] Synanon is one kind of therapeutic community offering to enhance human potential, and in the process, build a better society.

In contrast to retreat communes, service communes develop strong boundaries. Their boundaries are more affirmative than negative, more exclusive than inclusive, and more strict than permissive. Such boundary conditions derive from the existence of a strong central purpose, giving focus and meaning to the group, and providing it the means to distinguish clearly between desired and undesired members, or desired and undesired behavior. Its mission enables the group to set criteria for making choices, based on whatever will further the mission, and justifies its becoming a closed society. The boundary conditions of service communes, therefore, foster the development of commitment mechanisms that produce strong, coherent communities.

*Defining the Boundaries: Affirmation.* Service communes define themselves by their values, and by what positive steps they take to implement those values. They tend to have elaborate belief systems and integrating ideologies and to insist that all members share them. They are clear about who they are and what they are doing.

The group has at its center a purpose, and it often has an individual representation of this center in the person of a charismatic leader. The charismatic leader symbolizes the values of the group, representing the state of perfection that will be attained when the group's service is completed. He is the ultimate "helper," aiding the other helpers in the group. By affirming and believing in his guidance, one also affirms the purposes of the group, which supercede individual whims and fancies.

Cumbres, a New Hampshire growth community, illustrates how such affirmative boundaries help generate commitment mechanisms.[4] In 1969 Cesareo Palaez collected a group of former students and friends to form a community and staff a personal growth center. The purpose was to create an environment for enhancing human potential; community members would be growing and living a more spiritual life at the same time that they were communicating this spirit to paying guests. The name Cumbres is Spanish for "highest peak." This focus informed all aspects of daily life. Cumbres members participated in encounter groups, listened to lectures on psychology and religion, learned body awareness from visiting teachers, spent weekends on Zen meditation, and did the T'ai Chi Chuan (a Chinese moving meditation) every morning and evening. In Palaez's vision, even chores around the old New England inn housing the group were to play their part in the growth and development of members. When one of the young men working on the groups complained about the work, Palaez told him to read *Boyhood with Gurdjieff*, recounting an incident in which a boy had to mow the lawn for six months before the great spiritual master granted him an audience.

Palaez was a dramatic and forceful presence at Cumbres; he was everyone's teacher and guide. A former Cuban revolutionary, psychologist, and psychodramatist, he commanded great respect. When questioned by members about his dictates, he would often reply that he knew better than they what was good for them. Cumbres was built around affirmation of humanistic psychology and Eastern spiritualism, as chosen, interpreted, and preached by Palaez. Members unwilling to share this affirmation, primarily those near his own age (the mid-thirties) who were not willing to accord him the same reverence as the young, gradually left the community. The size of the group varied from twelve to twenty-five, with additional neighbors and guests swelling its ranks on weekends.

Because of the affirmative boundaries surrounding Cumbres, commitment mechanisms developed naturally. A sacrifice like giving up drugs was justified on spiritual grounds. As members were investing in something meaningful to them, they committed their resources and livelihood willingly. Cumbres' location seventy miles from Boston on ninety-five acres made the outside easier to renounce, and its isolation was reinforced by the monastic image that Palaez often advanced. A decision was made in the first summer not to open a branch in the city, for that would have detracted from the coherence of the community. Other kinds of renunciation flowed from the large number of activities at Cumbres and the energy required to sustain them. Though several couples shared their own houses, their time alone together was severely curtailed, and the emphasis on the free expression of affection extended relations beyond the couple to the whole group.

Communion was built in several ways. Chores were shared and rotated, and people often worked together as a group to complete a particular job. Undesirable as well as desirable work was shared, from running the office and stuffing envelopes to washing dishes. Meals were eaten in a central dining room in the inn, cooked and served by rotating crews. Members had several days a week for themselves, but during the rest of the week, every waking moment was infused with Cumbres — from T'ai Chi at 7 A.M. on the front lawn to evening coffee after group meetings at 10 or 11 P.M. On Zen meditation weekends, the Cumbres day started even earlier, at 5 A.M., to meditate before greeting the sunrise. The human potential movement and Eastern religions provided an abundance of rituals, symbols, and holy places, such as the daily T'ai Chi, exercises in which every group member was lifted and rocked, and blindfold walks by the stream in the woods. Special Cumbres celebrations were abundant. One weekend, members and guests participated in a pantomime circus; on another, some members erected a house of mystery and surprise, through which other members were led. Rituals to express appreciation of self and others were an important part of almost every group meeting at Cumbres, contributing to the love and warmth in the group.

Mortification and transcendance also flowed easily from Cumbres' sense that the community provided the path to

growth. Encounter groups offered confession, criticism, and
confrontation. Increased respect was given to those considered
by Palaez to be ready to guide others in growth. Philosophies
explaining the nature of human existence were read and discussed in seminars. Besides Palaez, others were considered as
teachers. They did not constitute a hierarchy, since Palaez
retained decision-making power, but they provided another
set of examples and models to emulate. Master Liang taught
T'ai Chi, Jan Kessler taught mime, and others came from Boston
and New York to impart their wisdom. Palaez, however,
remained the center, and he surrounded himself with much of
the same mystery and awe characteristic of nineteenth-century
charismatic leaders. His insight was considered magical by
members. His private quarters were almost sacred: he was not
to be disturbed at Cumbres, and in Boston he maintained an
apartment at a location unknown to most members and with an
unlisted phone.

Cumbres had another problem, however, which plagues many
service communes — financial constraints. The definition of
many service communes as businesses or organizations as well
as communal groups leads to tension. Cumbres was supported
by fees paid by guests, but these alone were not sufficient to
maintain the group. As a business, Cumbres had been heavily
financed by backers. Like the nineteenth century groups,
Cumbres had to weigh organizational against communal considerations. The decision not to move to Boston was made on
communal grounds, to preserve the isolation enhancing group
relations and learning, but it was a poor decision financially. As
finances continued to decline, Cumbres became even more
communal, the remaining members receiving greatly reduced
support and sharing property. But in the end, financial pressures
won out, the inn was sold to pay off investors, and Cumbres
closed after two years. The example of Cumbres illustrates
some of the limits as well as the strengths of service communes.
Service communes may find it easy to establish affirmative
boundaries around their purpose, but they are also subject to
two kinds of tensions: the need to maintain simultaneously an
organization and a community, and increased demoralization

and disruption if the group's service does not attract the constituency to which it is oriented.

*Across the Boundaries: Exclusion.* Service communes are also
exclusive in that they tend to have clearly defined membership
and to know, at any given moment, specifically who belongs
and who does not. They make positive choices as to membership. A person must be formally admitted by the group; he
must be explicitly defined as being "in." Positive steps must
also be taken to enter. Generally, the newcomer is a person
being "helped," as part of the constituency that the group
serves, and only gradually does he earn the right to become a
"helper" himself, one of the core members of the group. Formal
ceremonies and initiations may symbolize his admittance
across the boundaries of the group; he may have to demonstrate
his affirmation of the group through such acts as a financial
contribution.

Service communes are exclusive with respect to permitting
other movements across their boundaries as well. They do
not admit visitors as freely as retreat communes, and when
they do permit them, their activities are often monitored by
group members. For example, visitors may be escorted through
the community by an official spokesman for the group; they
may be asked to pay fees. Many service communes have formal
points of entry where visitors can legitimately gain access
without disturbing the community's control over its boundaries.
Reba Place, for instance, has a coffee house open once a week
as a place for members and visitors to interact, a clever device
which also ensures that visitors at least partially pay their way.
Cedar Grove operates a small adobe cafe on the road through
the community, run by a member and her daughter. Here
visitors can purchase lunch, buy crafts made by the school
children, and at the same time chat with community members.
The cafe represents only a very small source of income, but
it serves important boundary functions. Lama has open house
on Sunday, when visitors can freely roam the groups, participate in activities such as Sufi dancing, collect Lama literature,
and purchase such items as Tibetan prayer flags. At other
times outsiders may be invited to attend special seminars, with

the opportunity to camp on the hillsides for a contribution of
a few dollars. Other communes permit entry through their store,
such as the craft shop operated by Synergia to raise funds for
its ecological work, or through programs of education or
entertainment, such as Synergia's theatrical performances or
the concerts by music groups in other communes.

Service communes often control information across their
boundaries as part and parcel of their mission to serve. They
incorporate new information from the outside that will further
the group's ability to perform its service. Rather than finding
the continual intrusion of communication from American
society to be threatening, a service commune may consider it
useful "data." Such groups also send out to the environment
information that will meet the group's own purposes, by such
means as pamphlets and speakers. Reba Place, for example,
has a speaker service and several publications. In fact, one index
of how serious-minded and organized a group is about its
mission may be the amount of literature it produces. Service
communes tend to generate reams of paper, especially when
contrasted with retreat groups. These can include pamphlets
telling "The Cedar Grove Story," "Why We Live in Community,"
or "How To Make a Contribution"; mimeographed handouts
for members or guests on the latest philosophical input; books
by the major philosopher, such as Clarence Jordan of Koinonia's
"cotton patch" versions of the gospel; and even reprints of
newspaper or magazine articles about the group. All of this
indicates the community's intentionality and its eagerness to
assert control over its relation with society.

*Within the Boundaries: Strictness.* Whereas retreat communes
impose no limits, service communes that work effectively tend
to impose many limits. The model of direction and discipline is
an appropriate one. Service communes define behavior that is
acceptable; they make coherent choices of life style and expect
them to be adopted; they do not shy away from making demands, developing organization, and creating rules — though
not all the rules may be formalized. The group has work to
be done. Whether decisions are participated in by a whole
group or by single individuals acting for the group, it is important that decisions be made. Even helping individuals with their

own growth is interpreted as requiring the imposition of limits, the acceptance of order from the group. The examples of Cumbres and Synanon illustrate this discipline and order in two very different settings.

### Synanon: Can a Community Be Too Strong?

The boundary definitions of service communes permit the development of commitment mechanisms and in many cases produce highly committed members who are loyal, dedicated, obedient, and enthusiastic. Synanon represents an extreme case in this group, however, for its ex-addict members are so totally dedicated that critics have accused them of being "hooked on Synanon." But Synanon illustrates the ways in which the commitment mechanisms found in nineteenth century communes such as Oneida occur in modern dress. Synanon is also noteworthy for its extensive involvement with American society: not only has it helped many addicts who were not helped by traditional institutions (although many others abandoned the program before completing it), but its doors in several cities are open to its neighbors for recreation and entertainment, and it has accepted many recent non-addict members who seek a communal life-style and like Synanon's way. Synanon, though strict, is completely voluntary, and its doors are always open for members to leave. Inside the community, however, is discipline and a sense of mission.

The contrast with Oneida is revealing. There are superficial differences, such as a shift of scene from the 1880s to the 1960s, and from upstate New York to California, and in place of a group of radical Christians there is a conglomerate of ex-drug addicts, former alcoholics, and once lonely people. But many of the processes are the same. There are businesses: Oneida manufactured animal traps and silverware; Synanon sells gas and advertising. There are feedback and encounter sessions: in Oneida, mutual criticism; in Synanon, "games" and "stews." There is music: hymns in Oneida; jazz in Synanon. There is a leader, thought by some to be godlike; John Humphrey Noyes in Oneida, Charles Dederich in Synanon. The language is different; instead of "saving souls," Synanon cures "hangups."

Synanon is not called down by ministers for licentiousness but
by city officials for zoning violations. The context is different,
but many of the commitment mechanisms are the same.

Charles Dederich is the visionary behind Synanon. Many
members look upon him as a kind of religious leader, if not a
man of special inspiration, for he personifies many of the
ideals of the community. One adherent stated that, "Chuck
is my god, and Synanon is my religion." More modest worship-
ers claim that Dederich is not God but only Jesus. Others
describe him as a "modern Socrates," engaged in a "total war
against stupidity," of which "the present war against drug
addiction is of course only one tiny segment."[5]

Synanon's ideals are simple but have religious overtones. Every
morning at community meetings the Synanon prayer is read:

> *Please let me first and always examine myself.*
> *Let me be honest and truthful.*
> *Let me seek and assume responsibility.*
> *Let me have trust and faith in myself and my fellow man.*
> *Let me love rather than be loved.*
> *Let me give rather than receive.*
> *Let me understand rather than be understood.*[6]

Synanon abounds in rituals, special jargon, and symbols of the
group's existence. These particularly involve its campaign
against drugs, for newcomers must give up drugs immediately
on entrance; the community also bans alcohol and recently
waged a successful campaign against cigarette smoking. One
Synanon celebration is the Big Copout, stemming from the night
early in the group's history when the ex-addicts admitted
("copped") to taking an occasional fix, an incident that was
responsible for eliminating the last vestige of drugs from Synanon. Celebration of this event has become a tradition, initiated
by Dederich: "I got to musing on Synanon rituals . . . like
clean birthdays, Saturday night open houses, and the daily
reading of the philosophy. And it occurred to me that we
needed some kind of an annual Synanon celebration or taking
of stock."[7]

Synanon is communal not only in living arrangements but also in economy. New arrivals may pay an entrance fee, which is not refundable. No one in Synanon, at least in its early days, was paid, except for a few dollars a week of "walk-around money." Clothes and food are distributed equally, with meals eaten communally in large dining rooms, although older members have greater freedom and easier access to goods and services. Buildings and facilities such as cars are community-owned, but use of them is commensurate with members' responsibilities and group contribution. New ex-addict members enter at the bottom of the hierarchy; they contribute what resources they can and receive the lowest status chores to do, such as washing toilets and scrubbing floors, even if they had special skills or talents on the outside. For the first few months of their stay they may be prevented from seeing their outside families or leaving the house. Gradually, through participation in the community, they earn greater responsibility and can work their way up in the hierarchy, gaining even such major positions as director of a house, and they can again practice their special careers, such as art or music. Because Synanon's ideology specifies that "character is the only status" — character in the sense that Synanon defines it — as people show growth in commitment and contribution to the community, their status increases.

*the game*

The "game" is Synanon's word for its own form of mutual criticism or encounter, in which members attack the imperfections of each other's behavior in a verbal and emotional battle, venting whatever hostile or negative feelings they wish. This is the core activity of the group, described as a combination of group therapy, evening entertainment, a law court, and a town meeting. In the game there is no status: leaders as well as newcomers are subject to attack and scrutiny and similarly have the chance to examine and question others, with everyone meeting on an equal footing — although experienced game players of course have the advantage.

Synanon views the world outside its boundaries as sick, as a breeding ground for stupidity. To critics who argue that Synanon members become addicted to Synanon instead of drugs, members offer replies such as the following: "If a man works in the coal mines and comes down with tuberculosis, you cure him by sending him out to breathe clean air. After he is cured, do you then send him back to the coal mines?"

At one of its branches, on an isolated hilltop in rural Tomales Bay, California, Synanon has created the Academy, a community of about fifty people who are in training to be Synanon's future utopians. Here, the well-known Synanon game has grown into a full-time, round-the-clock activity with shifting membership, called the "perpetual stew," or stew for short. Members' lives at Tomales Bay are planned entirely around participation in work activities and in the stew. The quality of life there was described in a letter written by a member to his father in the summer of 1968:

June 25, 1968

Dear Dad,

Let me tell you a little about my daily life and what is going on here in Tomales Bay. I get up at 7:00 each morning, and I work from 8 to 4. We are building a building here; I am on the "tactical" squad, which takes care of vehicles, buildings, etc. The other day my boss was teaching me how to weld; yesterday I was building (with someone who knows what he was doing) a walkway around a building. I shovel a lot, and by the end of the day I'm happy and tired.

From 4 to 5 p.m. I clean up, and from about 5 to 7:30 (dinner) I'll talk, read, walk around the property, listen to music, etc. After dinner a group of us usually get together and listen to tapes, discuss concepts, or just talk. If Chuck [Dederich] is around he is usually talking and we'll sit around with him. Last nite for example, one of the fellows gave a talk about basic training in the Marines. Tonight we're going to cut up an Emerson essay.

That's my day . . . 6 days a week. Once a week I spend 24 hours in the stew. It has been going now for about a month, and it will keep going until??

The stew occupies its own building — about 100 yards from the main building. There are about 20 comfortable chairs, inside a large room — with special chairs for Chuck and Betty (his wife) and Dan Garrett (Director of Legal Affairs and #2 man in the [Synanon] Foundation). They come in and out at all hours of the day and night and play the Synanon game. WOW! Do they!

Every two hours several people leave and enter the stew. So there is a constant flow of traffic. Tomorrow morning at 10 I will enter the stew and leave at 10 a.m. on Wednesday morning. Besides playing the game, we will listen to tapes and maybe have a discussion. Chuck and Dan might conduct some Foundation business. For example, Chuck frequently meets visiting "Big Shots" in the stew and concludes agreements with them about property, or buildings, right there!

The game-playing is very good and very honest! Lots of ridicule is employed and everyone is pretty hostile. Most of the time anybody who gets the game put on them gets completely smashed. Imagine this – the game gets on you, someone indicts you, you defend, dodge, slide, try to get the game off you. In the usual 2-3 hr. game that might work! But two weeks ago the game was on me for three hours straight. You can't escape. Besides, you are tired – no sleep remember for 24 hrs. so your defenses aren't as good. SQUASH goes the image.

We got up here, we went into a "Cubic Day." A cubic day is the new Synanon life style. One type of cubic day is:

14 days "motion"
3 days pressure                    28 days (one month)
11 days vacuum

Let me explain . . . picture a cube, now divide it in half, giving you two rooms. One "room" is the motion room. It consists of (lets say) 14 days. In these 14 days, people work 12 hours a day, very hard – they do the work of two people. The other room is also 14 days, three of those days are called pressure – you *stew*. Then you have vacuum – no work, no responsibilities – finally back into motion.

When we arrived, we went right into "motion." I was in motion for about two weeks. Then I went into the perpetual stew:

30 hours in a stew
6 hours break
20 hou·s in a stew
6 hours break
10 hours stew – 60 hours of stewing, 72 hours total! WOW!

My sense of time was completely destroyed at times. I thought I had been in the room for years or five minutes. Through the window I could see the sun rising and falling, people yelling at each other. Chuck playing the game, he is the greatest, one of the most intelligent, funny, capable, manly, loving, human beings (the adjectives could go on and on forever.)

After I got out of the stew (the game was on me twice, both times I was completely smashed) I went back to vacuum. Since then I've been in for a 24 hour bit, and working 8 hours a day.

Starting tomorrow we will all be going back into the cubic day life style. Every day two or four people will go into it. Everyone in this plant has a counterpart, someone who can capably do their job, so tomorrow two girls from the house-keeping staff will be going into a cube. Gradually the entire plant will move onto that life style.

Perhaps you are wondering what about the Academy? (the school at Tomales Bay)

Chuck says that education is a quality of the academy; class-rooms, books, etc. have nothing to do with learning . . . they are tools used for a certain style of learning.

I am learning how to weld, how to work, how to listen, how to tell the whole truth, how to *trust*.

Chuck has told us that we won't be getting into books or ideas until we begin to trust each other, stop fighting and resisting, and have our contracts broken. Then we will proceed by massive dose. Using the stew setting, massive doses of information will be thrown at us. During vacuum we will read, talk, study.

Now our responsibility is to play the Synanon game, be honest, practice the Golden Rule. After the Fair (a money raising activity) is over we'll be moving full-bore on the building project. So far the foundations are down. The framework partially up, and a large steel roof erected. It's 120 feet by 120 feet! 2½ stories high . . .

Some interesting things, all the guys got ¼ inch haircuts a week ago. All of the Academy people are on a relationship/sex ban. We sleep in surplus army double bunks in the refinished attic of the main building.

Something else Synanon is going through . . . profound changes emanating from the Academy. Synanon I is changing into Synanon II.

The differences:

| Synanon I | Synanon II |
|---|---|
| —Cures dope fiends but creates anxious little children | —Cures dope fiends and creates adults |
| —Games | —Stews |
| —Typical middle class life | —Cubic days |

| *Synanon I* | *Synanon II* |
|---|---|
| —Concentration on integration with responsible community and no use of drugs | —Concentration on producing people capable of living the Synanon philosophy |
| —Hospital or institution | —Social movement |
| —Cure | —Education |

I don't know if that explains it, but there is a tremendous amount of pressure on everybody. Chuck wants to squeeze out all the "sickies" who are living at Synanon and no longer growing or contributing to the movement . . . He calls them retired dope fiends. Their symptoms (drug use, etc.) have been arrested, but they still are basically shit heads. They still lie, steal, cheat, etc. . .

That's why we are up here (31 of us):
to protect us from the B.S. of retired dope fiends.
to educate us in Synanon II and the Synanon game.
to accelerate us, so we can help run the Foundation.
to experiment on us, so Chuck can create a college.
to rid us of our own corruption, after all, we are as dirty as everyone else.
to give us a full education, the best in the country, information as well as a setting in which to apply it.
to teach us some skills, e.g., welding.
There are more, I'm sure but that's enough. . .

Please run my story and Synanon's story to any of my old friends willing to listen!
Onward!!!!!!!![8]

The commitment of Synanon's members has enabled the community to thrive and prosper to the extent that, as one member boasted, Synanon would like to see itself as "the oldest, richest and most successful commune in America." At various times in its history, Synanon has exemplified the use of a vast array of commitment-building processes. The most important sacrifice in Synanon (and its original *raison d'etre*) is complete abstinence from drugs and alcohol. Members, particularly in the early days, also lived an austere, nonindulgent, almost puritanical life. At Tomales Bay, they have constructed a whole village. Regardless of location, all Synanon members sacrifice their old careers, at least for a time. A musician may not be allowed to play his instrument or an artist to practice his art until he is considered completely integrated into the community. Investment is also a strong part of Synanon. Complete participation is necessary to reap any benefits of the commune. Members work on community economic enterprises and in turn derive their livelihood from Synanon. They contribute their money and property to the community, and the donation required for admission is not refundable. In many ways, members' futures become bound up with the success of the community.

Renunciation of the outside world is fostered, first, by Synanon's institutional completeness; it is a total community that offers everything within its own borders. If the nineteenth century communes could be considered villages, the new Tomales Bay facility may become a city. In addition, for the first months of their life in the community, members sometimes do not even step outside of Synanon. The outside world is condemned by Synanon, as are aspects of a member's previous life on the outside, particularly if he was an addict. Although Synanon tries to maintain good public relations, it is clear that the community considers its life style morally superior. Renunciation further occurs through the control Synanon maintains over movements across its boundaries, both of visitors coming in and members leaving. Special language, including the jargon of ex-addicts as well as new Synanon words and phrases ("stew," "cop out"), distinguish Synanon from the outside, as do special forms of dress sometimes adopted, such as the work overalls worn by all residents of Tomales Bay.

Renunciation of exclusive two-person intimacy is present to some extent, although Synanon also has many married couples. The community controls sexual relations through a highly puritanical attitude toward sex, particularly during members' early days, as well as by dormitory living that makes privacy difficult; many report that "courting" takes place on couches in the Synanon living rooms in full view of everyone. Occasional bans are placed on sex, such as the temporary celibacy rule at Tomales Bay; and the game serves to promote and enhance relations other than the couple. Renunciation of the family is fostered, first, by separation of new members from their biological families (a new person may not be allowed to communicate with his family for six months), and second, by communal dining and living. Even with separate apartments for families, meals are taken together in central facilities. In Tomales Bay and the Synanon school, children are raised communally, in their own quarters.

Communion, the strong group feeling that replaces renounced relationships, is strong at Synanon. Homogeneity is the first factor. Particularly in the early days, members had a common experience in the problem of addiction. Communal property and work arrangements also contribute to communion. The Synanon Foundation owns all property, supplying even the clothing. Jobs are rotated, with members moving from job to job and branch to branch, and there are also communal work efforts. Communal dwellings, ranging from large houses and apartment complexes to former hotels, as well as communal dining enhance group contact. There are regular group meetings, usually daily, from learning seminars to problem-solving meetings to games and "stews." There is much more group contact than privacy, and no matter is considered too private for group discussion in a game. Rituals are abundant, from the ritual functions of the game to the celebration of the Big Copout. Synanon has numerous symbols (one Synanon pamphlet is entirely devoted to translating the symbols), its own songs, music, and dances, and frequent concerts by its own jazz bands. It celebrates its own holidays and history. A sense of specialness and success pervade the group; any member will gladly tell any visitor how successful Synanon is. At the same time, the Synanon membership has shared in persecution and enmity from the outside, from Dederich's jailing in Santa Monica for a zoning violation to the arresting of two members for alleged parole violations, all in the early days.

Mortification is an important part of Synanon, justified as a tool in the program to tear down the dysfunctional character of the addict and rebuild a new identity. Confession, self-criticism, and frequently brutal mutual criticism are built into the games and stews that constitute Synanon's most routine and best-known activity. Members are differentiated on moral grounds and evaluated in terms of growth of character; rewards and punishments, such as the kinds of work a person is given, may flow from this evaluation. Rule breakers are publicly denounced and called to account in the game, and commitment is carefully examined. At one time, deviants were given haircuts as a visible sign of lost status. In keeping with the spiritual differentiation, old members become legendary figures, looked upon with awe by new people. De-differentiation of members also occurs, in two ways. First, a uniform life style is provided for all members. Second, old identities and statuses are taken away. New members start at the bottom of the ladder, doing such unpleasant jobs as scrubbing toilets until they earn their way to better chores by demonstrating growth and commitment. Statuses that members bring in from the outside count for nothing in Synanon; everyone starts new at zero-years-old and celebrates Synanon birthdays.

Transcendence involves the person in a higher meaning system, and Synanon is strong here too. The community has a firm sense of purpose and has developed a coherent philosophy incorporating many well-known thinkers, from Lao-tze to Ralph Waldo Emerson to Buckminster Fuller. Pamphlets and philosophic guides carry the message. New members "convert" to this ideology in classes and seminars. Leadership similarly fosters transcendence in the strong, awe-engendering figure of Charles Dederich. His godlike status is enhanced by his distance from most members and his special privileges, such as an expensive car and comfortable upholstered armchairs for his table in the dining hall at Tomales Bay. Under Dederich, there is a hierarchy of legendary figures, Synanon's own stable of heroes, to administer the Synanon communities. Any member may aspire to be part of that hierarchy. Finally, Synanon involves large sets of highly specific behavioral and moral prescriptions for members.

Synanon, then, has strong commitment mechanisms which generate high commitment. In thirteen years it has grown from a dozen to over a thousand members, and many more have participated in Synanon and "graduated" from it during that time. It has become large and prosperous, advancing almost as far from the small retreat commune back on the farm as General Motors has from the neighborhood stable.

As it prospers, Synanon may also become subject to some of

the influences pulling away from community that were faced
by the successful nineteenth-century utopian communities,
including an increased emphasis on running an efficient organization. The growing development of its own internal businesses
and a large bureaucracy may require organizational arrangements that will be detrimental to the communal structure.
Some members have also expressed concern that the community
may have difficulty surviving the eventual death of Dederich.
Its very strength raises many moral questions about Synanon.
For one thing, it goes further than did almost any nineteenth-
century community in instituting the most restrictive as well as
the most affirmative commitment mechanisms. Whereas no
nineteenth century group had all of the commitment mechanisms proposed, Synanon makes use of every one and more,
imposing controls on people that may go far beyond what is
necessary to build commitment. Whereas too little commitment
may generate stresses such as alienation or rootlessness, too
much commitment may deny the volition of the person. And
whereas people do indeed change dramatically in Synanon
and eventually occupy responsible positions, the process of
effecting that change may be more severe than necessary.

In its early days, Synanon was both radical and communal,
but now it is so large and centrally organized that concepts like
"total institution" may be more applicable than "commune"
to describe the present community. The size and hierarchial
power distribution of Synanon eliminate even the safety
valve afforded to people in the more authoritarian nineteenth-
century groups, that is, the possibility of exerting influence
through face-to-face interaction and by participating on committees making routine decisions. Synanon members reply
to this criticism that the game represents such a safety valve, in
that in the game hierarchy disappears, status dissolves, and
any member can influence and talk back to even top leaders like
Dederich. This answer makes sense up to a point, that point
being that power still resides at the top, and the movements of
individuals are still restricted. As a result, criticisms of Synanon
have been just as strong as the commitment of its members.
Whereas humanistic psychologist Abraham Maslow called Synanon a "eupsychia" or psychological utopia, Edgar Friedenberg

referred to its operations as "brainwashing" and as undermining some of the most important processes of a free society. Chuck Dederich has himself been called a "megalomaniac."[9] Synanon clearly arouses fierce objections as well as loyalty.

Retreat communes and service communes must be viewed as ideal types or extremes. Each of them may, in fact, draw on some aspects of the other, and they share the underlying idealizations of all communal life. Retreat communes, as ideal types, may go too far in imposing no order or limits, in building little commitment. Missionary communes such as Synanon, on the contrary, may go too far in imposing a tightly controlled order and in building more commitment than is possible for most people in this complex society. The examination of these two groups of communes illustrates an important paradox in social life: people often seek to create utopian communities in order to rid themselves of the authoritarian control of society and to gain a sense of mastery over their own destinies; but the survival of their utopian communities may depend on instituting their own authoritative system. Communes today struggle with this dilemma as they try to strike their own balance between freedom and control, mobility and permanence, variety and uniformity, inclusion and exclusion. These issues must to some extent affect all communes. Even the small urban "family" commune that sets out only to share a home may find that life together requires more commitment and more order than the limited involvement for which the group had bargained. It may even be impossible to derive the closeness and satisfaction of communal life without the limits.

*Among the communes that are functioning today, each following its separate star, it's extremely doubtful if any will survive. But if any one of these, or any other that may come afterward, proves a single new thing to the remainder of civilization, then the entire communal movement will have shown itself a valid alternative approach to enhancing the essential humanness of man within a society.*

—William Hedgepeth, *The Alternative: Communal Life in New America*

# 9   The Limits of Utopia

The utopian vision of the harmonious, integrated, loving community — the communal enclave of warm, close, supportive relationships — does not always occur according to scenario. Reality modifies the dream. But whether or not communes become permanent entities, legitimate and institutionalized "families" and settlements, they are important to examine and experience. The assumptions they make about what is possible and desirable in social life challenge the assumptions made by other sectors of American society. As experimental groups, they innovate with new forms of social organization, they imaginatively construct their own kind of collective being, and they strive for different and closer forms of human relationships. They attempt to repersonalize a society that they regard as depersonalizing and impersonal, making person-to-person relations the core of their existence.[1] Regardless of what kind of reconstruction of macroinstitutions they envisage, communal utopians put their emphasis on the small, face-to-face primary group.

Utopian communities are not without their limitations. Historically it has taken particular kinds of social arrangements to sustain them — arrangements not considered equally desirable by everyone. The experience of nineteenth century communes as well as the forms and variety of contemporary utopian movements raise questions not only about the possibilities for utopia but also about its limits and costs.

Today communes are often the subject of heated discussion, for the idea of collective living arouses a wide range of strong emotions. In the process, many criticisms have been leveled at utopian communities, some more valid and deserved than others. The questions raised will increasingly trouble the inventors and innovators, theorists and researchers of the communal movement as they face the realities of life in America's complex, urban society.

### Short-Lived or Sterile?

One major criticism reflects a belief that, despite evidence to the contrary, vital utopian communities are impossible. Critics argue that communes do not last over long periods of time, with most of them failing after only a short time, or that if they do survive, they immediately lose their vitality, institutionalizing static routines that become even less meaningful to later generations than they were to the first. This viewpoint involves a skepticism about the ability of communal orders to offer any solutions to the problems of society, suggested by its two somewhat contradictory premises: that communes cannot operate at all successfully over time, but that if they do work, they are sterile, unchanging, and by implication unsatisfactory. This is related to the argument that communes are only movements of withdrawal, which do not promote social change in the society at large.

The temporary quality of many communal ventures cannot be denied. In the past a large number dissolved while young. Some communes today deliberately form as temporary systems. Of these, some limit not only their projections for length of life but also their institutional scope; that is, members can maintain ties with other institutions while still belonging to the commune. One example is the small urban "family" commune living together while working outside. Harvey Cox described this possibility for flexible, segmented involvement as an advantage of urban life, permitting some people to enter completely into a comprehensive community, while others can innovate and implement communal ideals in just one or two spheres.[2]

Whether or not the group still constitutes a utopian community if it seeks to limit its scope both temporally and institutionally, given the fact that one utopian value is integration rather than fragmentation, some utopian thinkers would contend that the temporary quality of many communes is an advantage. It has been argued that the healthy community is one that can contemplate its own death when it no longer fulfills its members. According to this view, the very dissolution of a commune is a sign of its strength. A young woman in a political group in Washington once remarked, "Of course communes work − I'm in my fourth."

But the high mortality rate of American communes may indicate something other than a desire for mobile, dissolvable groups. It may indicate the difficulty of building viable communities that are sufficiently satisfying for members to be willing to invest themselves fully in support of the continued existence of the group. Some communes and utopian communities are temporary out of choice; others are short-lived because they do not organize in a way that builds commitment and fulfillment.

Even among those groups that officially claim to reject strong commitment and longevity, members' expectations may conflict, with some hoping that the group will continue and others eager to avoid long-range commitment. In a conversation at a New Mexican hippie commune, one member is reported to have said, "What we're doin', I suppose, is mainly just trying to live together and work out our lives." But another said, "I really don't see living here the rest of our lives, though, I don't know quite what exactly I'd like to be doin',"[3] Such discrepancies often reflect the group's own confusion or ambivalence over its goals.

There is still much to be learned about the personal consequences of having a series of temporary relationships and a constant turnover in one's social network. Does it add variety and richness and enhance the ability to relate meaningfully to many different people, or does it eliminate the depth and sharing that comes from mutual commitment? Does it promote strength or insecurity? One question is whether communes are indeed a solution to the alienation suffered by American society if they do not provide long-term relationships. Bennett Berger pointed out, for example, that even though child care duties may be supposedly shared on a commune, ultimate responsibility still devolves on the mother, so that men find it easier to run off, leaving mother and children behind.[4] The effects of this possibility on the child and the women are unclear.

Similarly, it is often demoralizing for a group — even the most "hang loose," "do your own thing" group — to face a continual turnover by losing members or to contemplate dissolution. It is too easy for those left behind to feel like failures, as I observed on one California commune, in that they failed to do whatever it might have taken to have kept the lost one. A member of Sunrise Hill also reported difficult feelings after many people had left at the end of the commune's first summer: "For those that remained, a fearful moment of truth came when we stood in that thinned group and recognized that it was, after all, just we few."[5] With a high turnover of members or rapid change of groups, the question occurs whether feelings of failure may be generated. This is an important area for investigation — how groups cope with the loss of members or with their own death, and how these situations affect the individuals in them. It is also important to learn about the consequences for intimacy, a major goal of many communes, when there is rapid turnover of relationships.

Another unresolved question is whether a group is still a utopian community, fulfilling utopian dreams, if it has a shifting membership, changing composition and even reshuffling or merging with other groups. Warren Bennis and Philip Slater argued that temporary relationships will probably be even more true of America of the future than they are today.[6] If that proves to be the case, then the chances for a group of people to constitute themselves as a utopian community and stay together for a substantial period of time may decline. But the decreased chance for endurance does not mean that some communal ventures, though temporary and short-lived, are not an important way to alleviate the loneliness and alienation symptomatic of the society or to redress economic imbalances through cooperative or socialist enterprises. At the very least, certain communes, like encounter groups, may help to educate people in the possibilities for alternative modes of living and relating. At most, a network of communes allowing for exchange of members may develop and survive.

Though many communes are short-lived, there have been a number of utopian communities in the past that lasted considerable periods of time with a relatively stable membership, and there are groups today, such as the Bruderhof, the Hutterites, Cedar Grove, and Koinonia Farm, that have maintained themselves successfully over time. There are over 220 Israeli kibbutzim, the first founded in 1910. Synanon, too, is growing and flourishing, with a stable core of people for whom the community is both permanent home and career, as well as a number of people who come for a short period just to participate in the program of re-education. These communities, being far from temporary, prove that viable utopian communities are indeed possible. Any assessment of such communities thus depends on what the observer chooses to observe — the "failures" or the "successes."

But other critics maintain that the very success of a commune means that it loses vitality. They contend that life in a stable utopian community requires settling down to a challenge-free, boring, and placid existence. If a commune does manage to develop a viable social organization, the costs of such a victory, according to these critics, are sterility and a loss of excitement. The "perfection" of utopia means an end to change and struggle. Once utopia is attained, one has nothing more for which to strive. Even Margaret Mead, otherwise a supporter of utopia and communal life, commented that descriptions of heaven are always much less interesting than descriptions of hell. And Wilbert Moore reported as the most frequent criticisms of utopias that they are unconscionably peaceable, millennialist, and static, missing the utility of conflict.[7]

The most vitriolic critic of utopian communities on these grounds was George Kateb in *Utopia and Its Enemies*. Condemning the nineteenth century communes as "depressing," he argued that any "perfect society" is ultimately unsatisfying.

people prefer not to be happy all the time

People need change, tension, and stimulation, conflict and war, to make life meaningful, he contended. People prefer not to be happy all the time. What Kateb pictured in the communes was a gray, lifeless, austere existence:

> Truly, what could be more depressing than the series of attempts to set up utopian communities in America in the nineteenth century? The coexistence of a community dedicated to an ideal of perfection and the great outside world could lead to nothing but a sense of isolation and strain in that community. Even to those living in the community, the quality of life inside had to be marked by artificiality and a feeling of *confinement*. The noble experiment had to conclude in a corrupting spiritual pride. The retreat from reality could not help attracting people who were merely eccentric; utopias could not help becoming havens for neurotics; the life lived could not help being meager in texture and lacking in complexity. For all these reasons, these utopian communities can excite contempt.[8]

Such contempt, however, is not supported by the evidence. It has not been shown that the levels of strain, artificiality, corruption, eccentricity, neurosis, or meagerness of life in nineteenth century utopias were any greater than those in the outside world. There is, in fact, some evidence to support the opposite conclusion — that utopian communities may reduce some of the traumatic consequences of life in America. Joseph Eaton and Robert Weil found in their study of mental health among the Hutterites that in many respects the Hutterites demonstrated fewer symptoms of pathology. Their reputation among physicians was one of relatively low manifestations of neurosis. Whereas Eaton and Weil found that their rate of psychosis was not lower than that of American society, the Hutterite communal organization offered an environment in which psychotics could be cared for without hospitalization. There is also impressionistic evidence that Oneida's systems of genetic mating (stirpiculture) and group child-rearing were at the least, not harmful to the adaptive growth to maturity of Oneida children, and at the most, they nurtured a group of people who later returned to Oneida after its dissolution as a commune to run it as a highly successful, well-managed

business. Similarly, from research on the kibbutz comes evidence
that kibbutz members have been leaders in Israeli society
out of proportion to their numbers and that kibbutz children
often become leaders in their army service.[9]
The consequences of life in utopian communities for mental
health, then, are far from negative, if indeed mental health
criteria and labels such as "neurotic" and "eccentric" can even
be applied to groups that challenge other definitions and
criteria of the wider society. In fact, it is the commune's
avoidance of pain rather than its experience of it that Kateb
considered most artificial, stressful, confining, and spiritually
corrupting. He championed the point of view that people
can find fulfillment only in misery and conflict. This idea is
underscored in Aldous Huxley's antiutopian novel *Brave New
World* in a bit of dialogue in which the Savage, an outsider,
refuses to become part of the utopian society in which all needs
are met and gratification is only a drug away. He chooses pain
over perfection:

"In fact," said Mustapha Mond, "you're claiming the right to be
unhappy."
"All right then," said the Savage defiantly, "I'm claiming the
right to be unhappy. Not to mention the right to grow old
and ugly and impotent; the right to have syphilis and cancer;
the right to have too little to eat; the right to be lousy; the
right to live in constant apprehension of what may happen tomorrow; the right to catch typhoid; the right to be tortured
by unspeakable pains of every kind."
There was a long silence.
"I claim them all," said the Savage at last.[10]

The fact is, though literary utopias may pretend to eliminate
pain or conflict, actual utopian communities have never succeeded in this respect. Some, both in the past and the present,
have come together for ends compatible with the Savage's
critique of the brave new world, that is, to be entitled to their
own unhappiness, as much or as little as they chose; to protest,
as many of today's communes do, someone else's definition
of what is "good" for them; and to share collectively whatever
suffering must be suffered and the ·eby reduce its impact.

The long-lasting communes of the past remained together through famines, floods, and fires; through successive migrations to new territories and the building of new communities; through persecution by their neighbors and agents of the wider soceity's morality (including a mob invasion of the Shakers); and through participation in social reform movements of the time. Creating a utopian group that is highly fulfilling and provides for all of a person's needs is not incompatible with that same group seeking adventure, challenge, or even struggle. The fixed or permanent social organization that is decried by critics of utopia — if any empirical group ever indeed becomes so internally rigid — still may interact as a unit with its environment in such a way as to promote or maintain challenge.

This helps to answer the question that many people ask about motivation in communal societies: why should anyone work in utopia? If one's welfare is ensured, why work? Kateb, for example, argued that utopias result in lowered exertion since they provide the blessings of life as one's due. The fact is that people work for causes and challenges beyond making sure they will eat or be paid. In a commune, they work to sustain the transcendent meaning of the community; they work because the effort may be intrinsically satisfying, may be chosen work; or they work because they are committed to the other people in the group and want, positively, to do their share to ensure the collective welfare and, negatively, to avoid the disapproval of people they love. Such a system does not operate perfectly, of course, and communal history is full of shirkers, idlers, and hangers-on. Contemporary communes in particular have this problem. But it would be interesting to undertake a study of the comparative rates of idleness and shirking and behind-the-scenes subversion in big bureaucracies versus utopian communities. To use one example where research has been done, the productivity of the Israeli kibbutzim has often been disproportionately higher than that of other kinds of agricultural ventures in Israel.[11]

Even if there can be external challenges and higher purposes, the question remains whether life inside a utopian community necessitates settling for a stable, placid, boring, austere, and lifeless existence, isolated from the rest of society. Need a

commune be, as Kateb suggested, "a closed world forever
without change"?[12] Given the large number and variety of
communal ventures, the answer depends both on the characteristics of the commune in question and on the point of view of
the observer, for what is boring and lifeless to one person
may be invigorating to another. Some communes, such as the
more austere religious communities of the past, essentially
cut themselves off from the changes and developments of the
society around them. Partly from choice on religious grounds,
partly of necessity in order to survive, such communities
sometimes form tight little islands in the midst of society. Their
children often leave to seek freedom and opportunity elsewhere.
Even some of the new generation of hippie communes wish
to disengage themselves from progress, change, and complexity in a similar way, by moving on to farms or into the
woods and creating a simple survival culture. But other utopian
communities have tried to find ways to incorporate change
and create dynamic, exciting environments in which new
elements can be introduced while maintaining the sense of a
warm, loving community. Oneida was decidedly experimental in
this sense. Neither the kibbutzim nor Synanon nor Twin Oaks
today cut themselves off from the rest of society; rather, they
search for ways to adopt new ideas and new technology to
their communal ethics.

The issue of austerity and sterility is even more complicated,
for just a simple look at a commune can be deceptive. A group
providing no outlets for the release or expression of tension
and strong emotion could not survive for long. All continuing
human groups strike a balance between asceticism and ecstacy,
and their social practices swing between the two, just as
commitment involves both giving up and getting.[13] Groups
whose most novel or striking characteristics are their asceticism
may have ecstacy lurking close behind, and vice versa. The
Shakers and Oneida, two nineteenth-century communes whose
life styles superficially appear quite different and seem to
represent the two opposite ends of the continuum, are cases in
point. The celibate Shakers, who worked in silence all day long
and gave up such vestiges of worldliness as art, burst out in
ecstatic fervor every evening in their ritual, rivaling any modern

encounter group in both imagined and realized sensuality. The free-loving Oneidans, accused by the surrounding society of "wanton licentiousness," in some respects led a life of rigorous self-control, exemplified by male continence in which men refrained from ejaculating. In today's communes are also seen swings between asceticism and ecstacy — the asceticism of withdrawal from the evil city to an untouched piece of nature, perhaps giving up meat, cars, television, electricity, or other creature comforts, and taking on difficult physical labor, combined with the ecstacy of freer sexual contact, nudity, and drugs.

To the extent that communities move back and forth between asceticism and ecstacy — as the Shakers did by working hard one moment, and the next abandoning themselves to frenzy — they may be generating cycles of renewal for themselves rather than boring routines. Members of one contemporary urban commune agree that their exhausting work during the day and their joyful encounters at night provide a rhythm and a renewing cycle to their lives. This issue, too, requires further investigation.

The argument about sterility and a lack of vitality in communes is related to another criticism — that utopian communities are anti-intellectual, often having a bias against art, reason, science, and technology. Many critics regard utopias as opposing technological development in particular, which they equate with progress and forward motion. Although communes often promise to reintegrate parts of a person, to use all of his capacities, and to create a group of "whole persons" relating to "whole persons," there has in fact been a tendency for communal groups to value the body more than the mind. The return to the land characteristic of many full-scale communities has meant that physical labor assumes a more legitimate place than intellectual effort. The farmer-intellectuals of Brook Farm in the last century found that the life of the mind and of art did not blend well with the demands of agriculture for sweat and toil. The asceticism of other communities has in part involved a devaluing of intellectual and artistic endeavors. Henrik Infield wrote of the Hutterites: "[They] want to live a simple life wherein all intellectual sophistication is prohibited. They show little or no interest in the fine arts. They read no fiction, see no shows, hear no orchestras, draw no pictures. Even history must not be studied, for it might bring the martial sounds of the outside world into this peaceful, purposely colourless society."[14] But this kind of austerity is unusual, and more commonly communes incorporate art, music, and entertainment.

Utopian groups have more often been characterized by a bias against science or intellect rather than one against art. Many small, rural hippie communes today reject modern science and technology as well as intellectual effort. Encounter groups, too, stress the expression of feelings over reason or analysis, to the extent that they have been accused of being anti-intellectual. The American "counterculture" in general has promoted a return to mysticism and spiritualism, through adopting such systems as astrology. It is natural, however, that many communal groups have devalued the intellectual, for groups tend to value what they need the most. Hence, land-based ventures subsisting at a simple level, organized around the soil and requiring constant physical effort, will value physical labor. Communes dependent on a suspension of disbelief and on ideological commitment, whose members must adopt wholeheartedly a set of not-always-rational or scientific principles, will value faith and unquestioning acceptance. Therapeutic groups attempting to make people open and vulnerable and sensitive to one another will value direct expressions of emotion. All groups concerned with struggling for their creation and survival will value doers more than thinkers. Creativity in such groups often has a practical cast, as in Shaker artistry that was channeled into making sturdy, simple furniture. The intellectual who sees several sides to every issue may also be out of place in a utopian community. Generally, the only "philosopher" permitted is the charismatic leader, who enunciates the guiding principles that give the group its focus. He is the modern equivalent of the "philosopher-king" described in Plato's *Republic*.

Though scientific and intellectual analysis have often had little place in utopian communities, and though the body and soul have often been developed to the exclusion of the mind, this condition has been for the most part a reaction to a society characterized by the opposite extreme. Moreover, there have been notable exceptions. Oneida stressed education and intellectual life and sent many of its children to universities. The life of the mind need not be incompatible with communal existence if it is well integrated into the fabric of the community. The wider issue of the effect of utopian communities on intellectuality and creativity is still largely uninvestigated.

Life in communal groups need not be unchanging or incompatible with social change. As planned or predicted societies, utopian communities are not necessarily unsuited to existence in a rapidly changing society, for what is planned may be a process that can remain despite shifting content. The process of discussion, of reflection, of criticism and feedback, and of decision-making can enable a group to incorporate new elements and engage in continual renewal. This is a challenge for the future — to build commitment to process rather than structure.

### The Issue of Relevance

Another major criticism of communes deals with their social significance and relevance. The issue concerns the relevance of utopian communities to the rest of society, and the number of people for whom they actually provide an alternative. Historically, most communal groups have maintained strong boundaries and have been concerned almost exclusively with life inside the community rather than with the outer world. For this reason many people consider utopias to be escapist or withdrawal movements, and many even accuse commune members of evading their social responsibilities. By retiring from established society, they are doing nothing to correct the problems which afflict that society.

Although this tendency may have been true of communities of the past, it is probably less true of present-day attempts. Synanon manifests great social concern, and in fact, by virtue of establishing a strongly bounded community, a "monastic" enclave within the urban jungle, it may be serving a very vital function for America by helping large numbers of drug addicts who are not helped elsewhere. The Shakers have always provided a home for orphans. Other utopian communities address themselves to important social problems as well. Camp Hill Village cares for the mentally retarded; Koinonia, New Communities, Inc., in Southwest Georgia, and other rural cooperative communities devote themselves to problems of rural poverty. In many ways the intense love and care, the close coordination of production and consumption, the participation in and sharing of power, the integration of home and work, and the elimination of private property often characteristic of fully developed utopian communities make them well suited to attacking problems of therapy, of integration and incorporation of minority groups and women, and of poverty.[15] The stress on cooperation and self-help makes the communal venture a good setting for grass-roots social change — change from the bottom of society up, change that operates by people organizing themselves.

Menachem Rosner pointed out that one of the differences between the Israeli kibbutzim and many utopian communities in the United States is that the kibbutz movement does not remain isolated from the rest of Israeli society. Martin Buber considered this one of the great strengths of the kibbutz movement, and in his book on utopia he referred to the kibbutz as "an experiment that did not fail."[16] The fact that over two hundred kibbutzim, though of varying ideological persuasions, have joined together in the Kibbutz Federation gives the movement the power of numbers and organization, which increases its significance as an alternative institution in a way not possible for isolated communal ventures. At one time about a third of the members of Knesset, the Israeli parliament, came from kibbutzim, so that the movement also had political significance. It is possible, therefore, that if communal ventures can combine into politically and socially significant units, they may have the potential to bring about social reform and to perform valuable change functions for the rest of society.

Yet it is still true that up to the present, American communes have not done much to change the society at large. For their members they may provide an intensely participatory group in which power is equitably shared, but they do not affect the power structure of the surrounding society. Internally they may

become totally cooperative or socialist, effecting a truly
equitable distribution of goods, but still do nothing to change
the inequitable resource allocation and income distribution
in American society. They may offer intensely loving relationships within a small group, but they do not erase the hatred,
violence, and conflict between peoples that exist outside their
boundaries. They have contributed to culture (the Shaker songs,
dances, and crafts) but not to politics. Like Koinonia, communes are generally isolated havens of peace and cooperation.
Utopians would argue that their usefulness is as a model for
others, and that by building the kinds of relations they value
among a small number of people, they prove to the rest of the
world that utopia is possible. When the rest of society comes to
recognize the worth of the communal model and begins to
adopt its practices, utopians argue, the macroinstitutions of
society will indeed change.

This dream was held in particular by nineteenth century
utopians like Robert Owen, whose communal village of New
Harmony was to be an example for the whole world to follow.
Similarly, the Oneidans regarded their community as a "shining
example" of the better world to come. Though Oneida survived
much longer than New Harmony, which failed dramatically
after two years, none of the nineteenth century utopias had
significant influence on American society. They were communal
curiosities, swimming against the great tide of industrialization
and urbanization. Groups today incorporating utopian ideas —
from encounter groups to communes to New Towns like
Columbia, Maryland — have a greater chance of persuading and
changing by example, partly because they are so much more
numerous than in the last century, partly because the mass
media and instant communication make them more visible,
partly because of the stronger need for them, and partly because
they exist in so many different forms and varieties, to almost
all of which planners and architects of the social environment
are giving serious attention. There are nevertheless vast segments
of the society still relatively untouched by the search for what,
after all, remains primarily a white middle class utopian vision,
pursued mostly by those unfulfilled by affluence who turn
to their emotions for salvation.

Involved with the concern that utopian communities are not relevant to social change on a large scale is the issue of size. Viable American utopian communities of the past had a modal size of about two hundred members — large enough to offer some variety, but small enough to manage easily. At one time the Shakers had six thousand members, but these were organized into eighteen villages located in different parts of the country. Kibbutz planners indicate that if a kibbutz becomes larger than a thousand, many problems ensue. The Hutterites have over ten thousand members, but they too are divided into villages of about one hundred each, and when any one village grows too large, another is started. Most extended-family communes in America have about eight to fifteen members, with the largest verging on thirty. Encounter groups and other growth communities typically consist of one to four groups of twelve each.

Some critics assert that it is no longer realistic to place hopes for utopia on the small communal ventures that, as self-contained societies, encompass only the tiniest fraction of the world's population and often turn their collective backs on the global village. Even at the turn of the century, utopian thinkers criticized the communitarians as isolationist, arguing that utopia lay in large- rather than small-scale social reconstruction, which aimed at total societies rather than villages, or even, as H. G. Wells wrote, at the planet itself: "No less than a planet will serve the purpose of a modern utopia." By the 1960s, Robert Boguslaw was referring to the systems engineers engaged in large-scale, computerized social planning as "the new utopians."[17] Whereas such concern for macrosocial reconstruction is appropriate in an urban age of large and complexly inter-related populations, its relevance to the utopian community is questionable. Its aims and ideals may not be translatable from groups of twenty or two hundred people to new cities or towns of upwards of ten thousand. The utopian community — never very large at most — may not be able to survive the transition from small group to urban community, from isolated retreat to complex society. Perhaps it cannot serve the greater numbers that new towns and other value-oriented community ventures are called upon to serve.

If the commune gets much larger than a few hundred members, its organization must change. Georg Simmel pointed out that pure socialistic societies have been possible only in very small groups, having failed in larger ones. In writing on the significance of numbers for social life, he stated: "The principle of socialism — justice in the distribution of production and reward — can easily be realized in a small group and ... can be safeguarded there by its members. The contribution of each to the whole and the group's reward to him are visible at close range; comparison and compensation are easy. In the large group they are difficult, especially because of the inevitable differentiation of its members, of their functions and claims."[18] In other words, as a group, even a utopian group, gets larger, it increases in complexity, differentiation, distance between members, and potential for inequality. Only the division of labor, according to Simmel and other theorists, can provide the interdependence to integrate a large group; but such a division of labor may give rise to the specialization and separation that are antithetical to communal ideals. Other social scientists argue that these same communal ideals, even if they could survive in a complex, highly-differentiated urban community, may not be particularly desirable over large populations. Homogeneity may be a commitment-building asset in a small commune, but heterogeneity and diversity are exciting components of urban life. Full participation and close contact are laudatory in a communal group; these same practices may be unwieldly, inefficient, and sometimes frustrating in very large communities, or they may not provide the same sense of political ownership, involvement, closeness, and emotional support that they do in small groups. It is clear, in any event, that communes cannot be built on the scale of urban communities, or even of component parts of such communities, such as neighborhoods, merely by retaining the communitarian social institutions viable for populations of two hundred and simply increasing the number of people. Larger size necessitates differences in social organization that may violate utopian ideals.

Perhaps utopian communities are relevant for very large urban populations if that large number is divided into rather small units, each of which becomes the communal enclave. But then questions arise of intergroup coordination and cooperation that have never been addressed in the prior history of utopian experiments, and which are today being addressed by the Kibbutz Federation in only a limited way, as compared to the vast and complex American urban existence. There are no answers in the experience of utopian communities of the past or present to the problem of building large and complex structures out of very small ones – especially when the small ones may need their distinctiveness and identity in order to survive as close communities. In fact, history suggests that the process by which large social systems are constructed out of small, intimate ones is the very process by which Gesellschaften (societies or complex organizations or cities) are created out of Gemeinschaften (close, familylike communities). How communal and utopian ideals can be translated to large-sized units is therefore a difficult question, one that will be faced often by social planners of the future.

One answer to the question of size may be the same as that for acquiring political significance – a federation of small communes. Many communes in union have the potential to create cooperative facilities and organizations that are suitable to urban life, such as schools, day care centers, food cooperatives, or shared enterprises that employ commune members, while at the same time preserving the small size of each "family." Several such federations have been begun: in northern California an attempt was made by several communes to build a free school; in Vermont a health collective services area communes; in Boston a federation of twenty communes has operated a food cooperative and a commune-matching service. Still another Boston group has an arrangement with New Hampshire farm communes to produce organic food for urban communes. There is much promise in these cooperative ventures, but also some difficulty. The Israeli kibbutzim could federate because of the many shared values among them, and because they always saw themselves as part of a larger movement; but even so, there are four separate kibbutz movements of varying ideological persuasions. Commune federations creating viable alternative institutions will have to work on the problems of developing common values and goals among communes and of dealing with possible conflicts. How to build intergroup cooperation without bureaucratization or centralized control by a federation will be a major issue for the future.

Finally, critics assert that utopian communities are insulated from many of the realities of life in the wider society, while at the same time being highly dependent on the existence of that society. They contend that utopian communities can exist only as a counterculture within a society organized on very different principles, but which can make available to the commune goods and services it cannot provide for itself. Many communes today reject technology but benefit from its products. Personal growth groups can create close, warm, loving relations just because they avoid dealing with power relations or with decision-making issues that create strain in relations outside encounter groups. There is also some truth to the argument that utopian groups need to have the larger society to fight against or complain about, in order to coalesce around a shared rejection. It is a social psychological canon that extra-group conflict heightens intragroup cohesiveness, that having an external enemy gives a group added strength. It is unknown how many utopian communities have survived in fact because they were persecuted, but emnity of some kind with the outside society has been a fact of life for practically every utopian community on record.

Some of these criticisms of utopian communities today stem from the perceived limitations of utopian experiments. Others reflect skepticism that the small, close, homogeneous, loving community can have anything but a deviant place in a highly technological, diverse urban society. Paul Goodman has argued, however, that utopian dreams should be retained, with a new community model, more similar to the kibbutz than to American communities, substituted:

In our era, to combat the emptiness of technological life, we have to think of a new form, the conflictful community. Historically, close community has provided warmth and security, but it has been tyrannical, antiliberal, and static (conformist small towns). We, however, have to do with already thoroughly urbanized individuals with a national culture and a scientific technology. The Israeli kibbutzim offer the closest approximation. Some of them have been fanatically dogmatic according to various ideologies, and often tyrannical; nevertheless, their urban Jewish members, rather well educated on the average, have inevitably run into fundamental conflict. Their atmosphere has therefore been sometimes unhappy but never deadening, and they have produced basic social inventions and new character-types. Is such a model improvable and adaptable to cities and industrial complexes? Can widely differing communities be accommodated in a larger federation? How can they be encouraged in modern societies? These are utopian questions.[19]

The utopian questions Goodman raised cannot yet be answered, because despite all the debates on communes and utopias, there has been little systematic research addressed to these critical issues.

## Group Pressure and Social Control

The final important critical question about communal groups concerns their internal organization, particularly the role of group pressure and social control. If communal orders do succeed, critics contend, it is because they substitute one form of coercion for another. The argument runs that when communal groups effect harmony between members and develop a smooth, intimate, cooperative life, they often achieve this at a terrible cost to the individual. Though communes may remove the repressive control of distant, impersonal institutions, they replace it with the control of the intimate, face-to-face group of peers, which is perhaps a more benign kind of coercion, but coercion nonetheless. Such critics also point out that in the past the longest-lived communes have been those apparently most "authoritarian" in the sense of having strong leaders or a leadership hierarchy, many formal rules or informal group norms, and continual demands on the individual for "spiritual improvement" as defined by the group.

The question of controls is a complex one, pondered by philosophers and social theorists from the Greeks to the present. It asks, among other things, whether social life can be sustained

without social control, what makes social control and group
pressure coercive, whether groups and individuals are doomed
to be antagonists, and in what ways the group either represses
the individual or promotes his growth. To the extent that these
issues bear on communal orders, it is important to remember
the general features of communes: they are voluntary social
orders, based on free entrance and exit, regardless of how much
pressure the group may put on the individual to stay; their
social practices tend to reflect the choices of the members
themselves; they usually reject the use of physical violence; they
frequently employ practices of mutual criticism and feedback,
in which whoever is playing the role of leader is also subject
to the criticism of others; they often rotate positions and have
frequent meetings in which to share information, so that all
members are highly involved in the life and decision-making of
the group; and whatever power there is is usually highly visible,
for no matter how much figures such as charismatic leaders
are infused with mystery, special privilege, and social distance,
they are still physically present and highly accessible to members. It is also important to remember that a certain amount of
order seems to be necessary for sustained social life, and
communes, at least, often attempt to find ways to establish
order that are as equitable as possible. In some ways, order is
merely another name for clarified expectations, and structure
is another name for an agreement on the part of a group. The
importance of clear expectations and group agreements is
stressed by even the most anarchistic commune theorists.
Finally, people probably vary in their personal requirements
and tolerance for structure and group control, just as communes
vary among themselves in the amount they provide. As long
as there are a variety of communes, perhaps people can choose
the level of order and communality they prefer. In the last
century Oneidans and Shakers visited back and forth and were
sympathetic to each other, but they also probably chose that
community in which they were personally most comfortable.

It is undeniable, however, that group pressure plays a large
part in the life of communal orders. Eaton and Weil pointed out
with respect to the Hutterites that in place of the many symptoms of estrangement and alienation in the wider society,

such as alcoholism, drug addiction, and insomnia, members of
the Hutterite communes often suffer from acute guilt feelings
when they feel they have violated the norms of the group.
In Synanon, group pressure is the primary form of social control,
responsible not only for the cohesion of the community but
also for the striking and dramatic changes in members. Even in
anarchistic communes that reject any formal organization or
demands on members, informal group pressure still constitutes
a powerful influence for conformity, and members often report
a great unease at "letting down the group," that is, failing
to live up to the standards of the community. One of the major
criticisms of personal growth centers and encounter groups,
whether embryonic or actual communes, is that the individual
is placed in a coercive situation where he is vulnerable to the
pressures of the group. Such pressures, critics assert, may
require him to violate his own inner nature in the interests of
being a "good group member." Going even further, right-wing
critics have accused sensitivity groups, such as those used by
communes, of "brainwashing" and "thought control," of
preparing people for the "dictatorial control which is the essence of Nazism and all Socialism." Synanon, too, has been
attacked by Edgar Z. Friedenberg for "brainwashing."[20]
   Some of this concern is legitimate, and all communal groups
are subject to the danger of crossing the point at which a
close, warm, loving group becomes an instrument for inducing
conformity. But part of the concern also lies in the American
fear of being swallowed up by a group, a fear of suffocation
of the individual, a fear of loss of freedom and privacy. Americans are generally pictured as friendly, gregarious, and expansive,
but other evidence suggests that instead they shy away from
intimacy. D. K. Weisberg presented data to indicate that
Americans maintain more physical distance in interaction than
French or Latin Americans and do much less touching. Abraham
Maslow cited Kurt Lewin's and Walter Toman's arguments
that Americans need so many more therapists than the rest of
the world because they just do not know how to be intimate.
As Philip Slater forcefully argued in *The Pursuit of Loneliness*,
it is this very American protection of individualism to the
exclusion of cooperation and community that may be in large

measure responsible for many of the psychological crises in
our society today.[21]

It is true that those communities have worked best which
manage to generate commitment and loyalty in their members,
which immerse people in a strong group that often asks them
to make sacrifices, renounce other relationships, and open
themselves to criticism by the group. In some cases the community stops there, having created the conditions for harmony
and cooperation, and desires little more than to retain its
members. Other groups wish to promote self-reliance and
responsibility as well, so as to develop strong individuals
capable of meeting or suspending their own needs in the context of a loving community. Synanon, for example, has transformed some former drug addicts into responsible members
of the community. Carl Rogers suggested that the end states of
encounter groups are "more personal independence, fewer
hidden feelings, more willingness to innovate, more opposition
to institutional rigidities."[22]

But the issue need not necessarily be phrased as the group
versus the individual, as community or privacy, as organization
or freedom. Rather, the question for the future is how to promote the growth of the individual and to respect his privacy
in the context of a close loving community that also has the
degree of organization needed to continue to meet the needs of
the individuals within it. There are trade-offs to be made here:
a certain amount of one thing may be exchanged for a measure
of the other. For example, many members of contemporary
communes have reported in interviews that they did give up
some of their privacy when they joined the communes. However, they also assert either that they do not miss it, that
they do not need as much privacy as they had thought, that
they have learned to live without it, or most significantly,
that the rewards they find in intimacy and closeness far outweigh the cost in privacy. All human groups may need to strike
balances, for social life is full of such trade-offs.

### The Importance of Utopias and Communes

Some of the criticisms directed against utopian communities
are concerned with valid social, political, and philosophical

issues in the life of communal orders. Others, however, stem
from the American ideology rooted in a Puritan conscience,
which values pain over gratification and regards deprivation and
suffering as prime human motivators; which prefers "progress"
and linear movement forward to cyclical activity; which values
change for its own sake; which considers movements that
lack immediate or apparent social utility to the wider society
as "escapist"; and which views the separateness and isolation
of the individual as superior to close group relationships. Not
only does communal life challenge many of these assumptions,
but the current movement may have some impact on reshaping
them.

In any human group there is a gap between what works or
has functional or organizational value, and what is desirable
or has personal or social value. Utopian communities attempt to
narrow this gap between the practical and the ideal, but they
are not always successful. Measures that some communes
have found to be practical, their critics do not feel are ideal.
Methods that other communes chose as ideal were pragmatically
impossible. The life of communes, therefore, like other groups,
has its limits and costs as well as its benefits and advantages.
Utopian communities are not the answer to everything. They
are difficult to create, even more difficult to sustain. They
exact a dedication and an involvement that many people find
unappealing. They sometimes have shortcomings that make
them fail of the perfection they promise. But as thoughtful,
concerned people have discovered, they do supply partial
answers. Erich Fromm, for example, described communal
orders as one of the roads to sanity that will reassert the dignity
of humanity.[23]

Utopian communities are in fact possible, within limits. Even
though they may provide less than they promise, communes
and alternative communities are increasing in number today as
more and more Americans seek more fulfilling social relations.
Most of these new ventures will probably not last very long,
but as rapidly as some communes dissolve, others spring up. The
impact of communes and new communities on American society
cannot be predicted, but it is no longer possible to regard them
merely as interesting aberrations. As an independent movement,
they may be difficult to sustain in this society, but they will

undoubtedly affect the future organization of the family, of religion, of work, and of therapy. Their existence has raised a new set of options for Americans, which may influence expectations about the quality of life. For example, children reared in communal ventures, even for part of their lives, may grow up desiring different life styles and social institutions than do those raised in isolated nuclear families.[24]

Utopian communities are important not only as social ventures in and of themselves but also as challenges to the assumptions on which current institutions are organized. The work organization of nineteenth century groups, for example, with its job rotation, communal work efforts, mutual criticism, shared ownership, equality of compensation, participatory decision-making, infusion with spiritual values, and integration with domestic life, may provide alternative models for contemporary work organizations. Nineteenth century communes are also a rich source of ideas for developing decentralized communities in which production and consumption as well as domestic and economic life are closely linked. Synanon and other communes dealing with societal outcasts offer one alternative to mental hospitals and prisons. Koinonia represents an alternative model for dealing with rural poverty and racial tension. The Shakers, Oneida, Amana, and the kibbutzim in Israel offer models for the alternative organization of highly efficient but cooperative agricultural or industrial enterprise. Small communes are alternatives to the isolated nuclear family. Therapeutic communities based on utopian notions are alternatives to traditional one-to-one, pathology-oriented therapies. The utopian community itself represents a model for a different kind of community organization, one from which community planners can derive a useful set of options.

The importance of considering the potential for utopias thus transcends the more limited issue of whether or not individual communes work. Utopian visions of social reconstruction supply an antidote to the pervasive assumption that "sick" or deviant individuals are both the source and the symptom of social problems, and that the individual must therefore be changed. Utopian thinking and experimentation are aimed at structural reform, at the creation of new social worlds or communities where the old problems no longer arise. Social problems, according to this view, are a function of structural defects in society and can be solved only by constructing a new society or by reshaping social institutions. Although some utopian experiments are more successful than others, and some succeed in eliminating particular problems only to introduce others, the mode of thinking that goes into the invention of a utopian community should be encouraged. It strives to implement ideals of a better way of living and relating, to consider options and alternatives, to become structurally inventive, and to experiment with the creation of wholly new social worlds. Utopian communities are society's dreams.

Regardless of their form or stability, today's communes, like those of the past, tend to reflect, by their very formation, a romantic, optimistic, utopian vision of human potential. They believe that by living together, people can overcome loneliness; by generating and respecting shared dreams, life can become more meaningful; by creating small, cooperative, group-run communities, individuals can gain a sense of personal control; and by returning to the simple, uncomplicated, "organic" sources of sustenance, basic human satisfactions can be achieved. A communal vision assumes the best of people: that they are willing to sacrifice and share, and that they can work out their differences so as to live together in harmony, peace, and love. As John Leonard expressed it in 1971: "The romantic notion of the perfectibility of man is really all we have to sustain us, no matter how illusory it may prove to be . . . The rest is rhetoric, and the romantics have the best rhetoric."

# Sample and Methodology for Study of Nineteenth Century Communes

The first issue in studying historical communes is defining the range of the phenomenon. The utopian community represents an extreme case of a system seeking to institutionalize communal, primary, and expressive relations, while at the same time it is organized as a corporate group to meet production goals and carry on relations with external systems for its participants. Utopian communities in the past resembled total social orders in that for the most part their members never needed to go outside the boundaries of the community for the necessities of life; the organizational structure took into account practically all of the social roles members played, such as their economic, religious, sexual, familial, and political functions, — even including the role of citizen in the larger society. In addition, utopian communities were often demarcated spatially, in terms of their functioning as a centrally planned and controlled residential unit, which explicitly organized living, sleeping, and eating patterns. It was through one central organization that members related to a variety of environments and external systems. Thus, utopian communities are just as clearly defined and ordered by their *Gesellschaft* nature — the fact that members relate to one another in the context of their organizational tasks — as they are by their communal goals.

This conception of utopian communities, which stresses their organizational functions, departs markedly from previous formulations. Utopias have been defined as communistic or socialistic societies, as communal social systems, as value-oriented social movements, and as movements of social withdrawal. None of these perspectives, however, quite captures the totality of a utopia's system properties.

Generally, historians have defined utopian communities as communistic or socialistic societies because they often affect property relations by instituting some form of joint holding. Thus, John Noyes, Charles Nordhoff, William Hinds, Charles Gide, and others classed together those communities having a historically striking property, a characteristic that generally differentiated them from other settlements.[1] However, there

are several reasons why this is a limited concept. In the first place, a utopian community differs greatly in the extent of communistic sharing — in
whether it includes production, distribution, or consumption, how it limits
collective ownership, and who holds actual title to property, whether
the community, leaders, or individuals. Some American utopias were
actually joint stock companies, owned by their investors, some of whom
resided in the community, while others did not. It would not be accurate
to define these systems as communistic or socialistic when they really
represented an organizational innovation more characteristic of capitalistic
economic systems. Finally, to define utopian communities in terms of
their property relations or work relations (which actually varied greatly) is
to ignore their other meaningful organizational characteristics, such as
their stress on brotherhood and interpersonal involvement, and their
political, religious, residential, and extrasystem relations. While not a
defining characteristic of a utopian community, however, communistic
organization may be a functional characteristic, for various kinds of
economic sharing may facilitate mutual expressiveness.

Some sociologists have defined utopian communities as communal
systems, or as Gemeinschafts in the more traditional sense of the term. Ivan
Vallier, who treated them as such, defined communal systems in the
following manner: they are designed as an ideal moral order oriented to
noninstrumental goals; their consciously limited membership interacts on a
primary group basis; they voluntarily separate from the larger society;
they are organized in terms of nonspecific, generally interchangeable roles;
and they operate as fused structural contexts within which members act
in overlapping, general roles.[2] Some of these characteristics do indeed
describe persisting communal systems, but others are merely secondary
features that may support such a system or may be associated with it for
other reasons. The degree of separation from the larger society, the
extent of conscious limitation of membership, the extent to which roles
are diffuse and generally interchangeable — all of these are empirical
questions for communal systems rather than theoretically defining values,
and can be examined only in the context of concrete empirical systems.
These issues are problematic, leading to questions such as: Do communal
systems of long duration exhibit separation from the larger society while
those of short duration do not? Do successful communal systems have
more primary-type interaction than unsuccessful ones? Do persisting communal systems limit membership while unsuccessful ones do not? In
other words, communal systems should be defined on the basis of one
central characteristic, their mutually expressive goals, while their other
secondary properties remain problematic rather than fixed, so that
research can discover the effects of the absence or presence of such secondary features on the maintenance of communal systems. What Vallier
described is not the ideal typical communal system but rather the successfully maintained communal system.

Even when Vallier's definition of such systems is pared down, however,
it is evident that characterizing utopian communities as communal

systems is limited. This view considers only one side of a utopia, which definitely has another side. One of the most striking characteristics of such systems is that they are fully organized Gesellschafts. Though utopias wish people to interact on a communal basis, this is generally in the context of other goals related to establishing a political and economic order. In fact, many historical utopias were more or less explicitly founded for economic rather than communal purposes. The Fourierite communities in the United States are an example, and they even referred to themselves as associations. The communal goals of such organizations were at least partially derived from the expression of common instrumental purposes and economic organizations.

Utopian communities have also been treated in the literature on value-oriented social movements. Neil Smelser, for example, included them among other "collective attempts to restore, protect, modify, or create values in the name of a generalized belief." Ralph Turner and Lewis Killian describe value-oriented movements in a similar way.[3] It is true that utopian communities are undeniably interested in values, but they are also to a great degree oriented to practical considerations stemming from associational exigencies, such as the necessity of dealing with environments. Moreover, a social movement generally characterizes a social system at a particular organizational stage, namely, mobilization. Utopian communities, on the other hand, exist in a relatively established and institutionalized form. A minimal amount of organization is assumed in order to define a utopian community at all. In addition, some utopian communities in the past lasted long enough to become in effect part of the established order, having an institutionalized position in the larger society. Other communes did not derive from social movements but evolved slowly out of established groups. In fact, utopias vary greatly in the amount and duration of organization prior to their founding, as well as the degree to which they are part of the established institutional order.

Writers have also asserted that utopian communities belong among movements of social withdrawal, defined as "collective protests . . . made effective by actively withdrawing from either all or most of the contacts with the offending society and seeking the ultimate reconstruction of that society."[4] However, not all utopian communities meet these criteria. It is true that they are separatist in the sense that they establish their own set of systems to meet the environmental needs of their members, but these political and economic systems may have a great deal of contact with the rest of society, through trade or proselytizing, for example. In fact, many utopian communities in the past founded their own economic, political, religious, and social organizations in preference to those in operation in society, but continued to maintain contact via society's systems. Whether utopian communities seek the ultimate reconstruction of society is similarly problematic. Many are established only to meet the needs of their members and more fully express their values with little interest in changing the outside. The Harmony Society in nineteenth-century America is one example. That communes often move to spatially isolated locations is not de facto evidence that they are movements of social withdrawal, for many other groups seek isolated locations, and groups of all kinds seek the opportunity for a fresh start that the frontier offers.

For a variety of reasons, therefore, utopian communities do not fit neatly into any of the categories into which they have traditionally been placed, although each of these categories describes some aspect of their organization. It is doubtful that utopian communities are communistic, separatist, derived from social movements, or oriented to the reconstruction of society, as revealed by research on nineteenth-century American communes.

## Choosing the Sample

The nineteenth-century utopian communities examined for this study are those founded in the United States between the Revolutionary and the Civil Wars (approximately 1780 to 1860). By choosing groups from a single society in one historical period, I am controlling for variations in the environment, holding external conditions constant while testing the differential effects of various organizational strategies.[5]

In selecting a sample of American utopian communities established between 1780 and 1860, I faced several problems. Foremost was the unit problem, determining what represents a single instance of a utopian community. Some communities changed location several times, some had branches in different locations, and others established branches that were relatively independent from the mother community. Historian Arthur Bestor arrived at a list of 124 cases based on the assumption that the unit was a single location. Thus, the Shakers appear on his list twenty-two times, for at various times there were twenty-two Shaker villages in separate locations in the United States. Hinds listed even more distinct social systems involving the Shakers, for he counted each of the "families," the semiautonomous, segregated units within Shaker villages, as single instances of communal experiments. Similarly, Bestor listed the Harmony Society or Rappites three times, for they changed location twice, and he included separately Oneida and its branch at Wallingford, Connecticut. The fact that utopian communities were sometimes known only by the name of their location facilitates the tendency to consider a separate location as the test of a distinct utopia. But location need not be a sociologically meaningful variable, nor does it necessarily provide a criterion for independent status. Harmony maintained its general organizational pattern and personnel through all three locations, and Oneida's branch had no distinctive structure, taking its direction entirely from the mother community. Though each Shaker village had its own authority structure, all were founded on a single model, often by personnel from other Shaker villages, adhered to the same ideology, and took orders from a central authority with jurisdiction over all the villages. Neither individual Shaker villages nor the three locations of Harmony nor the branch of

Oneida, therefore represent independent instances of utopian communities.[6]
Identity of organization, with some centralized control over simultaneou:
or successive locations, is a better test of a unit utopia. By employing
this criterion, I reduced Bestor's list of 124 experiments to 91.[7] These 91
utopian communities, representing the entire population founded in
the United States between 1780 and 1860, include 11 "successful"
utopias, 79 "unsuccessful" ones, and one case that proved to be unclassi-
fiable (Icaria). Success was measured by length of time in existence; a
system had to exist as a utopian community for at least twenty-five years,
the sociological definition of a generation, in order to be considered
successful. A case was regarded as a utopian community if all relevant
relations among members were centrally controlled by a single organization. For example, Oneida was considered to have been ended as a utopian
community when it shifted to a conventional economic system and
gave up jurisdiction over its members' social and marital relations. Its duration as a utopian community was thirty-three years, even though as
some kind of social system it has persisted over one hundred twenty years.
When the utility of the twenty-five-year criterion was tested on the entire
list, it was found that only one successful utopia lasted less than thirty-
three years, and no unsuccessful case lasted more than sixteen years.
From this list of utopian communities a "sample" of 9 successful and 21
unsuccessful cases was selected. The sample consisted of communities
for which there were at least two independent sources of information. Of
the 11 successful cases in the entire population, only 2 could not be
included in the sample, because of a scarcity of information on their social
organization (although some data on one of them was collected). Of the
79 unsuccessful utopias, 9 cases on which some data had been collected
were omitted from the sample for lack of information. Availability of data
was not the only criterion used for selection of the 21 unsuccessful cases
in the sample, however, for an attempt was also made to achieve representa-
tiveness and independence. All major types and time periods were included
in the sample, and most of those not studied were either similar in
type and ideology to those examined or very small in size and short in
duration — the average life of all unsuccessful cases being less than two
years. The problem of independence arose with respect to the Fourierist
communes. There were 22 Fourierist phalanxes, all unsuccessful. Most of
these were planned on the basis of a single model of organization. Six
phalanxes in New York State even formed a confederation for a time,
known as the American Industrial Union, and there was a national
Fourierist association, as well as clubs in many cities.[8] Although there was
no central control over the communities, so that each of the 22 organizations may be considered a different unit, they were clearly less than
independent. For this reason, the Fourierist phalanxes were deliberately
undersampled, with only the three included for which the most information could be gathered. Within the sample of unsuccessful cases, those

of relatively longer duration were also overrepresented, owing partly to the availability of materials, for the longer a community's existence, the greater the likelihood of its attracting notice. But the emphasis on duration was also deliberate, designed to increase the meaningfulness and validity of the comparison between successful and unsuccessful cases. Social organization does not usually arise suddenly and *in toto*, but often requires a slow period of organization. To include only 3 communities of less than two full years' duration and 14 of at least three full years tends to ensure that the differences between successful and unsuccessful cases are not owing to differences in their stage of organizational development but rather to differences in the kinds of organization they do establish. The following communities were studied, listed in order of longevity:

## Successful Communities

*The Shakers* 184 years. 1787–present. Grew out of a sect, the United Society of Believers, founded by Ann Lee. First Shaker Village established by Joseph Meachem after her death. About 500 original members; at height, 1830–1840, 6,000 members in 18 villages throughout the Northeast.

*The Harmony Society*. 100 years. 1804–1904. German separatists led by George Rapp. Settled first in Harmony, Pennsylvania, then New Harmony, Indiana, then Economy, Pennsylvania. 600–700 original members; 800 in 1811.

*Amana*. 90 years. 1843–1933. The Society of True Inspiration, a German sect. Settled first in Ebenezer, New York, then established seven communal villages in Iowa. 800 original members; 1,800 in 1880.

*Zoar*. 81 years. 1817–1898. The Society of Separatists, a German group led by Joseph Bimeler. Settled in Ohio. 300 original members; 500 in 1853.

*Snowhill*. 70 years. 1800–1870. Seventh Day Baptists. An offshoot of the Ephrata Community in Pennsylvania.

*Saint Nazianz*. 42 years. 1854–1896. A Catholic commune established in Wisconsin by German immigrants led by Father Ambrose Ochswald. 28 original members; 450 in 1866.

*Bethel* and *Aurora*. 36 years. 1844–1880. Established in Missouri and Oregon, by followers of William Keil. Bethel was founded first; later Keil and part of the group moved to Aurora.

*Oneida*. 33 years. 1848–1881. American Perfectionists led by John Humphrey Noyes, implementing "Bible communism" in upstate New York. For a time, branches elsewhere, principally in Wallingford, Connecticut. 40 original members in Putney, Vermont. 104 members in Oneida in 1849; 288 in 1880. (Thirty-three years is a conservative figure for Oneida's duration, for the core group actually started five years earlier in Putney, and when the community was transformed in to a joint-stock company in 1881, it retained strong communal overtones and a residential base.)

*Jerusalem*. 33 years. 1788–1821. New York community established by followers of Jemimah Wilkinson, the "Universal Friend." 250 members in 1800. (Thirty-three years is a conservative figure for Jerusalem's duration, since a core of the community remained together another twenty-two years under the guidance of Rachel Malin, Jemimah's appointed successor.)

## Unsuccessful Communities

*Hopedale.* 15 years. 1841–1856. Practical Christian community in Massachusetts founded by Adin Ballou, a leading nonresistor. 28 original members; 229 in 1853.

*Modern Times.* 15 years. 1851–1866. An anarchist commune on Long Island, with which Josiah Warren was associated.

*Bishop Hill.* 14 years. 1846–1860. A Swedish religious sect led by Eric Janson, settled in Illinois. 400 original members; 1,500 by 1854.

*North American Phalanx.* 13 years. 1843–1856. A leading Fourierist phalanx and the longest-lived, established in New Jersey. Albert Brisbane and Horace Greeley were associated with it. 30–40 original members; 112 in 1852.

*Communia.* 8 years. 1847–1855. A socialist experiment in Iowa. Wilhelm Weitling and other German Marxists were involved. 12 original families; 79 people in 1853.

*Oberlin.* 8 years. 1833–1841. Christian community in Ohio, by which Oberlin College was founded. Led by John Shiphard and composed of religious group organized for the purpose of founding a community. About 11 families.

*Brook Farm.* 6 years. 1841–1847. A community near Boston established by a group of Transcendentalist intellectuals led by George Ripley. Nathaniel Hawthorne lived in it for a time. 20 original members; no more than 100 at any one time. Became a Fourierist phalanx.

*Wisconsin Phalanx.* 6 years. 1844–1850. A Fourierist phalanx led by Warren Chase. 71 original members; 180 in 1846.

*Northampton.* 4 years. 1842–1846. The Northampton Association of Education and Industry, a Massachusetts community. Started with 21 adults and 20 children; 180 people in 1843.

*Utopia.* 4 years. 1847–1851. Established in Ohio. The second attempt at founding a community by the anarchist Josiah Warren, who wished to substitute for money a scheme of "equitable commerce" based on labor credits. 6 original families; 12 families in 1849.

*Kendal.* 3 years. 1826–1829. The Friendly Association for Mutual Interests at Kendal, an Ohio community established around the philosophy of Robert Owen. 150 people at largest.

*Nashoba.* 3 years. 1825–1828. Tennessee commune founded by Frances Wright for emancipated slaves. 20 people at largest.

*Order of Enoch.* 3 years. 1831–1834. The First United Order among the Mormons, their first experiment in a total, collective commune, established at Independence, Missouri.

*Skaneateles Community.* 3 years. 1843–1846. New York community

founded by John Collins, an anarchist. 36 original members; 90 in 1844.
*Iowa Pioneer Phalanx.* 2 years. 1844–1846. Fourierist phalanx. 50 members.
*Jasper Colony.* 2 years. 1851–1853. German sect in Iowa led by Hermann Diekhoner. 10 families at largest.
*New Harmony.* 2 years. 1825–1827. Robert Owen's Indiana experiment. 1,000 people by the end of 1825.
*Preparation.* 2 years. 1853–1855. Schismatic Mormons in Iowa led by Charles Thompson. Over 50 families at largest.
*Blue Spring.* 1 year. 1826. Little-known Owenist venture in Indiana. 27 people at largest.
*Fruitlands.* 8 months. 1843. Established by Bronson Alcott and Charles Lane in Massachusetts. 16 people at most. Louisa May Alcott lived there.
*Yellow Springs.* 6 months. 1825. Owenist commune in Ohio. Led by Daniel Roe, it grew out of a group of Swedenborgians. 75–100 families joined.

These two types of nineteenth-century utopian communities, successful and unsuccessful, provided the data for testing hypotheses about the kinds of practices that build commitment to a community and thus make utopia a flourishing practical reality. It was assumed that the nine successful much more than the twenty-one unsuccessful groups would organize in ways that promote and sustain commitment.

## Data Collection

Data were collected from four kinds of sources: central members, such as leaders; peripheral members, such as deviants and apostates; visitors and first-hand observers; and historians. In addition, a number of documents, such as constitutions and financial records, were examined. Information from these sources pertaining to a large number of variables was recorded as though it represented responses to a nonfixed, nonordered interview schedule. Data were then sorted into categories representing answers to questions suggested by theory and by hypotheses about the following variables and their changes over time:

Background, prior history, conditions of founding
Location, physical characteristics
Population size
Recruitment
Adult socialization
Child socialization
Ideology
Authority structure
Decision-making process
Leadership prerogatives
Members' feelings about leaders
Behavioral rules and formal codes

Social controls and sanctions
Deviance
Finances
Property relations
Work arrangements
Differentiation and stratification
Sexual, familial, and friendship relations
Members' feelings about each other
Group contact vs. individuality and privacy
Funeral practices
Religion and religious practices
Concept of community by members
Concept of the outside
Dress
Language, slang
Outside's attitude toward community
Members' visits outside
Outsiders' visits to community
Relations with neighbors
Relations with other utopias
Relations with local, state, and national government
Legal status and transactions
Influence of and responsiveness to the outside
Natural disasters and response to them
Dissension, sect formation, challenges to authority
Defections
Life style
The end of the community, its dissolution or transformation

   When data bore on more than one set of variables, it was included in all
relevant categories. Whenever possible, the information was given a
time-referrent, so that the study could take into account the period of the
utopia's history for which the data held true.
   Potential bias in the data was one of the most serious methodological
problems faced. Accounts of community life are often written by persons
with interests other than historical accuracy. Some descriptions are
autobiographical (often by the founder or leader), some are propagandistic
or pedagogical, and others are saturated with political or religious ideology.
Furthermore, some accounts make reference to still other reports for
specific facts and thus offer a tangled combination of primary and
secondary material. To minimize these difficulties, the following precau-
tions were taken. First, information on all critical variables was taken
as often as possible from at least two independent sources and from two
informants who represented different perspectives, such as a member
of the community and a nonmember visitor or historian. Second, once
information had been categorized, internal checks were used to determine

whether other related data tended to confirm or discredit the information. These internal checks were made by independent judges who did not know the hypotheses of the study. For example, celibacy would seem to be necessarily associated with some sort of separate sleeping arrangement for men and women; if this condition were not met, the judgment that the system was celibate would have problematic status, unless confirmed by other information.

Once the data was assembled and ordered in terms of the concepts to which it related, it was necessary to devise a data reduction technique so that hypotheses could be tested quantitatively. Toward this end, a data summary was constructed. It consisted of a series of questions dealing with practices, occurrences, rules, and procedures in which the concepts and variables bearing on the hypotheses were operationally defined. The data summary form transformed the hypotheses into concrete and therefore measurable terms. It included 260 questions about particular events and organizational strategies.

The data summaries for all thirty-one utopian communities in the sample were completed by five independent judges who had sociological training but did not know the hypotheses of the study. Interjudge agreement was $r = .79$. For no community did the agreement fall below .71, and it ranged up to .85. Essentially the procedure was analogous to having informants fill out questionnaires, but in this case the information was provided by judges who had studied the information supplied by many informants. Thus, a three-step process of data reduction was employed: information from informants and documents was collected; it was then sorted into conceptually meaningful categories; and the resulting data were summarized in terms of the presence or absence of particular theoretically critical practices, procedures, and events in each utopian community. This procedure made it possible for indexes to be constructed and quantitative comparisons to be made.

Several general sociological postulates informed the selection of the specific practices designated as commitment mechanisms. First, all aspects of a group, no matter how trivial to the common sense observer, were viewed as having consequences for commitment. The study of commitment mechanisms thus involved a total case analysis of every unit in the sample, to the extent that the information could be found. Second, for commitment purposes certain strategies that appear quite different phenomenologically may be functionally alternative. While more than one strategy may serve the same function, the same strategy might have more than one functional consequence. As a result, my list of mechanisms was not exhaustive or analytically pure. Finally, the primary interest was in function rather than cause.[9] Instead of asking why a community did something or what the stimuli were to which it responded, I asked whether the arrangement, once chosen, was functional for the maintenance of a group. For its theoretical purposes this study did not, for example, ask why the Shakers forbade their members to visit outside the community,

or why Brook Farm did not. Instead, it investigated whether or not
such a decision, regardless of its origin, contributed to group success. The
data protocols constructed for each community answered such questions.

## Data Summary Form

(1) Card number

(2–4) Name of community _____

(5–7) Date founded _____

Date dissolved _____

_____years in existence

Background

(8) Did the utopian community derive from a prior
organization or organized group?

(9) Was the prior organized group a

1. Religious sect, church, or cult?
2. Economic or production organization?
3. Political group or political party?
4. Social, intellectual, or literary group?
9. N.A.
0. There was no prior organized group.

(10) Was the prior organized group in existence

1. More than 50 years before the utopian community was founded?
2. Twenty to fifty years before?
3. Ten to nineteen years?
4. Four to nine years?
5. Less than four years?
9. N.A.
0. There was no prior organized group.

(11) Was the utopian community founded principally
by one person?

Location

(12–19) If the community had more than one successive location (the entire community moved to
a different place), how long did the community
stay in each location?

(20–21) If the community had more than one simultaneous location, what was the largest number of
simultaneous locations it had at any one time?

(Answer the following for the longest location of the
community, its principal or central location.)

(22) How far away were neighbors, neighboring farms,
or neighboring towns?

1. Five miles or more
5. Less than five miles
9. N.A.

(23) Was the community on a waterway?

(24) Was the community on a railroad?

Size          Give the population of the community for all dates for which it is known, in chronological order.

(25-27) How many original members were there, i.e., those who lived in the community at its founding?

(28-31) What is the largest number that ever belonged to the community and its branches at any one time?

(32-34) What is the largest number that ever resided at any one location of the community at any one time?

Recruitment    (35) Did the original members have a common religious background?

    1. Yes, they all shared a religion or religious beliefs

    2. Yes, most of them shared a religion

    5. No, they belonged to several different religions

    9. N.A.

(36) Did the original members share political views or affiliations?

(37) Did the original members have a similar socio-economic status, class, or educational background?

(38) Did the original members have a common national origin?

(39) Were the original members acquainted with one another before they joined (formed) the community? (See also Background)

(The following refer to recruits.)

(40) Was a financial contribution, a donation to community of money or property, required for admission?

    1. Yes, it was required

    2. Yes, it was preferred, though not required

    5. No, it was not required or preferred

    9. N.A.

(41) Was a recruit asked to sign over his property to the community?

(42) Was a recruit expected to make any kind of financial investment?

(43) Was conversion to the community's ideology required for admission?

(44) Was the recruit expected to take any vows, agree to any changes in his behavior, or exhibit any behavior modifications? List them.

(45) Was a particular national origin or ethnic group membership required for admission?

(46) Were special skills, artistry, intelligence, or technical expertise ever desired for admission?

(47) Did the community have a procedure for deciding if a prospective member was acceptable?

(48) Did the community ever reject prospective members as unacceptable?
1. Yes, frequently
2. Yes, occasionally
5. No, very infrequently
9. N.A.

(49) Did the community recruit by personal contact or by impersonal means (e.g., advertisements)?
1. Community recruited by personal contact throughout its history
2. Community recruited by personal contact during most of its history
5. Community did most of its recruiting impersonally, e.g., by advertising in newspapers or publishing propaganda
9. N.A.
0. The community never recruited

(50) Was there a formal probationary period, during which a prospective member could participate in the community to a limited extent without the rights of full membership? (See also Socialization: New Members)
1. Yes, throughout community's history
2. Yes, for part of its history. Give dates _____
5. No
9. N.A.

Socialization:
New Members

(51) Were new members given instruction in the community's doctrines?

(52) Were new members given lists of rules to learn, books, pamphlets, etc., to study?

(53) Were new members at all segregated from old members?

Socialization:
Children

(54) Did the community run its own schools?

(55) Was the school licensed by the state?
1. Yes
5. No
9. N.A.
0. The community did not run its own schools

(56) Did the children live in the school?
1. Yes, throughout community's history
2. Yes, for part of its history. Give dates _____
5. No, they did not live there
9. N.A.

0. The community did not run its own schools

(57) Did the school that community children attended (whether run by the community or not) include outside children as well as community children?
1. Yes, throughout community's history
2. Yes, for part of its history. Give dates _____
5. No
9. N.A.

(58) Were children automatically accorded full membership status in the community on reaching adulthood, or did they have to meet some tests (e.g., of faith) or some of the criteria for new members (e.g., knowledge of ideology)?
1. Children had to meet some criteria before gaining adult membership status
5. Children were automatically accorded full membership status on attaining a certain age
9. N.A.

Ideology

(59) Did the community's ideology include explanations of human nature or the essential character of man?
1. Yes, throughout community's history
2. Yes, for part of its history. Give dates _____
5. No
9. N.A.

(60) Was the community's ideology a complete, elaborated philosophical system touching on many aspects of man's relation to the world?
1. Yes, throughout community's history
2. Yes, for part of its history. Give dates _____
5. No
9. N.A.

(61) Did the ideology offer explanations for human misery and suffering that either justified and rationalized them or provided solutions for their alleviation?
1. Yes, throughout community's history
2. Yes, for part of its history. Give dates _____
5. No
9. N.A.

(62) Did the ideology provide for the investing of power in persons with particular qualities (e.g., wisdom, experience, spirituality, inspiration, creativity, or age)?

(63) Did the ideology legitimate demands made of members by reference to a higher principle (e.g., justice, the will of the people, the will of nature, or God)?

(64) Did the ideology impute magical or special powers to any members of the community (e.g., great insight, wisdom, gift of prophecy, ability to see or know things other people can't see or know)?

(65) Was possession of these or other magical or special powers ever taken as evidence of a person's good standing in the community?

(66) Did the ideology describe the community as conjunctive or disjunctive with the events of history, e.g., as a next step in a logical evolution or as a radical break with the past? (See also View of Community)

(67) Did the ideology view the community as progressive or regressive, e.g., as moving forward in history, to the future, or backward to a glorious past, recapturing that past? (See also View of Community)

(68) Did the ideology relate the community to any figures of historical importance, e.g., Christ, the Apostles, or George Washington? (See also View of Community)

**Authority Structure**

(The following refer to top leaders or the single top leader, those with power over many areas of community life.)

(69) Was there a hierarchy of top leaders, or did members receive instructions directly from the top leader and take complaints directly to him?
1. There was a hierarchy throughout community's history.
2. There was a hierarchy for part of its history. Give dates _____
5. Members received instructions from the top and took complaints there; there was no hierarchy
9. N.A.

(70) Were top leaders responsible for the founding of the community or else chosen by their predecessors in the top positions and groomed for leadership by them?
1. Yes, they were either responsible for the founding or chosen by their predecessors throughout community's history
2. Yes, for part of community's history. Give dates _____
5. No, they were chosen by other means throughout community's history
9. N.A.

(71) Did members or leaders ever step forward and

announce themselves as the appropriate next
leader?

(72) Did members participate in the choosing of top
leaders?

1. No, members did not participate in the choosing
of top leaders
2. Yes, members indicated their approval of some
of the leaders selected elsewhere, but not the
very top leaders
3. Yes, members elected some of the leaders, but
not the very top leaders
4. Yes, members indicated their approval of all of
the top leaders selected elsewhere
5. Yes, members elected all of the top leaders
9. N.A.

(73) If members participated in choosing leaders, was
there ever more than one candidate for any top
leadership position?

1. No, only one candidate per position
4. Yes, occasionally, at least once
5. Yes, frequently
9. N.A.
0. Members did not participate

(74) Did members have impeachment or recall privileges
over leaders?

1. No, they did not have such privileges
2. Yes, they had these privileges over some of the
leaders, but not the very top leaders, for part
of the community's history. Give dates _____
3. Yes, they had these privileges over some of the
leaders, but not the very top leader, throughout
the community's history
4. Yes, they had these privileges over all of the
leaders, for part of the community's history.
Give dates _____
5. Yes, they had these privileges over all of the
leaders, throughout the community's history
9. N.A.

(75) Was there ever a single leader with complete power,
absolute rule, in the community?

(76–78) How many chief executives did the community
have in its history? List them, their positions, and
dates, in chronological order.

(1) Card number
(2–4) Community identifying number

Leadership
Prerogatives

(5) Did the top leaders enjoy special privileges that the membership at large did not enjoy?
1. Yes, some privileges, throughout the community's history. List privileges.
2. Yes, some privileges, for part of community's history. Give dates _____
List privileges _____
5. No
9. N.A.

(6) Did the top leaders enjoy immunity from any community obligations or social controls (e.g., confession, mutual criticism, or obligation to work the fields)?

(7) Did the top leader(s) live in a residence separate from most of the community membership?

(8) If the leader had his own residence, was this residence different from or better than that of the ordinary membership?

(9) Were top leaders addressed differently than community members, called by a different name, or their name always prefaced with a special title (e.g., king, father, elder, generalissimo, or fuhrer)?

Decision-
Making

(10) Were community decisions ever based on mystery, irrationality, inspiration, or intuition (as opposed to logic, scientific reasoning, pragmatism, or democratic consent)?
1. Yes, decisions had an irrational base frequently throughout community's history
2. Yes, decisions had an irrational base frequently during one period of community's history, but not at other times. Give dates _____
3. Yes, decisions had an irrational base occasionally throughout community's history
4. Yes, decisions had an irrational base occasionally during one period of community's history, but not at other times. Give dates _____
5. No, practically all decisions were based on logic, scientific reasoning, pragmatism, or democratic consent
9. N.A.

(11) Was the ultimate justification for decisions generally ideology (values) or practical concerns?
1. Generally ideology throughout community's history
2. Generally ideology for part of its history. Give dates _____

5. Generally practical concerns throughout its history
9. N.A.

(12) Were decisions of top leaders generally accepted without question, or did they have to be justified or explained to the membership?

(13) Were general organizational decisions about the structure of the community generally made by top leaders, or did most members participate in making them?

(14) Did members participate in making everyday, routine community decisions?

Rules

(15) Was there a somewhat fixed daily routine that menbers followed; i.e., were certain things (eating, working, sleeping) always done at certain times?

(16) Was this daily routine (if present in even one period) specified in a great deal of detail, accounting for almost every minute of the members' day?

(17) Did the community have personal conduct rules for members (e.g., deportment, bearing, how a member walked, talked, or conducted himself)?

(18) Did the community have many codified behavioral rules?

(19) Did the number of rules of any kind increase over time?

(20) Did the number of rules decrease over time, or alternatively, was there increased tolerance for the violation of rules?

(21-22) In what year of existence did the community first have a constitution?

(23-24) How many times was the community reorganized, the name changed, the constitution revised, or a new constitution written? If more than one of these things happened at the same time, count it only once. List constitutions, reorganizations, revisions, or name changes, and dates, in chronological order.

Social Control

(25) Did the community require regular "confession" of personal misconduct, failings, or weaknesses?

(26) Did the community require "confession" of the past or of misconduct from new members upon joining?

(27) If the community required either of these confessions, was the confession public, before the entire community?

(28) Did the community practice "mutual cirticism," with members telling each other of their or

the others' weaknesses, failings, and points that
needed improvement?

(29) If the community had "mutual criticism," were
members told of their good points as well as
their bad?

(30) Did the community practice "mutual surveilance,"
with members checking each other's conduct
or being required to report another's misconduct,
in a kind of "honor system"?

(31) Did the community leader(s) practice surveillance,
e.g., observe members' behavior from secret,
have a means for coming upon members unexpec-
tedly, or just watch the behavior of members at
any opportunity?

(The following questions refer to sanctions. See also
Deviance.)

(32) Was public denouncement ever used as a sanction,
e.g., calling the deviant to the attention of the
whole community on a public occasion?

(33) Was removal of a privilege of membership for a
period of time ever used as a sanction?

(34) Was a deviant ever punished by not allowing him
to participate in some community activity?

(35) Did the community ever use force, physical
restraint, or physical coercion in handling a
deviant?

(36) Was expulsion from the community ever used as a
sanction?

(37) Were deviants more often expelled from the
community or just punished within it?

(38) Did the deviant lose status in the eyes of the community, was he thought less of, by virtue of his
rule-breaking?

(39–41) List briefly all known incidents of deviance and
their dates.

Finances     (42–44) List for all known years the community's assets,
profits, and debts, in chronological order.

Property     (45) Did the community as a whole own the land on
Relations          which the community was situated, as opposed to
members owning the land individually?

(46) Did the community as a whole own all buildings
on the land, as opposed to members owning
buildings individually?

(47) In whose name was title to ownership of both land
and buildings?

1. The community as a corporation or legal
authority

2. The leader's name
5. Individual members' names
7. Others. Specify _____
9. N.A.

(48) Did the community as a whole own furniture, tools, and equipment, as opposed to members owning these things individually?

(49) Did the community as a whole own clothing and personal effects, as opposed to members owning these things individually?

(50) Was a record kept of any money, property, or goods that members contributed to or invested in the community upon joining or later? (See also Recruitment)

(51) Was it official policy to reimburse members who defected or withdrew for their contribution or investment of money, property, or goods, regardless of actual practice? (See also Defections)

(52) In practice were members reimbursed? (See also Defections)

(53) Were members paid in any way for their labor in the community — in the form either of wages or of credit toward purchases and community services? (See also Work)

(54) If labor was paid or given credit, did all jobs in the community carry the same amount of pay or credit for the same amount of time? (See also Work)

(55) Were all community services provided free of charge, or did members have to pay for them with money·or labor credit?

(56) If a member received money for any reason (e.g., sold something, worked or performed a service for someone on the outside, received a gift), was he required or expected to turn it over to the community?

(57) Was it official policy to reimburse members who withdrew or defected for their years of service to the community and their labor for the community, regardless of actual practice? (See also Defections)

(58) In practice were members reimbursed for labor or service? (See also Defections)

Work and Work
Arrangements

(59–61) List community work activities used by the community to support itself (excluding household tasks such as laundry, cooking, cleaning), and give approximate dates the activities were begun, in chronological order.

(62) Were jobs rotated among people as a rule, or did the same people always do the same jobs?

(63) Were people assigned to jobs on the basis of skill?

(64) Did the community hire outside labor?

(65) Did hired labor constitute a relatively large number, considering the community's size, or a relatively small number?

(66) Was hired outside labor menial and manual (just another pair of hands) or technically and expertly skilled (a manager, scientist); i.e., was it physical or mental labor?

(67) Did the community's work aimed at self-support require selling something on the outside?

(68) If the work required selling, did community members do the selling, or did the community employ agents (outsiders) to sell for them?

(69) Did the community provide medical services in any form (including faith healing, if no other healing was used)?

Stratification

(70) Were members distinguished on spiritual or moral grounds, i.e., the extent to which they exemplified ideal traits of membership or the extent of their commitment to the community, with the more spiritual, moral, committed, or zealous members receiving more deference?

(71) Was the deference formally structured or informal?

(72) Were members distinguished on the basis of skill, intelligence, or expertise, with the more skilled, intelligent, and expert members receiving more deference?

(73) Was the deference formally structured or informal?

(1) Card number

(2–4) Community identifying number

Family, Living Arrangements, Sexual Relations

(5) Did members live in a central community building or buildings, as opposed to each having separate, private residences?

(6) Did members eat in a community dining hall; i.e., were meals centrally prepared and served?

(7) Did all members eat the same meals, or was there a choice, with members being able to eat different things (including any special, idiosyncratic diets)?

(8) Did families share a dwelling unit, e.g., live together in the same house or in the same apartment within a community building?

(9) If families did not live together, did individual members have private rooms or did they share rooms with other members?

(10) Did the community practice free love or complex marriage?

(11) If the community practiced free love, did the community place any restrictions or controls on it, affecting aspects such as the quality of sexual relations, who could or could not have relations, contraception and self-control?

(12) Did the community require celibacy?

(13) If the community required celibacy, how much separation of sexes did it enforce?
1. A great deal
2. Some
4. Just a little
5. None at all
9. N.A.
0. Community practiced free love or complex marriage or regular marriage

(14) Did the community encourage or prefer celibacy, while still allowing marriage?

(15) If celibacy was preferred or encouraged while marriage was allowed, did celibate members gain a more spiritual status or receive approbation, or did married members lose status at least for a while?

(16) Were children separated from their parents?

(17) If yes, at what age?
1. Birth
2. One to three years old
3. Four to six years old
4. Six to twelve years old
5. Fourteen to seventeen years old
9. N.A.
0. Children never separated from parents

Members' Feelings about Each Other

(18) According to members and observers, did most members of the community appear to like each other, exhibit affection for each other, and consider other members friends or potential friends?

Funerals

(19) Were funerals simple or elaborate?

(20) Was there a period of mourning for departed members?

(21) Were graves simple or elaborate?

(22) Did all members have the same grave and markings (excluding the leader)?

(23) Did leaders have a different grave and markings?

(24) Did the community's funeral practices and grave markings change over time?

Group Contact   (25)  Did the entire community or most of the members ever get together in a communal effort to perform community tasks (e.g., harvesting, cleaning, building, "bees")?

(26) How frequent were these communal work sessions?

(27) Were there frequent group meetings or occasions on which the entire community (or most of the members) got together?

(28) How frequent were these meetings?
1. Daily
2. Almost daily
3. Weekly
4. Almost weekly
5. Monthly
6. Bimonthly
9. N.A.
0. No frequent group meetings

(29) What kind of meetings were they in general?
1. Religious ceremonies
2. Educational meetings, lectures, or instruction
3. Social occasions, parties, or casual group get-togethers
4. Political or business meetings
8. Others. Specify _____
9. N.A.

(30) When the members got together for a meeting, did they perform any rituals (recurring events of symbolic importance)?

(31) Was the entire group meeting ritualized?

(32) Did the community have songs about itself or about the membership?

(33) Did the community celebrate special community occasions or important dates in community history?

(34) Did the community do any group singing?

(35) Did the community celebrate national holidays?

(36) Was there much opportunity for privacy in the community; were there many places a member could go to be alone?
1. Very little opportunity or place for privacy
3. Some opportunity and place for privacy
5. A great deal of opportunity and place for privacy
9. N.A.

(37) Approximately how much of a member's waking day was spent with other people?
1. More than two-thirds

3. One-third to two-thirds
5. Less than one-third
9. N.A.

**Members'**
**Concept**
**of Community**

(38) How satisfied did members appear to be with the community?
1. Satisfied throughout community's history
2. Satisfied for most of its history. Give dates ____
_____
3. Neither satisfied nor dissatisfied
4. Fairly dissatisfied for most of community's history. Give dates _____
5. Fairly dissatisfied throughout its history
9. N.A.

(39) How important did members (as distinguished from top leaders) think the community was; how much importance did they attribute to its success or failure?
1. Great importance throughout community's history
2. Great importance for most of its history
3. Neither particularly important or unimportant
4. Little importance for most of community's history
5. Little importance throughout its history
9. N.A.

(40) Did the community conceive of itself as the wave of the future, as anticipating important future developments?

(41) Did the community conceive of itself as setting an example for the rest of society?

**Members'**
**Concept**
**of Outside**

(42) Did the community have a special name for the outside, referring to it by that term most of the time?

(43) What was the nature of the outside, from the community's viewpoint?
1. Evil and wicked
2. Dangerous and tempting, but temptations could be avoided
3. Misguided and misdirected
4. Just different
5. Not essentially different ("people are the same all over")
9. N.A.

(44) Did community leaders go on public relations tours or speaking tours?

(45) What was the purpose of such tours?
1. To proselytize, gain converts

2. To get contributions of money
3. To justify the community and apologize for it
4. Just to inform the outside world about the community
9. N.A.
0. Leaders did not go on public relations, speaking tours

(46) Did the community publish propaganda about the community, such as books, pamphlets, or newspapers?

(47) What was the purpose of such propaganda?

Distinguishing Characteristics

(48) Did the community require a uniform style of dress, different from that of the outside world?

(49) Even if a uniform was not required, did there tend to be a uniform style of dress, different from that of the outside world?

(50) Did the community speak a language other than English?

(51) Was this language taught to the children?

(52) Did the community use any slang, jargon, or esoteric terminology not in common use on the outside?

Attitudes of Outside Toward Community

(53) Was the community ever the victim of physical persecution, mob violence, or other use of force?

(54) Was the community ever publicly denounced in newspapers, books, etc?

(55) Was the community ever the victim of economic discrimination?

(56) Was the outside tolerant of the community?

(57) Did people on the outside ever give financial support to the community?

Members Going Outside

(58) How often did the average member (other than leaders) leave the community?
1. Less often than yearly
2. Yearly
4. Monthly
5. Daily
9. N.A.

(59) If he left only yearly or less than yearly, did the rules forbid members to leave?

(60) Did a member have to ask permission of leaders or superiors in order to leave the community?

(61) Did the community give members funds for travel, or were funds for travel easily accessible?

(62) Could members leave to visit their families on the outside?

(63) Did members leave primarily to secure services

(medical, etc.) not available in the community?

(64) Did members leave in the service of the community? (e.g., to sell goods or products, propagandize, secure a new location)

(65) Were members who left accompanied by another member?

(66) Did the community impose social controls on the traveler (e.g., the whole community gathering to send the member off, the member confessing before leaving and after returning, the member met by the whole community or some representative of it on his return?

(67) Could a person be a nonresident member? (See also Recruitment)

Visitors

(68) How often did outsiders visit the community?
   1. Less often than yearly
   2. Yearly
   3. Bimonthly, semiannually
   4. Monthly
   5. Weekly
   6. Daily or almost daily
   9. N.A.

(69) What kinds of visitors came to the community?
   1. Propagandists, revivalists, ideologists
   2. Tourists (for a vacation, rest, or curiosity)
   3. Salesmen
   4. Other utopians
   8. All of the above
   9. N.A.

(70) Did visitors at any one time constitute a relatively large number, considering the community's size, or a relatively small number?
   1. Relatively small number
   5. Relatively large number
   9. N.A.

(71) Were visitors asked to conform to community rules?

(72) Did the community have rules covering members' interaction with visitors, restricting it in any way, or informing members on how to behave with visitors?

(73) Were there any rituals centered around visitors, such as preparing the community for the arrival of visitors or responding to the presence of outsiders after they had left?

(74) Were visitors prohibited from viewing any aspects of the community?

Neighbors (75) How often did the community come into contact
with its neighbors?
1. Very often, throughout community's history
2. Fairly often, or for only part of its history
4. Once in a while
5. Hardly ever, rarely
9. N.A.

(1) Card number
(2–4) Community identifying number

Relations with (5) Did the community vote in national, state, and
Government local elections?
(6) Did eligible members of the community fight in
any wars?
(7) Was the community pacifist?

The Community (8) What was the legal status of the community?
and the Law 1. Incorporated as a town
2. Incorporated as a business, company, or
organization
3. Incorporated as a church, religious group, or
charitable organization
4. Unincorporated
9. N.A.
(9–12) What litigation was the community involved in?
1. Suits by individuals (former members) to
recover property
2. Suits by heirs to recover property
3. Suits challenging the legal status of the community
4. Legal investigations of the community and its
activities
5. Suits by relatives of members charging the
community with mistreating them
6. Prosecutions of the community for violating
the law

Influence of (13) Did the community read outside newspapers?
the Outside

Natural (14–16) List all known fires, floods, famines, epidemics
Disasters (outbreaks of disease), and other disasters,
with their dates, in chronological order.

Challenges to (17–22) List incidents of challenge to authority, such as
Authority other men claiming leadership, sects and parties
with different views, schisms (breaks from the
community, secessions), with dates, in chronological order
(23) Were there many ideological controversies in the
community's history, disagreements over inter-

pretation of ideology, or conflicts over values?

(24) Were there any schisms in the community's history, in which a group of members seceded together, broke off, and perhaps founded a new community?

**Defections**

(25) Did members defect for economic reasons, to find a better opportunity elsewhere?

(26) Did members defect for social reasons, because of felt incompatibility with other members or dislike of them?

(27) Did members defect for reasons of personal indulgence, because the community lacked luxuries or the member had given up too much to belong?

(28) Did members defect to do something the community forbade, such as getting married?

**Austerity/ Luxury**

(29) Did the community have to build its own buildings?

(30) Did the community forbid certain indulgences, e.g., tobacco, alcohol, or meat?

(31-32) What other things, not necessarily forbidden, did members have to do without?

**Demise**

(33) Did the community die slowly (e.g., less than five members left at the end), or was it formally dissolved while a fair percentage of its membership still belonged?
   1. Died slowly
   5. Formally dissolved
   9. N.A.

(34) If formally dissolved, what incident precipitated the dissolution?

(35) The community then became
   1. An economic organization or business
   2. A religious organization or church
   3. A territorial unit, such as a township or village, with no central economic or religious organization
   4. A combination of the above. Specify _____
   _____
   5. Nothing; everyone left or the community just ceased
   9. N.A.
   0. Community not yet over (Shakers)

**Miscellaneous**

(36) Did people reside in the community or in the immediate community area who were not members?

(37) Did all members pitch in on work, doing their share, or did some have no work, or refuse to work, remaining idle or lazy?
1. All worked and shared, throughout community's history
4. Some idled and shirked, for part of its history
5. Some idled and shirked, throughout its history
9. N.A.

# Bibliography

Abramson, E., H. A. Cutler, A. W. Kautz, and M. Mendelson. "Social Power and Commitment: A Theoretical Statement," *American Sociological Review,* 23 (February 1958), 15-22.

Albertson, Ralph. "A Survey of Mutualistic Communities in America," *The Iowa Journal of History and Politics,* 34 (October 1936), 375-444.

Alcott, Louisa May. "Transcendental Wild Oats: A Chapter from an Unwritten Romance," in *Bronson Alcott's Fruitlands,* comp. Clara Endicott Sears. Boston and New York: Houghton Mifflin, 1915, pp. 145-174.

Allen, Edward J. *The Second United Order among the Mormons.* New York: Columbia University Press, 1936.

*The Amana Society: a Bit of the Old World Set Down in the New.* Amana, Iowa: Amana Products, c. 1936.

*American Avatar.* Publication of the Fort Hill Community, Roxbury, Mass. 1968-1970.

Andorn, Miriam Cramer. "Shakerism for Today," in *Selected Papers.* Cleveland: The Shaker Historical Society, 1957, pp. 1-9.

Andressohn, John C., ed. "Three Additional Rappite Letters," *Indiana Magazine of History,* 45 (June 1949), 184-188.

——. "Twenty Additional Rappite Manuscripts," *Indiana Magazine of History,* 44 (March 1948), 83-108.

Andrews, Edward Deming. *The Gift To Be Simple: Songs, Dances and Rituals of the American Shakers.* New York: Dover Publications, 1962.

——. *The People Called Shakers: A Search for the Perfect Society.* New York: Dover Publications, 1963.

Arndt, Karl J. R. "The Genesis of Germantown, Louisiana; or the Mysterious Past of Louisiana's Mystic, Count de Leon," *The Louisiana Historical Quarterly,* 24 (April 1941), 378-433.

——. *George Rapp's Harmony Society, 1785-1847.* Philadelphia: University of Pennsylvania Press, 1965.

——. "George Rapp's Petition to Thomas Jefferson," *American-German Review,* 7 (October 1940), 5-9, 35.

——. "The Life and Mission of Count Leon," *American-German Review,* 6 (June 1940), 5-8, 36-37; (August 1940), 15-19.

Aumann, F. R. "A Minor Prophet in Iowa," *The Palimpsest,* 8 (July 1927), 253–260.

Bailie, William. *Josiah Warren.* Boston; Small, Maynard, 1906.

Baker, Russell. "Observer: Lord Sean's Wives and Fellow Husbands," *The New York Times,* April 5, 1970.

Ballou, Adin. *History of the Hopedale Community, from Its Inception to Its Virtual Submergence in the Hopedale Parish,* ed. William S. Heywood. Lowell, Mass., 1897.

Banta, Richard E. "New Harmony's Golden Years," *Indiana Magazine of History,* 44 (March 1948), 25–36.

Barnes, Sherman B. "An Icarian in Nauvoo," *Journal of the Illinois State Historical Society,* 34 (June 1941), 233–244.

Becker, Howard S. "Notes on the Concept of Commitment," *American Journal of Sociology,* 66 (July 1960), 32–40.

Bek, William G. "The Community at Bethel, Missouri, and Its Offspring at Aurora, Oregon," *German American Annals,* 7 (September 1909), 257–276, 306–328; 8 (April 1910), 15–44, 76–81.

———. "A German Communistic Society in Missouri," *Missouri Historical Review,* 3 (October 1908), 52–74; (January 1909), 99–125.

Bendix, Reinhardt. *Max Weber: An Intellectual Portrait.* Garden City, N.Y.: Doubleday, 1960.

Bennett, Michael. "The Alternative," *The Mother Earth News,* 1 (September 1970), 32–34.

Bennis, Warren and Philip E. Slater. *The Temporary Society.* New York: Harper and Row, 1968.

Ben-Yosef, Avraham C. *The Purest Democracy in the World.* New York and London: Herzel Press and Thomas Yoseloff, 1963.

Berger, Bennett, and Bruce Hackett. "Child Rearing Practices of the Communal Family." Progress report to NIMH, Washington, D.C., 1970. Mimeographed.

Bernard, L. L., and Jessie L. Bernard. *Origins of American Sociology: The Social Science Movement in the United States.* New York: Russell & Russell, 1965.

Berne, Eric. *The Structure and Dynamics of Organizations and Groups.* New York: Grove Press, 1966.

Bestor, Arthur Eugene, Jr. "American Phalanxes: Fourierist Socialism in the United States." Ph.D. dissertation, Yale University, 1938.

———. *Backwoods Utopias: The Sectarian and Owenite Phases of Communitarian Socialism in America, 1663–1829.* Philadelphia: University of Pennsylvania Press, 1950.

———, ed. *Education and Reform at New Harmony: Correspondence of William Maclure and Marie Duclos Fretageot, 1820–1833.* Indianapolis: Indiana Historical Society, 1948.

———. "The Evolution of the Socialist Vocabulary," *Journal of the History of Ideas,* 9 (June 1948), 259–302.

———. "Fourierism in Northampton: A Critical Note," *The New England Quarterly,* 13 (March 1940), 110–122.

Bittner, Egon. "Radicalism and the Organization of Radical Movements,"

*American Sociological Review,* 28 (December 1963), 928–940.

Blau, Peter M., and W. Richard Scott. *Formal Organizations: A Comparative Approach.* San Francisco: Chandler, 1962.

Blumer, Herbert. "Collective Behavior," in *Principles of Sociology,* ed. A. M. Lee. New York: Barnes & Noble, 1953, pp. 167–222.

Boguslaw, Robert. *The New Utopians: A Study of System Design and Social Change.* Englewood Cliffs, N.J.: Prentice-Hall, 1965.

Boisen, Anton T. "Economic Distress and Religious Experience: A Study of the Holy Rollers," *Psychiatry,* 2 (May 1939), 185–194.

Bole, John Archibald. *The Harmony Society: A Chapter in German American Culture History.* Philadelphia: Americana Germanica Press, 1904.

Bremer, Fredrika. *The Homes of the New World: Impressions of America,* trans. Mary Howitt. Vols. I and II. New York, 1853.

Brisbane, Albert. *A Concise Exposition of the Doctrine of Association.* New York, 1843.

———. *A Mental Biography, with a Character Study by His Wife Redelia Brisbane.* Boston, 1893.

Brown, Katharine Holland. "The Icarian Community," *Harper's Monthly Magazine,* 110 (December 1904), 141–146.

Brown, Roger. *Social Psychology.* New York: Free Press, 1965.

Buber, Martin. *Paths in Utopia,* trans. R. F. C. Hull. Boston: Beacon Press, 1958.

Cabet, Etienne. "History and Constitution of the Icarian Community," trans. Thomas Teakle. *Iowa Journal of History and Politics,* 15 (April 1917), 214–286.

Calverton, V. F. *Where Angels Dared To Tread.* Indianapolis: Bobbs-Merrill, 1941.

Cantril, Hadley. *The Psychology of Social Movements.* New York: John Wiley, 1941.

Carden, Maren Lockwood. *Oneida: Utopian Community to Modern Corporation.* Baltimore: The Johns Hopkins Press, 1969. Also in paper. New York: Harper & Row, 1971.

Chase, Daryl. "The Early Shakers: An Experiment in Religious Communism." Ph.D. dissertation, University of Chicago, 1936.

Cheney, Ednah, D., ed. *Louisa May Alcott: Her Life, Letters and Journals.* Boston, 1890.

Clark, Burton R. "Organizational Adaptation and Precarious Values," *American Sociological Review,* 21 (June 1956), 327–336.

Codman, John Thomas. *Brook Farm: Historic and Personal Memoirs.* Boston, 1894.

Cohen, Elie. *Human Behavior in the Concentration Camps.* London: Jonathan Cape, 1954.

Conkin, Paul K. *Two Paths to Utopia: The Hutterites and the Llano Colony.* Lincoln: University of Nebraska Press, 1965.

Cooley, Charles Horton. *Social Organization: A Study of the Larger Mind.* New York: Schocken Books, 1962.

Coser, Lewis A. *The Functions of Social Conflict.* New York: Free Press, 1964.

——. "Greedy Organizations," *European Journal of Sociology*, 8 (October 1967), 196–215.

——. "Sects and Sectarians," *Dissent*, 1 (Autumn 1954), 360–369.

Cross, Whitney R. *The Burned-over District: The Social and Intellectual History of Enthusiastic Religion in Western New York, 1800–1850*. New York: Harper and Row (Harper Torchbooks), 1965.

Cox, Harvey. *The Feast of Fools*. Cambridge, Mass.: Harvard University Press, 1969.

Curtis, Edith Roelker. *A Season in Utopia: The Story of Brook Farm*. New York: Thomas Nelson, 1961.

Davidson, Sara. "Open Land: Getting Back to the Communal Garden," *Harper's Magazine*, 270 (June 1970), 91–102.

Davies, James C. "Toward a Theory of Revolution," *American Sociological Review*, 27 (February 1962), 5–19.

Demerath, N. J., and Victor Thiessen. "On Spitting Against the Wind: Organizational Precariousness and American Irreligion," *The American Journal of Sociology*, 71 (May 1966), 674–687.

Diamond, Sigmund. "From Organization to Society: Virginia in the 17th Century," *American Journal of Sociology*, 63 (March 1958), 457–475.

Dills, R. S. *History of Green County*. Dayton, Ohio, 1881.

Dixon, William Hepworth. *Spiritual Wives*. Vol. II. London, 1868.

Dobbs, Catherine R. *Freedom's Will, the Society of Separatists of Zoar: An Historical Adventure of Religious Communism in Early Ohio*. New York: William-Frederick Press, 1947.

Donham, Parker. "Town Wants Commune Closed," *The Boston Globe*, Oct. 12, 1970.

Dornbusch, Sanford. "The Military Academy as an Assimilating Institution," *Social Forces*, 33 (May 1954), 316–321.

Dow, Edward F. "A Portrait of the Millenial Church of Shakers," *The Maine Bulletin*, 34 (August 1931), University of Maine Studies, Second Series, no. 19.

Durkheim, Emile. *The Division of Labor in Society*, trans. George Simpson. Glencoe, Ill. Free Press, 1949.

——. *The Rules of Sociological Method*. Glencoe, Ill.: Free Press, 1938.

——. *Socialism and Saint-Simon*, ed. Alvin W. Gouldner, trans. Charlotte Sattler. Yellow Springs, Ohio: Antioch Press, 1958.

Eastman, Hubbard. *Noyeism Unveiled: A History of the Sect Self-Styled Perfectionists, with a Summary View of Their Leading Doctrines*. Brattleboro, Vt. 1849.

Eaton, Joseph W. "Controlled Acculturation: A Survival Technique of the Hutterites," *American Sociological Review*, 17 (June 1952), 331–340.

——, and Robert J. Weil. *Culture and Mental Disorders*. Glencoe, Ill.: Free Press, 1955.

Edmonds, Walter D. *The First Hundred Years, 1848–1948*. Oneida, N.Y.: Oneida, 1948.

Egbert, Donald Drew, and Stow Persons, eds. *Socialism and American Life*. Vols. 1 and 2. Princeton, N.J.: Princeton University Press, 1952.

Ellis, John B. *Free Love and Its Votaries; or American Socialism Unmasked,*

*Being an Historical and Descriptive Account of the Rise and Progress of Various Free Love Associations in the United States and of the Effects of Their Vicious Teachings upon American Society.* New York, 1870.

Ellsworth, Richard C. "Northern New York's Early Co-operative Union," *Proceedings of the New York State Historical Association,* 27 (1929), 328–332.

Ely, Richard T. "Amana: A Study of Religious Communism," *Harper's Monthly Magazine,* 105 (October 1902), 659–668.

———. *Recent American Socialism.* Johns Hopkins University Studies in Historical and Political Science. Baltimore, 1885.

Endore, Guy. *Synanon.* Garden City, N.Y.: Doubleday, 1968.

Engels, Friedrich. "Socialism: Utopian and Scientific," in Lewis S. Feuer, ed., *Marx and Engels: Basic Writings on Politics and Philosophy.* Garden City, N.Y.: Doubleday (Anchor), 1959, pp. 68–111.

Erdahl, Sivert. "Eric Janson and the Bishop Hill Colony," *Journal of the Illinois State Historical Society,* 18 (October 1925), 503–574.

Estlake, Allan (Abel Easton). *The Oneida Community: A Record of an Attempt To Carry Out the Principles of Christian Unselfishness and Scientific Race-Improvement.* London: George Redway, 1900.

Etzioni, Amatai. *A Comparative Analysis of Complex Organizations.* New York: Free Press, 1961.

———. "Two Approaches to Organization Analysis: A Critique and a Suggestion," *Administrative Science Quarterly,* 5 (September 1960), 257–278.

Evans, Frederick W. *Shakers: Compendium of the Origin, History, Principles, Rules and Regulations, Government, and Doctrines of the United Society of Believers in Christ's Second Appearing, with Biographies of Ann Lee, William Lee, James Whittaker, J. Hocknell, J. Meacham, and Lucy Wright.* New York, 1859.

Fairchild, James H. *Oberlin: The Colony and the College, 1833–1883.* Oberlin, Ohio, 1883.

Fairfield, Dick. *Communes, U.S.A.* San Francisco: Alternatives! Foundation, 1971.

Federal Writers' Project. *The Harmony Society in Pennsylvania.* Philadelphia: William Penn Association, 1937.

Feldman, Kenneth A. "Family Antecedents of Commitment to Social Norms." Ph.D. dissertation, University of Michigan, 1965.

Festinger, Leon, and J. Merrill Carlsmith. "Cognitive Consequences of Forced Compliance," *Journal of Abnormal and Social Psychology,* 58 (March 1959), 203–210.

Fishman, Aryei, ed. *The Religious Kibbutz Movement: The Revival of the Jewish Religious Community.* Jerusalem, Israel: Religious Section of the Youth and Hehalutz Department of the Zionist Organization, 1957.

Fletcher, Robert S. "The Government of the Oberlin Colony," *The Mississippi Valley Historical Review,* 20 (September 1933), 171–190.

Fourier, Francois Marie Charles. *Selections from the Works of Fourier,* intro. Charles Gide, trans. Julia Franklin. London-Swan Sommenschein, 1901.

"Fourierist Colony in Iowa," *Annals of Iowa*, 17 (January 1930), 233-236.

Fox, Wendell P. "The Kendal Community," *Ohio Archaeological and Historical Quarterly*, 20 (1911), 176-219.

Freeman, Linton C., and Robert E. Winch. "Societal Complexity: An Empirical Test of the Typology of Societies," *American Sociological Review*, 62 (March 1956), 461-466.

Freud, Sigmund. *Civilization and Its Discontents*, trans. and ed. James Strachey. New York: W. W. Norton, 1962.

——. "The Group and the Primal Horde," in *Readings on the Sociology of Small Groups*, ed. Theodore M. Mills and Stan Rosenberg. Englewood Cliffs, N.J.: Prentice-Hall, 1970.

Friedenberg, Edgar Z. "The Synanon Solution," *Nation*, 200 (March 8, 1965), 256-261.

Fromm, Erich. *The Sane Society*. New York: Holt, Rinehart and Winston, 1955.

Gallaher, Ruth A. "Icaria and the Icarians," *The Palimpsest*, 2 (April 1921), 97-112.

Gardner, Hamilton. "Communism among the Mormons," *The Quarterly Journal of Economics*, 37 (November 1922), 134-174.

——. "Cooperation among the Mormons," *The Quarterly Journal of Economics*, 3 (May 1917), 461-499.

Gardner, Hugh. "Your Global Alternative: Communes, Experiments, Jails, and Hidey-Holes," *Esquire*, 74 (September 1970), 106-109.

Geddes, Joseph A. *The United Order among the Mormons (Missouri Phase)*. Salt Lake City, Utah: Deseret News Press, 1924.

Gide, Charles. *Communist and Cooperative Colonies*, trans. Ernest F. Row. London: George G. Harrap, 1930.

Gillin, John L. "A Contribution to the Sociology of Sects," *The American Journal of Sociology*, 16 (September 1910), 236-252.

Goffman, Erving. *Asylums*. Garden City, N.Y.: Doubleday (Anchor), 1961.

Gollomb, Naftali. "Kibbutz Administration." Mimeographed. Jerusalem, Israel: 1964.

——. "Kibbutz Organization from a Managerial Aspect." Mimeographed. Department of Kibbutz Management Service, Israel Department of Agriculture, 1966.

Goode, William J. "The Theoretical Importance of Love," *American Sociological Review*, 24 (February 1959), 38-47.

Goodman, Paul. *Utopian Essays and Practical Proposals*. New York: Vintage Books, 1964.

Gouldner, Alvin W. "The Norm of Reciprocity: A Preliminary Statement," *American Sociological Review*, 25 (April 1960), 161-179.

Gouldner, Helen P. "Dimensions of Organizational Commitment," *Administrative Science Quarterly*, 4 (December 1960), 468-487,

Gray, Charles. "The Icarian Community," *Annals of Iowa*, 6 (July 1903), 107-114.

Green, Calvin, and Seth Y. Wells. *A Summary View of the Millenial Church, or United Society of Believers (Commonly Called Shakers): Comprising the Rise, Progress and Practical Order of the Society; Together with the*

*General Principles of Their Faith and Testimony.* Albany, 1823.

Gross, Henry. *The Flower People.* New York: Ballantine Books, 1968.

Gross, Neal, and William E. Martin. "On Group Cohesiveness," *American Journal of Sociology,* 57 (May 1952), 546–564.

Gunn, Alexander. *The Hermitage: Zoar Notebook and Journal of Travel.* New York, 1902.

Gustatis, Rosa. *Turning On.* New York: Macmillan, 1969.

Guthe, Carl E. "The Shakers," *House and Garden,* 87 (March 1945), 103–106.

Halter, Marilyn B. "What Must We Do To Be Saved?" Senior honors thesis, Brandeis University, 1971.

Haraszyi, Zoltan. *The Idyll of Brook Farm, as Revealed by Unpublished Letters in the Boston Public Library.* Boston: Trustees of the Public Library, 1937.

Harmer, Richard. "Bedrock." Mimeographed. Cambridge, Mass.: Harvard Business School, 1970.

Haskett, William J. *Shakerism Unmasked.* Pittsfield, Mass., 1828.

Hawley, Charles A. "A Communistic Swedenborgian Colony in Iowa," *The Iowa Journal of History and Politics,* 33 (January 1935), 3–26.

————. "The Historical Background of the Attitude of the Jasper Colony Toward Slavery and the Civil War," *The Iowa Journal of History and Politics,* 34 (April 1936), 172–197.

Hawthorne, Manning. "Hawthorne and Utopian Socialism," *The New England Quarterly,* 12 (December 1939), 726–730.

Hawthorne, Nathaniel. *The Blithedale Romance.* 1851.

Heald, Edward Thorton. *The Stark County Story.* Canton, Ohio: The Stark County Historical Society, 1949.

Heberle, Rudolf. "The Sociology of Ferdinand Tonnies," *American Sociological Review,* 2 (February 1937), 9–25.

Hedgepeth, William, and Dennis Stock. *The Alternative: Communal Life in New America.* New York: Macmillan, 1970.

Hendricks, Robert J. *Bethel and Aurora, an Experiment in Communism as Practical Christianity with Some Account of Past and Present Ventures in Collective Living.* New York: The Press of the Pioneers, 1933.

Hendrickson, Walter B. "An Owenite Society in Illinois," *Indiana Magazine of History,* 45 (June 1949), 175–182.

Hillquit, Morris. *History of Socialism in the United States.* 5th rev. and enl. ed. New York: Funk and Wagnalls, 1910.

Hinds, William Alfred. *American Communities and Cooperative Colonies.* New York: Corinth Books, 1961. First published 1878. 2nd rev. ed., Chicago: Charles H. Kerr, 1908.

Hine, Robert V. *California's Utopian Colonies.* New Haven: Yale University Press, 1966.

*History of Monoma County, Iowa.* Chicago, 1890.

Hobsbawm, E. J. *Primitive Rebels: Studies in Archaic Forms of Social Movement in the 19th and 20th Centuries.* Manchester, Eng.: Manchester University Press, 1959.

Hoffer, Eric. *The True Believer: Thoughts on the Nature of Mass Movements.* New York: Time, 1963.

Holloway, Mark. *Heavens on Earth: Utopian Communities in America, 1680-1880.* London: Turnstile Press, 1951.

Hopper, Rex D. "The Revolutionary Process: A Frame of Reference for the Study of Revolutionary Movements," *Social Forces,* 28 (March 1950), 270-279.

Houriet, Robert. *Getting Back Together.* New York: Coward, McCann and Geoghegan, 1971.

——. "Life and Death of a Commune Called Oz," *The New York Times Magazine,* Feb. 16, 1969, pp. 30-31, 89-103.

Hulme, Kathryn. *The Nun's Story.* Boston: Little Brown, 1956.

Huxley, Aldous. *Brave New World and Brave New World Revisited.* New York: Harper (Colophon Books), 1965.

"Icarians at Nauvoo," *Annals of Iowa,* 6 (July 1904), 424.

Infield, Henrik F. *Cooperative Communities at Work.* New York: Dryden Press, 1947.

——. *Cooperative Living in Palestine.* New York: Dryden Press, 1944.

——. *Utopia and Experiment: Essays in the Sociology of Cooperation.* New York: Praeger, 1955.

"An Iowan Utopia," *The Literary Digest,* 52 (April 1, 1916), 932-933.

Jacobs, Ruth Harriet. "Emotive and Control Groups as Mutated New American Utopian Communities," *Journal of Applied Behavioral Science* 7 (March-April 1971), 234-251.

Jacobson, Margaret E. "The Painted Record of a Community Experiment: Olaf Kraus and His Pictures of the Bishop Hill Colony," *Journal of the Illinois State Historical Society,* 34 (June 1941), 164-176.

Jacoby, John E. *Two Mystic Communities in America.* Paris: Les Presses Universitaires de France, 1931.

James, Henry Ammon. *Communism in America.* New York, 1879.

Johnson, Theodore E., ed. "A Sketch of the Life and Religious Experiences of Richard W. Pelham," *The Shaker Quarterly,* 9 (Summer 1969), 53-64.

Jones, Susan Spragg. "Communes and Social Change: Thoughts on Communal Living Based on Interviews with Communes in the Boulder-Denver Area." Mimeographed. May 1970.

Jordan, Philip D. "The Iowa Pioneer Phalanx," *The Palimpsest,* 16 (July 1935), 211-225.

Kanter, Rosabeth Moss. "Commitment and Social Organization: A Study of Commitment Mechanisms in Utopian Communities," *American Sociological Review,* 33 (August 1968), 499-517.

——. "Commitment Mechanisms in Utopian Communities." Paper read at meeting of the American Sociological Association, San Francisco, August 1967. Mimeographed.

——. "Communes," *Psychology Today,* 4 (July 1970), 56-70.

Kateb, George. *Utopia and Its Enemies.* New York: Free Press, 1963.

Katz, Daniel. "The Motivational Basis of Organizational Behavior," *Behavioral Science,* 9 (April 1964), 131-146.

———, and Robert L. Kahn. *The Social Psychology of Organizations*. New York: Wiley, 1966.

Kelman, Herbert C. "Compliance, Identification, and Internalization: Three Processes of Attitude Change," *Journal of Conflict Resolution*, 2 (March 1958), 51–60.

Kennedy, J. H. *Early Days of Mormonism: Palmyra, Kirtland, and Nauvoo*. New York, 1888.

Kent, Alexander. "Cooperative Communities in the United States," *Bulletin of the Department of Labor*, 35 (July 1901), 563–646.

Killian, Lewis. "Social Movements," in *Handbook of Modern Sociology*, ed. Robert E. L. Faris. Chicago: Rand McNally, 1964, pp. 426–455.

King, C. Wendell. *Social Movements in the United States*. New York: Random House, 1956.

Knoedler, Christiana F. *The Harmony Society, a 19th Century Utopia*. New York: Vantage Press, 1954.

Laidler, Harry W. *A History of Socialist Thought*. New York: Thomas Y. Crowell, 1927.

———. *Social-Economic Movements: An Historical and Comparative Survey of Socialism, Communism, Co-operation, Utopianism, and Other Systems of Reform and Reconstruction*. New York: Thomas Y. Crowell, 1947.

Lamott, Kenneth. "Doing Their Own Thing at Morningstar," *Horizon*, 10 (Spring 1968), 14–19. Reprinted in *Utopias: Social Ideals and Communal Experiments*, ed. Peyton E. Richter. Boston: Holbrook Press, 1971, pp. 155–164.

Lamson, David Rich. *Two Years' Experience among the Shakers: Being a Description of the Manners and Customs of That People, the Nature and Policy of Their Government, Their Marvelous Intercourse with the Spiritual World, the Object and Uses of Confession, Their Inquisition, in Short, a Condensed View of Shakerism as It Is*. West Boylston, Mass. 1848.

Lassiter, William L. "The Shaker Legacy," *House and Garden*, 87 (March 1945), 45, 120, 122, 134.

Leopold, Richard William. *Robert Dale Owen: A Biography*. Cambridge, Mass.: Harvard University Press, 1940.

Lindley, Harlow, ed. *Indiana as Seen by Early Travelers: A Collection of Reprints from Books of Travel, Letters and Diaries Prior to 1830*. Indianapolis: Indiana Historical Commission, 1916.

Linn, William Alexander. *The Story of the Mormons, from the Date of Their Origin to the Year 1901*. New York: Macmillan, 1923.

Linton, Ralph. *The Study of Man*. New York: D. Appleton-Century, 1936.

Lipset, Seymour Martin. *Agrarian Socialism: The Cooperative Commonwealth Federation in Saskatchewan, a Study in Political Sociology*. Berkeley and Los Angeles: University of California Press, 1950.

Lockwood, George B. *The New Harmony Communities*. Marion, Ind.: Chronicle, 1902.

———. *The New Harmony Movement*. New York: D. Appleton, 1905.

Lockwood, Maren. "The Experimental Utopia in America," *Daedalus*, 94 (Spring 1965), 401–418.

——. "The Oneida Community: A Study of Organizational Change." Ph.D. dissertation, Harvard University, 1962.

Lofland, John, and Rodney Stark. "Becoming a World-Saver: A Theory of Conversion to a Deviant Perspective," *American Sociological Review*, 30 (December 1965), 862–875.

Loomis, Charles P. *Social Systems: Essays on Their Persistence and Change.* Princeton, N. J.: D. Van Nostrand, 1960.

Ludlum, David M. *Social Ferment in Vermont, 1791–1850.* New York: Columbia University Press, 1939.

Lyman, H. S. "The Aurora Community," *Oregon Historical Society Quarterly*, 2 (March 1901), 78–93.

McBee, Alice Eaton. "From Utopia to Florence: The Story of a Transcendentalist Community in Northampton, Mass., 1830–1952," *Smith College Studies in History*, 32 (1947).

Macdonald, A. J. "Materials for a History of Communities in the United States." New Haven, Yale University Library, Manuscripts and Collections.

Macdonald, Donald. "The Diaries of Donald Macdonald, 1824–1826," *Indiana Historical Society Publications*, 14 (1942), 142–379.

McIntosh, Montgomery E. "Cooperative Colonies in Wisconsin," *Proceedings of the State Historical Society of Wisconsin*, 1903, pp. 99-117.

McKinley, Kenneth William. "A Guide to the Communistic Communities of Ohio," *The Ohio State Archaelogical and Historical Quarterly*, 46 (January 1937), 1–15.

MacLean, J. P. *Shakers of Ohio: Fugitive Papers Concerning the Shakers of Ohio with Unpublished Manuscripts.* Columbus, Ohio: F. J. Heer, 1907.

Maine, Henry Sumner. *Ancient Law.* New York, 1885.

Mannheim, Karl. *Ideology and Utopia: An Introduction to the Sociology of Knowledge,* trans. Louis Wirth and Edward Shils. New York: Harcourt, Brace and World, 1936.

Manuel, Frank E., ed. *Utopias and Utopian Thought.* Boston: Houghton Mifflin, 1966.

March, James G., and Herbert A. Simon. *Organizations.* New York: Wiley, 1958.

Marks, C. R. "Monona County, Iowa, Mormons," *Annals of Iowa*, 7 (April 1906), 321–346.

Matineau, Harriet. *Society in America.* London, 1837.

Maslow, Abraham H. *Eupsychian Management: A Journal.* Homewood, Ill. Irwin-Dorsey, 1965.

——. "Synanon and Eupsychia," *Journal of Humanistic Psychology,* 7 (Spring 1967), 28–35.

——. *Toward a Psychology of Being.* Princeton, N.J.: D. Van Nostrand, 1962.

Mead, Margaret. "Towards More Vivid Utopias," *Science*, 126 (Nov. 8, 1957), 957–961.

Meadows, Paul. "Movements of Social Withdrawal," *Sociology and Social Research*, 29 (September-October 1944–1945), 46–50.

Melcher, Marguerite Fellows. *The Shaker Adventure.* Cleveland, Ohio: Press of Western Reserve University, 1960.

Merton, Thomas. *Mystics and Zen Masters.* New York: Dell, 1969.

Messinger, Sheldon L. "Organizational Transformation: A Case Study of a Declining Social Movement," *American Sociological Review,* 20 (January 1955), 3–10.

Mikkelson, Michael A. "The Bishop Hill Colony, a Religious Communistic Settlement in Henry County, Illinois," *Johns Hopkins University Studies in Historical and Political Science,* 10 (January 1892), 1–80.

Miller, Ernest L. "Some Tennessee Utopias." M.A. thesis, University of Tennessee, 1941.

Miller, I. G. "The Icarian Community in Nauvoo, Illinois," *Illinois State Historical Library Publications,* 11 (1906), 103–107.

*The Modern Utopian.* San Francisco: Alternatives! Foundation,

Moore, Wilbert E. "The Utility of Utopias," *American Sociological Review,* 31 (December 1966); 765–772.

Naegele, Kaspar D. "The Institutionalization of Action," in *Theories of Society,* ed. Talcott Parsons, Edward Shils, Kaspar D. Naegele, and Jesse R. Pitts. Vol. I. New York: Free Press, 1961, pp. 183–190.

Neal, Julia. *By Their Fruits: The Story of Shakerism in South Union, Kentucky.* Chapel Hill: University of North Carolina Press, 1947.

Newman, Kristine, and Henry Wilhelm. "Twin Oaks — The Great Farm Revolution," *The Mother Earth News,* 1 (January 1970), 56–59.

Nichols, Thomas L. *Forty Years of American Life.* Vol. I and II. London, 1864.

Niebuhr, H. Richard. *The Social Sources of Denominationalism.* Cleveland and New York: World (Meridian Books), 1957.

Nixon, Edgar B. "The Zoar Society: Applicants for Membership," *The Ohio State Archaelogical and Historical Quarterly,* 45 (October 1936), 341–350.

Noe, Charles Fred. "A Brief History of the Amana Society, 1714–1900," *Iowa Journal of History and Politics,* 2 (April 1904), 162–187.

Nordhoff, Charles. *The Communistic Societies of the United States; from Personal Visit and Observation: Including Detailed Accounts of the Economists, Zoarites, Shakers, the Amana, Oneida, Bethel, Aurora, Icarian, and Other Existing Societies, Their Religious Creeds, Social Practices, Numbers, Industries, and Present Condition.* New York: Schocken Books, 1965. First published 1875.

Noyes, John Humphrey. *History of American Socialisms.* New York: Hillary House, 1961. First published 1870.

——. *Male Continence.* Oneida, N.Y., 1877.

Noyes, Pierrepont. *My Father's House: An Oneida Boyhood.* New York: Farrar and Rinehart, 1937.

O'Brien, Harriet E. *Lost Utopias: A Brief Description of Three Quests for Happiness, Alcott's Fruitlands, Old Shaker House, and American Indian Museum, Rescued from Oblivion, Recorded and Preserved by Clara Endicott Sears on Prospect Hill in the Old Township of Harvard, Massachusetts.* Boston: Perry Walton, 1929.

O'Dea, Thomas F. *The Mormons.* Chicago: University of Chicago Press, 1957.

Oneida Community. *Handbook of the Oneida Community.* Wallingford, Conn., 1867.

——. *Mutual Criticism.* Oneida, N.Y., 1876.

Otto, Herbert A. "Communes: The Alternative Life Style," *Saturday Review,* 54 (April 24, 1971), 16–21.

Owen, Robert Dale. *The Life of Robert Owen, By Himself.* London: G. Bell, 1920.

——. *A New View of Society, and Other Writings.* London and Toronto: J. M. Dent, 1927.

——. *Threading My Way: Twenty-Seven Years of Autobiography.* London, 1874.

Parker, Robert Allerton. *A Yankee Saint: John Humphrey Noyes and the Oneida Community.* New York: G. P. Putnam's, 1935.

Parks, Edd Winfield. "Dreamer's Vision — Francis Wright at Bashoba (1825–'30)," *Tennessee Historical Magazine,* series 2, vol. 2 (January 1932), 75–86.

Parsons, Talcott. "The Pattern Variables Revisited," *American Sociological Review,* 25 (August 1960), 467–483.

——. *The Social System.* Glencoe, Ill.: Free Press, 1951.

——. *Societies: Evolutionary and Comparative Perspectives.* Englewood Cliffs, N. J.: Prentice-Hall, 1966.

——. *Structure and Process in Modern Societies.* Glencoe, Ill.: Free Press, 1960.

——. and Edward A. Shils, eds. *Toward a General Theory of Action.* New York: Harper and Row, 1962.

Pears, Thomas Clinton, Jr., ed. *New Harmony, an Adventure in Happiness: Papers of Thomas and Sarah Pears.* Indianapolis: Indiana Historical Society, 1933.

Pedrick, S. M. "The Wisconsin Phalanx, at Ceresco," *Proceedings of the State Historical Society of Wisconsin,* 1902, pp. 190–226.

Perkins, William Rufus, and Barthinius L. Wick. *History of the Amana Society or Community of True Inspiration.* State University of Iowa Publications. Iowa City, 1891.

Perlmutter, David M. "Commitment to Norms and Social Control in Shaker Society. B.A. honors thesis, Harvard University, 1959.

Pfautz, Harold. "The Sociology of Secularization," *American Journal of Sociology,* 61 (September 1955), 121–128.

Piercy, Harry D. "Shaker Medicines," in *Selected Papers.* Cleveland: Shaker Historical Society, 1957, pp. 11–31.

Piotrowski, Sylvester A. *Etienne Cabet and the* Voyage en Icarie: *A Study in the History of Social Thought.* Washington, D.C.: Catholic University of America, 1935.

Plath, David W. "The Fate of Utopia: Adaptive Tactics in Four Japanese Groups," *American Anthropologist,* 68 (October 1966), 1152–1162.

——. "Utopian Rhetoric: Conversion and Conversation in a Japanese Cult," in *The Verbal and Visual Arts: Proceedings of the Annual Spring*

*Meeting of the American Ethnological Society,* ed. June Helm. Forthcoming.

Podmore, Frank. *Robert Owen: A Biography.* New York: D. Appleton, 1924.

Price, Realto E. *History of Clayton County, Iowa.* Chicago: Robert O. Law, 1916.

Randall, E. O. *History of the Zoar Society, from Its Commencement to Its Conclusion: A Sociological Study in Communism.* Columbus, Ohio: Fred J. Heer, 1904.

"Reader's Glossary: A Concise Compendium of Characteristic Shakerisms," *House and Garden,* 87 (March 1945), 46–47.

Richardson, Patsy. "No More Freefolk," *The Modern Utopian,* 4 (Summer-Fall 1970), 3.

Ricker, Alan W. *The Amana Society: A Study in Cooperation from the Viewpoint of a Socialist.* Girard, Kan.: A. W. Ricker, 1911.

Rieff, Philip. *The Triumph of the Therapeutic: Uses of Faith after Freud.* New York: Harper Torchbooks, 1968.

Robinson, Charles Edson. *A Concise History of the United Society of Believers Called Shakers.* East Canterbury, N.H., 1893.

Rogers, Carl. *Carl Rogers on Encounter Groups.* New York: Harper and Row, 1970.

Rosner, Menachem. "Communitarian Experiments, Self-Management Experience, and the Kibbutz," Mimeographed. 1970.

Rourke, Constance Mayfield. *Trumpets of Jubilee: Henry Ward Beecher, Harriet Beecher Stowe, Lyman Beecher, Horace Greeley, P. T. Barnum.* New York: Harcourt Brace, 1927.

Sachse, Julius Friedrich. *The German Sectarians of Pennsylvania, 1742–1800: A Critical and Legendary History of the Ephrata Cloister and the Dunkers.* Philadelphia, 1900.

Sagarin, Edward. *Odd Man In: Societies of Deviants in America.* Chicago: Quadrangle Books, 1969.

Sams, Henry W., *Autobiography of Brook Farm.* Englewood Cliffs, N.J.: Prentice-Hall, 1958.

Samuels, Gertrude, "For Squares: Open House at Synanon," *The New York Times,* Sept. 6, 1970.

Sanborn, F. B., and William T. Harris. *A. Bronson Alcott: His Life and Philosophy.* Boston, 1893.

Schafer, Joseph. "The Wisconsin Phalanx," *The Wisconsin Magazine of History,* 19 (June 1936), 454–474.

Schulz-Behrend, G. "The Amana Colony," *American-German Review,* 7 (December 1940), 7–9, 38.

Schuster, Eunice Minnette. "Native American Anarchism: A Study of Left-Wing American Individualism," *Smith College Studies in History,* 17 (October 1931–July 1932).

Scott, W. Richard. "Theory of Organizations," in *Handbook of Modern Sociology,* ed. Robert E. L. Faris. Chicago: Rand McNally, 1964, pp. 485–529.

Sears, Clara Endicott. *Bronson Alcott's Fruitlands*. Boston and New York: Houghton Mifflin, 1915.

———. *Gleanings from Old Shaker Journals*. Boston and New York: Houghton Mifflin, 1916.

Sears, John van der Zee. *My Friends at Brook Farm*. New York: Desmond FitzGerald, 1912.

Selznick, Philip. "Foundations of the Theory of Organization," *American Sociological Review*, 13 (February 1948), 25–35.

———. *TVA and the Grass Roots*. New York: Harper Torch-books, 1966.

"The Shakers," *Life*, 62 (March 17, 1967), 59–70.

"Shaker; The Shaker Look: Shaker Made; Shaker Furniture; Shaker Storage," *House and Garden*, 87 (March 1945), 36–45, 116–118.

Shambaugh, Bertha M. H. "Amana," *The Palimpsest*, 2 (July 1921), 193–228.

———. *Amana, the Community of True Inspiration*. Iowa City: State Historical Society of Iowa, 1908.

———. "Amana — In Transition," *The Palimpsest*, 17 (May 1936), 149–184.

———. *Amana That Was and Amana That Is*. Iowa City: State Historical Society of Iowa, 1932.

Shaw, Albert. "Cooperation in the Northwest," *Johns Hopkins University Studies in Historical and Political Science*, 6 (1888), 199–359.

———. *Icaria, a Chapter in the History of Communisn*. New York and London, 1884.

Shepard, Herbert A. "Changing Interpersonal and Intergroup Relationships in Organizations," in *Handbook of Organizations*, ed. James G. March. Chicago: Rand McNally, 1965, pp. 1115–1143.

Shepard, Odell, *The Journals of Bronson Alcott*. Vol. I. Port Washington, N. Y.: Kenniket Press, 1966.

———. *Pedlar's Progress: The Life of Bronson Alcott*. Boston: Little, Brown, 1937.

Shils, Edward. "Charisma, Order, and Status," *American Sociological Review*, 30 (April 1965), 199–213.

Siegel, Jules, "West of Eden," *Playboy*, 17 (November 1970), 173–174, 240–254.

Simmel, Georg. *Conflict*, trans. Kurt H. Wolff. New York: Free Press, 1964.

———. "On the Significance of Numbers for Social Life" and "The Secret Society," in *The Sociology of Georg Simmel*, ed. Kurt H. Wolff. New York: Free Press, 1964, pp. 87–104, 345–376.

Simon, John E. "Wilhelm Keil and Communist Colonies," *The Oregon Historical Quarterly*, 36 (June 1935), 119–153.

Simons, Richard. "A Utopian Failure," *Indiana History Bulletin*, 18 (February 1941), 98–114.

Simpson, R. L., and W. H. Gulley. "Goals, Environmental Pressures and Organizational Characteristics," *American Sociological Review*, 27 (June 1962), 344–351.

Skinner, B. F. "Design of Experimental Communities," in *International Encyclopedia of the Social Sciences*. Forthcoming.

Slater, Philip E. *Microcosm: Structural, Psychological, and Religious Evolution in Groups*. New York: Wiley, 1966.

———. "On Social Regression," *American Sociological Review*, 28 (June 1963), 339–364.

———. *The Pursuit of Loneliness*. Boston: Beacon Press, 1970.

Small, James Louis. "A Mid-Western Experiment in Catholic Community Life," *The Catholic World*, 114 (March 1922), 793–802.

Smart, George K. "Fourierism in Northampton: Two Documents," *The New England Quarterly*, 12 (June 1939), 370–374.

Smelser, Neil J. *Theory of Collective Behavior*. Glencoe, Ill.: Free Press, 1963.

Smith, David E. "Millenarian Scholarship in America," *American Quarterly*, 17 (Fall 1965), 535–549.

Sparks, Edwin Erle. "The Expansion of the American People," *The Chautauquan*, 31 (May 1900), 151–167.

Spiro, Melford E. *Kibbutz: Venture in Utopia*. Cambridge, Mass.: Harvard University Press, 1956.

Stearns, Bertha-Monica. "Two Forgotten New England Reformers," *The New England Quarterly*, 6 (March 1933), 59–84.

Stinchcombe, Arthur. "Social Structure and Organization," in *Handbook of Organizations*, ed. James G. March. Chicago: Rand McNally, 1965, pp. 142–191.

Stonehill, Judy. "As It Is in Heaven, or So They Thought." Senior honors thesis, University of Michigan, 1967.

Stunkard, Albert. "Some Interpersonal Aspects of an Oriental Religion," *Psychiatry*, 14 (November 1951), 419–431.

Swan, Norma Lippincott. "The North American Phalanx," *Monmouth County Historical Association Bulletin*, 1 (May 1935), 35–65.

Swanson, Roy W. "Iowa of the Early Seventies as Seen by a Swedish Traveler," *The Iowa Journal of History and Politics*, 27 (October 1929), 564–581.

Sweet, William Warren. *Religion in the Development of American Culture, 1765–1840*. Gloucester, Mass.: Peter Smith, 1963.

———. *Revivalism in America*. Nashville: Abingdon Press, 1944.

Swift, Lindsay. *Brook Farm: Its Members, Scholars and Visitors*. New York: Corinth Books, 1961.

Thomas, John L. "Romantic Reform in America, 1815–1865," *American Quarterly*, 17 (Winter 1965), 657–681.

Toch, Hans. *The Social Psychology of Social Movements*. Indianapolis: Bobbs-Merill, 1965.

Tocqueville, Alexis de. *Democracy in America*. New York: Knopt, 1945.

Todd, Richard. " 'Walden Two'; Three? Many More?" *The New York Times Magazine*, March 15, 1970, pp. 24–25, 114–126.

Toennies, Ferdinand. *Community and Society*, trans. Charles P. Loomis. East Lansing: Michigan State University Press, 1957.

———. "Gemeinschaft and Gesellschaft," trans. Charles P. Loomis, in *Theories of Society*, ed. Talcott Parsons, Edward A. Shils, Kaspar D. Naegele, and Jesse R. Pitts. Vol. I. New York: Free Press, 1961, pp. 191–201.

Trollope, Mrs. Francis M. *Domestic Manners of the Americans*. Vol. I. London, 1832.

Turner, Ralph H., and Lewis M. Killian. *Collective Behavior*. Englewood Cliffs, N. J.: Prentice-Hall, 1957.

Tyler, Alice Felt. *Freedom's Ferment: Phases of American Social History from the Colonial Period to the Outbreak of the Civil War*. New York: Harper and Row (Harper Torchbooks), 1962.

"Twin Oaks: On to Walden Two," *Time*, 98 (September 20, 1971), 48–49.

Udy, Stanley H., Jr. "The Comparative Analysis of Organizations," in *Handbook of Organizations*, ed. James G. March. Chicago: Rand McNally, 1965, pp. 678–709.

Vallier, Ivan A. "Production Imperatives in Communal Systems: A Comparative Study with Special Reference to the Kibbutz Crisis," Ph.D. dissertation, Harvard University, 1959.

———. "Structural Differentiation, Production Imperatives, and Communal Norms: The Kibbutz in Crisis," *Social Forces*, 40 (March 1962), 233–241.

Vidich, Arthur J., and Maurice R. Stein. "The Dissolved Identity in Military Life," in *Identity and Anxiety: Survival of the Person in Mass Society*, ed. Maurice R. Stein, Arthur J. Vidich, and David Manning White. Glencoe, Ill.: Free Press, 1960, pp. 493–505.

Warren, Roland, L. "German *Parteilieder* and Christian Hymns as Instruments of Social Control," *Journal of Abnormal and Social Psychology*, 38 (January 1943), 96–100.

Waterman, William. "Frances Wright," *Columbia University Studies in History, Economics, and Public Law*, 115, no. 1. (1924).

Webber, Everett. *Escape to Utopia: The Communal Movement in America*. New York: Hastings House, 1959.

Weber, Max. *The Theory of Social and Economic Organization*, trans. A. M. Henderson and Talcott Parsons. Glencoe, Ill.: Free Press, 1947.

Weis, Virginia. "With Hands To Work and Hearts to God," *The Shaker Quarterly*, 9 (Summer 1969), 35–46.

Weisberg, Deborah Kelly. "A Cross-Cultural Study of Social Interaction." Senior honors thesis, Brandeis University, 1971.

Wells, Lester Grosvenor. *The Skaneateles Communal Experiment, 1843–1846*. Syracuse, N. Y.: Onondaga Historical Association, 1953.

Williams, Aaron. *The Harmony Society at Economy, Pennsylvania*. Pittsburgh, 1866.

Williams, Mentor L. "Paulding Satirizes Owenism," *Indiana Magazine of History*, 44 (December 1948), 355–365.

Wilson, Bryan R. "An Analysis of Sect Development," *American Sociological Review*, 24 (February 1959), 1–15.

Wittke, Carl. *The Utopian Communist: A Biography of Wilhelm Weitling*,

*Nineteenth Century Reformer.* Baton Rouge: Louisiana State University Press, 1950.

Wolfe, Burton H. *The Hippies.* New York: Signet Books, 1968.

Wolfe, Leonard, ed. in collaboration with Deborah Wolfe. *Voices from the Love Generation.* Boston: Little, Brown, 1968.

Wolski, Kalikst. "A Visit to the North American Phalanx," trans. Marion Moore Coleman, *Proceedings of the New Jersey Historical Society,* 83 (July 1965), 149–160.

Woods, John. "Two Years' Residence in the Settlement on the English Prairie, in the Illinois Country, United States, June 5, 1820–July 3, 1821," in *Early Western Travels, 1748–1846,* ed. Reuben Gold Thwaites. Cleveland, Ohio: Arthur H. Clark, 1904, pp. 179–357.

Woolsey, Theodore D. *Communism and Socialism, in Their History and Theory.* New York, 1880.

Wooster, Ernest S. *Communities of the Past and Present.* Newllano, La.: Llano Colonist, 1924.

Yablonsky, Lewis, *Synanon: The Tunnel Back.* Baltimore: Penguin Books, 1967.

Yamura, Barbara S., in collaboration with Eunice W. Bodine. *A Change and a Parting. My Story of Amana.* Amana: Iowa State University Press, 1960.

Yaswen, Gordon, "Sunrise Hill Community: Post-Mortem." Mimeographed. Available from author, Star Route, Montague, Mass. 01351.

Yinger, J. Milton. "Contraculture and Subculture," *American Sociological Review,* 25 (October 1960), 625–635.

Youngs, Benjamin Seth. "An Expedition Against the Shakers," *Ohio Archaeological and Historical Society Publications,* 21 (1912), 403–415.

Zablocki, Benjamin. *The Joyful Community.* Baltimore: Penguin, 1971.

*Zoar, an Ohio Experiment in Communalism.* Columbus: Ohio State Archaeological and Historical Society, 1952.

# Notes

## 1. A Refuge and a Hope

1. In 1680 a group of Protestant mystics, the Labadists, founded a community in northern Maryland.

2. America's origins, too, can be conceptualized in utopian terms. According to Henry Bamford Parkes, "the conception of the United States as a land of messianic nation destined by God or by the processes of history to be the scene of a new and better social order which would be an example to the rest of the world, has always been a significant element in the national consciousness." Introduction to William Alfred Hinds, *American Communities and Cooperative Colonies* (New York, 1961), p. v. For a fuller discussion of religious utopias, see Alice Felt Tyler, *Freedom's Ferment* (New York, 1962); Stow Persons, "Christian Communitarianism in America," in Donald Drew Egbert and Stow Persons, ed., *Socialism and American Life* (Princeton, 1952), I, 125–151.

3. William G. Bek, "The Community at Bethel, Missouri, and Its Offspring at Aurora, Oregon," *German American Annals*, n.s. 7 (September 1909), 263.

4. *Zoar, an Ohio Experiment in Communalism* (Columbus, Ohio, 1968), p. 7.

5. Tyler, *Freedom's Ferment*, p. 217. For a fuller discussion of politico-economic utopias, in addition to Tyler, see T. D. Seymour Bassett, "The Secular Utopian Socialists," in Egbert and Persons, *Socialism and American Life*, pp. 153–211.

6. Preamble to the Constitution of the Friendly Association for Mutual Interests at Kendal, Ohio. Wendall P. Fox, "The Kendal Community," *Ohio Archaeological and Historical Quarterly*, 20 (1911), 176–219.

7. Pierrepont Noyes, *My Father's House*, (New York, 1937), pp. 17–18; Robert Allerton Parker, *A Yankee Saint*, (New York, 1935), p. 230.

8. P. Noyes, *My Father's House*, p. 4; Oneida Community, *Handbook of the Oneida Community* (Wallingford, Conn., 1867), pp. 10–11.

9. Oneida song, quoted in Mark Holloway, *Heavens on Earth* (New York, 1966), p. 179.

10. Maren Lockwood, "The Oneida Community," Ph.D. diss., Harvard University, 1962, p. 171.

11. Oneida Community, *Handbook*, pp. 12–14.

12. Oneida Community, *Handbook*, p. 20.

13. Walter D. Edmonds, *The First Hundred Years, 1848–1948* (Oneida, N.Y.: 1948), p. 19.

14. Lockwood, "Oneida," p. 169.

15. John Humphrey Noyes, *History of American Socialisms* (New York, 1961), pp. 624–629. P. Noyes, *Father's House*, pp. 8–9.

16. Allan Estlake, *The Oneida Community* (London, 1900), pp. 72, 60–63; Lockwood, "Oneida," p. 84.

17. Parker, *Yankee Saint*, pp. 257, 259–260.

18. P. Noyes, *Father's House*, pp. 39, 66–67; Edmonds, *First Hundred Years*, p. 26.

19. P. Noyes, *Father's House*, pp. 104–106.

20. Edmonds, *First Hundred Years*, p. 20.

21. Parker, *Yankee Saint*, pp. 217–218.

22. Oneida Community, *Handbook*, p. 14; Oneida Community, *Mutual Criticism* (Oneida, N. Y., 1876), p. 52; Lockwood, "Oneida," p. 78.

23. Estlake, *Oneida*, p. 67.

24. Parker, *Yankee Saint*, pp. 257, 268; Ellis, *First Hundred Years*, p. 50; Estlake, *Oneida*, p. 50.

25. Estlake, *Oneida*, pp. 59, 60–61.

26. Lockwood, "Oneida," pp. 51–52.

27. Information on Twin Oaks comes primarily from personal visits and interviews with members, supplemented by a questionnaire and Twin Oaks archives and documents. See also Richard Todd, " 'Walden Two'; Three? Many More?" *The New York Times Magazine*, March 15, 1970, pp. 24–126; Robert Houriet, *Getting Back Together* (New York, 1971), pp. 277–325; Kristine Newman and Henry Wilhelm, "Twin Oaks – The Great Farm Revolution," *The Mother Earth News*, 1 (January 1970), 56–59; Dick Fairfield, *Communes, U.S.A.* (San Francisco, 1971); "Twin Oaks: On to Walden Two," *Time*, 98 (September 20, 1971), 48–49; Kat Griebe, "Kat's Book," unpub. ms.

28. The behavior code is quoted in a Twin Oaks brochure.

29. Note pinned to a bulletin board, November 1971.

30. "Kat's Book," p. 30.

## 2. Society's Maternal Bed: Idealizations of Communal Life

1. Charles Horton Cooley, *Social Organization* (New York, 1962), p. 30.

2. Cooley, *Social Organization*, p. 38, and Philip Rieff's Introduction, p. xi.

3. Henry Gross, *The Flower People* (New York, 1968), p. 90.

4. Harry W. Laidler, *Social-Economic Movements* (New York, 1947),

p. 57. See also Franscois Marie Charles Fourier, *Selections from the Works of Fourier*, trans. Julia Franklin (London, 1901).

5. Everett Webber, *Escape to Utopia* (New York, 1959), p. 356.

6. Parker Donham, "Town Wants Commune Closed," *Boston Globe*, Oct. 12, 1970.

7. Burton H. Wolfe, *The Hippies* (New York, 1968), p. 79.

8. Paul K. Conkin, *Two Paths to Utopia* (Lincoln, 1965), p. 135.

9. *American Avatar*, publication of Fort Hill Community, Roxbury, Mass., 1968.

10. *Avatar*.

11. Quoted in Henry Ammon James, *Communism in America* (New York, 1879), p. 13.

12. Alan W. Ricker, *The Amana Society* (Girrard, Kan., 1911), p. 39.

13. Webber, *Escape to Utopia*, p. 322.

14. Gross, *Flower People*, p. 89; Robert V. Hine, *California's Utopian Colonies* (New Haven, 1966), p. 49

15. Wolski, Kalikst, "A Visit to the North American Phalanx," trans. Marion Moore Coleman, *Proceedings of the New Jersey Historical Society*, 83 (July 1965), 156.

16. Wolfe, *Hippies*, p. 85.

17. Gross, *Flower People*, pp. 71-72.

18. Daryl Chase, "The Early Shakers," Ph.D. diss., University of Chicago, 1936, p. 14.

19. Other communes strike visitors as grim, serious, and humorless. This observation was made of the Shakers as well as some contemporary communes. Few utopian groups allow the luxury of laughing at themselves, although some share laughter and joy in other ways.

20. Hine, *California*, p. 49.

21. Robert Allerton Parker, *A Yankee Saint* (New York, 1935), p. 250.

22. Chase, "Early Shakers," p. 12.

23. Webber, *Escape to Utopia*, pp. 326-327.

24. Philip E. Slater, *Microcosm* (New York, 1966).

25. Sigmund Freud, "The Group and the Primal Horde," in *Readings on the Sociology of Small Groups*, ed. Theodore M. Mills and Stanley Rosenberg (Englewood Cliffs, N. J., 1970), p. 76.

## 3. Commitment: The Problem and the Theory

1. William Warren Sweet, *Revivalism in America* (New York, 1944); Whitney R. Cross, *The Burned-over District* (New York, 1965).

2. Alexis de Tocqueville, *Democracy in America*.

3. On Owenite groups, see Arthur Eugene Bestor, Jr., *Backwoods Utopias* (Philadelphia, 1950). On anarchism, see Eunice Minette Schuster, "Native American Anarchism: A Study of Left-Wing American Individualism," *Smith College Studies in History*, 17 (October 1931-July 1932). Among the leaders of utopian communities included in Schuster's study are John Humphrey Noyes of Oneida; Adin Ballou of Hopedale; Josiah

Warren of Equity, Utopia, and Modern Times; Frances Wright of Nashoba and New Harmony; and Wilhelm Weitling of Communia. As for Marxism, nineteenth-century American communes had at least two connections with it. Wilhelm Weitling, who had met Marx and Engels, was a leading figure in Communia, Iowa. Carl Wittke, *The Utopian Communist* (Baton Rouge, 1950). For a time in the 1870s it also appeared that the Icarian community at Corning, Iowa, might become a center of the First International in the United States, and Marxian exiles of the Paris Commune of 1871 were gathering there. T.D. Seymour Bassett, "The Secular Utopian Socialists," in *Socialism and American Life*, ed. Donald Drew Egbert and Stow Persons (Princeton, 1952), I, 207.

4. The entire sample of thirty communities studied is described in the Appendix.

5. Georg Simmel, "The Secret Society," in *The Sociology of Georg Simmel*, ed. Kurt H. Wolff (New York, 1964), p. 366.

6. This definition bears some similarity to Talcott Parson's notion of "institutionalization."

7. Although recruitment would seem at first glance to be as important as retention of people for continuation of a system, the two problems are distinct, requiring for solution different kinds of organizational strategies. Recruitment does not necessarily require commitment but may be accomplished in many other ways with noncommitted actors (for example, birth, accident, and external organizational phenomena may serve to recruit uncommitted individuals). However, once a person has performed any single act within a system, the problem arises of committing him to further and future participation. Thus, the commitment necessary for continuation involves retaining participants, and recruiting them is not a commitment problem (though of course the ways in which they are recruited have implications for commitment). In very complex systems, it might also seem likely that group cohesiveness would be limited to peer groups. However, if cohesiveness is defined not in terms of sociability and mutual attraction but rather in terms of the ability to withstand disruptive forces and threats from outside the group ("sticking together"), it applies to systems of any degree of complexity. See Neal Gross and William Martin, "On Group Cohesiveness," *American Journal of Sociology*, 57 (December 1952), 533–546.

8. Talcott Parsons and Edward A. Shils, eds., *Toward a General Theory of Action* (New York, 1962), pp. 4–6, 11.

9. Social control is possible without moral commitments, of course, but it should not be as efficient or effective.

10. Howard S. Becker, "Notes on the Concept of Commitment," *American Journal of Sociology*, 66 (July 1960), 32–40.

## 4. Live in Love and Union: Commitment Mechanisms in Nineteenth Century Communes

1. Leon Festinger and J. Merrill Carlsmith, "Cognitive Consequences of Forced Compliance," *Journal of Abnormal and Social Psychology*, 58 (March 1959), 203–210.

2. Martin Buber, *Paths in Utopia* (Boston, 1958), p. 134.

3. Harry D. Piercy, "Shaker Medicines," in *Selected Papers* (Cleveland, 1957), pp. 11-31.

4. Maren Lockwood, "The Experimental Utopia in America," *Daedalus,* 94 (Spring 1965), 408.

5. Christiana F. Knoedler, *The Harmony Society, a 19th Century Utopia* (New York, 1954), p. 10.

6. "An Iowan Utopia," *The Literary Digest,* 52 (April 1, 1916), 932-933.

7. Knoedler, *Harmony,* p. 149.

8. Theodore E. Johnson, ed., "A Sketch of the Life and Religious Experiences of Richard W. Pelham," *The Shaker Quarterly,* 9 (Summer 1969), 56.

9. Though the Shakers permitted nonresident probationary members in the novitiate, they allowed no nonresident full members in the junior and senior families.

10. Egon Bittner, "Radicalism and the Organization of Radical Movements," *American Sociological Review,* 28 (December 1963), 938; Lewis A. Coser, "Sects and Sectarians," *Dissent,* 1 (Winter 1954), 362.

11. Bryan R. Wilson, "An Analysis of Sect Development," *American Sociological Review,* 24 (February 1959), 11; Ralph H. Turner and Lewis M. Killian, *Collective Behavior* (Englewood Cliffs, N. J., 1957), p. 481.

12. Arthur Stinchcombe, "Social Structure and Organizations," in *Handbook of Organizations,* ed. James G. March (Chicago, 1965), p. 186.

13. William Alfred Hinds, *American Communities and Cooperative Colonies* (New York, 1961), pp. 86-87.

14. Alan Estlake, *The Oneida Community* (London, 1900), p. 11.

15. Philip E. Slater, "On Social Regression," *American Sociological Review,* 28 (June 1963), 348; Sigmund Freud, *Civilization and Its Discontents,* trans. and ed. James Strachey (New York, 1962), pp. 60-61.

16. See also Lewis A. Coser, "Greedy Organizations," *European Journal of Sociology,* 8 (October 1967), 196-215.

17. John Humphrey Noyes, *Male Continence* (Oneida, N. Y., 1877).

18. Lockwood, "Experimental Utopia," p. 409.

19. Slater, "Social Regression."

20. Edward Deming Andrews, *The Gift To Be Simple* (New York, 1962), p. 20. Emphasis added.

21. *Zoar, an Ohio Experiment in Communalism* (Columbus, Ohio, 1968), p. 41.

22. Andrews, *Gift To Be Simple,* p. 109.

23. John Archibald Bole, *The Harmony Society* (Philadelphia, 1904),p. 9.

24. Edward Deming Andrews, *The People Called Shakers* (New York, 1963), pp. 106-114.

25. Aaron Williams, *The Harmony Society at Economy, Pennsylvania* (Pittsburgh, 1866), pp. 41-42.

26. Norma Lippincott Swan, "The North American Phalanx," *Monmouth County Historical Association Bulletin,* 1 (May 1935), 35-65.

27. Virginia Weis, "With Hands To Work and Hearts to God," *The Shaker Quarterly,* 9 (Summer 1969), 45, 43.

28. Lockwood, "Experimental Utopia," p. 406.

29. Anton T. Boisen, "Economic Distress and Religious Experience," *Psychiatry*, 2 (May 1939), 185-194; Herbert Blumer, "Collective Behavior," in *Principles of Sociology*, ed. A. M. Lee (New York, 1953), pp. 208-210.

30. Roland L. Warren, "German *Partelieder* and Christian Hymns as Instruments of Social Control," *Journal of Abnormal and Social Psychology*, 38 (January 1943), 96-100.

31. Karl J. R. Arndt, *George Rapp's Harmony Society, 1785-1847* (Philadelphia, 1965), p. 255.

32. Andrews, *Shakers*, pp. 164-165.

33. David M. Perlmutter, "Commitment to Norms and Social Control in Shaker Society," B.A. honors thesis, Harvard University, 1959, p. 81.

34. Daryl Chase, "The Early Shakers," Ph.D. diss., University of Chicago, 1936, p. 14.

35. Turner and Killian, *Collective Behavior*, p. 399. See also Georg Simmel, *Conflict*, trans. Kurt H. Wolff (New York, 1964); Lewis A. Coser, *The Functions of Social Conflict* (New York, 1964); Blumer, "Collective Behavior"; and Freud, *Civilization*, p. 61.

36. Erving Goffman, *Asylums* (Garden City, N.Y., 1961). See also Kathryn Hulme, *The Nun's Story* (Boston, 1956); Albert Stunkard, "Some Interpersonal Aspects of an Oriental Religion," *Psychiatry*, 14 (November 1951), 419-431.

37. Eric Hoffer, *The True Believer* (New York, 1963), p. 66.

38. Andrews, *Gift To Be Simple*, pp. 79, 81.

39. William G. Bek, "The Community at Bethel, Missouri, and Its Offspring at Aurora, Oregon," *German American Annals*, n.s. 7 (September 1909), 276.

40. Perlmutter, "Commitment," pp. 82-83.

41. Barbara S. Yamura, *A Change and a Parting* (Ames, Iowa, 1960), p. 135. See also Bertha Maud Shambaugh, *Amana That Was and Amana That Is* (Iowa City, 1932), p. 245.

42. Yamura, *Change and Parting*, p. 215.

43. John Humphrey Noyes, *History of American Socialisms* (New York, 1961), pp. 64-65.

44. Buber, *Paths*, pp. 140, 7.

45. Max Weber, *The Theory of Social and Economic Organizations*, trans. A. M. Henderson and Talcott Parsons (Glencoe, Ill., 1947), pp. 358-363; Edward Shils, "Charisma, Order, and Status," *American Sociological Review*, 30 (April 1965), 200, 202, 206.

46. Shils, "Charisma," p. 204.

47. Hinds, *American Communities*, p. 54.

48. Nordhoff, *Communistic Societies*, p. 133; John B. Ellis, *Free Love and Its Votaries* (New York, 1870), p. 133; Allan Estlake, *The Oneida Community* (London, 1900), p. 54; Hinds, *American Communities*, pp. 132, 131; William G. Bek, "The Community at Bethel, Missouri, and Its

Offspring at Aurora, Oregon," *German American Annals*, n.s. 7 (September 1909), 264.

49. Turner and Killian, *Collective Behavior*, p. 473.

50. Robert Allerton Parker, *A Yankee Saint* (New York, 1935), p. 218.

51. Webber, *Escape to Utopia*, p. 67.

52. Hinds, *American Communities*, p. 592.

53. Frank Podmore, *Robert Owen* (New York, 1924), pp. 291-292.

## 5. The Comforts of Commitment: Issues in Group Life

1. Martin Buber, *Paths in Utopia* (Boston, 1958), p. 140.

2. William Alfred Hinds, *American Communities and Cooperative Colonies* (New York, 1961), p. 38.

3. Georg Simmel, "The Secret Society," in *The Sociology of Georg Simmel*, ed. Kurt H. Wolff (New York, 1964), pp. 360, 361; Philip E. Slater, *Microcosm* (New York, 1966).

4. Buber, *Paths*, p. 135.

5. Simmel, "Secret Society", p. 374.

6. Sigmund Freud, "The Group and the Primal Horde," in *Readings on the Sociology of Small Groups*, ed. Theodore M. Mills and Stan Rosenberg (Englewood Cliffs, N. J., 1970), p. 77.

7. Slater, *Microcosm*.

8. Simmel, "Secret Society".

9. Richard Harmer, "Bedrock," mimeo., Harvard Business School, p. 7.

10. William Hedgepeth and Dennis Stock, *The Alternative* (New York, 1970), p. 115.

11. David Smith, "Millenarian Scholarship in America," *American Quarterly*, 17 (Fall 1965), 544.

## 6. Away from Community

1. Aaron Williams, *The Harmony Society at Economy, Pennsylvania* (Pittsburgh, 1866), pp. 72-81.

2. Joseph W. Eaton, "Controlled Acculturation: A Survival Technique of the Hutterites," *American Sociological Review*, 17 (June 1952), 331-340.

3. Bertha Maud Shambaugh, *Amana That Was and Amana That Is* (Iowa City, 1932), pp. 362, 354, 346.

4. Maren Lockwood, "The Oneida Community," Ph.D. diss., Harvard University, 1962, p. 93.

5. James Louis Small, "A Mid-Western Experiment in Catholic Community Life," *The Catholic World*, 114 (March 1922), 793-802.

6. See Ferdinand Toennies, *Community and Society*, trans. Charles P. Loomis (East Lansing, Mich., 1957); Max Weber, *The Theory of Social and Economic Organization*, trans. A.M. Henderson and Talcott Parsons (Glencoe, Ill., 1947); Emile Durkheim, *The Division of Labor in Society*, trans. George Simpson (Glencoe, Ill., 1938). For a comprehensive discus-

sion on the *Gemeinschaft/Gesellschaft* dichotomy and my own reformulation, see Rosabeth Moss Kanter, "Utopia: A Study in Comparative Organization," Ph.D. diss., University of Michigan, 1967, pp. 1-27.

7. Shambaugh, *Amana*, p. 380.

8. Lockwood, "Oneida", p. 89.

9. Lockwood, "Oneida," p. 41.

10. This concept was first suggested to me by Albert J. Reiss, Jr.

11. Eaton, "Controlled Acculturation." This is similar to what has been identified as the process of secularization. However, I wish to divorce the ideas presented here from any notion of a fixed developmental sequence. I am saying only that value indeterminism aids Gesellschaft purposes, not that it must arise as the result of an inevitable process, such as that described in the literature on secularization.

12. Richard T. Ely, *Recent American Socialism*, Johns Hopkins University Studies in Historical and Political Science (Baltimore, 1885), p. 15; Charles Gide, *Communities and Cooperative Colonies*, trans. Ernest F. Row (London, 1930), p. 12.

13. Ralph Albertson, "A Survey of Mutualistic Communities in America," *The Iowa Journal of History and Politics*, 34 (October 1936), 440.

14. Recently Oneida, Ltd., sold stock publicly for the first time.

## 7. Retreat from Utopia

1. Herbert A. Otto, "Communes: The Alternative Life Style," *Saturday Review*, 54 (April 24, 1971), 17.

2. Alice Felt Tyler discusses nineteenth century unrest in *Freedom's Ferment* (New York, 1962). For revivalism, see Marilyn B. Halter, "What Must We Do To Be Saved?" Senior honors thesis, Brandeis University, 1971.

3. Personal communication.

4. Warren G. Bennis and Philip E. Slater, *The Temporary Society* (New York: Harper and Row, 1968).

5. In the spring of 1971, the town of Arlington, Mass., set up hearings for the purpose of defining a "family," so that they could establish zoning regulations that would exclude communes.

6. Eric Berne, *The Structure and Dynamics of Organizations and Groups* (New York, 1966), pp. 233, 238.

7. Patsy Richardson, "No More Freefolk," *The Modern Utopian*, 4 (Summer-Fall 1970), 3.

8. Georg Simmel, "The Secret Society," *The Sociology of Georg Simmel*, ed. Kurt H. Wolff (New York, 1964), p. 361.

9. See Gordon Yaswen, "Sunrise Hill Community," Mimeographed (Montague, Mass.); Robert Houriet, "Life and Death of a Commune Called Oz," *The New York Times Magazine*, Feb. 16, 1969, pp. 30-31, 89-103. Information on Tolstoy Farm comes from questionnaires and personal visits, supplemented by Dick Fairfield, *Communes, U.S.A.* (San Francisco, 1971), pp. 130-132; Sara Davidson, "Open Land: Getting

Back to the Communal Garden, *Harper's Magazine*, 270 (June 1970), 91-102. Information on Morningstar comes from personal observation and Kenneth Lamott, "Doing Their Own Thing at Morningstar," in *Utopias*, ed. P. E. Richter (Boston, 1971), pp. 155-164; Rasa Gustatis, *Turning On* (New York: Macmillan, 1970). All information on "Paper Farm" (a pseudonym employed to protect the group), comes from questionnaires interviews, and personal visits.
10. Houriet, "Oz," p. 100.
11. Personal interviews.
12. Bennett Berger, personal communication; Houriet, "Oz," p. 89.
13. Personal interviews.
14. Lamott, "Morningstar," p. 162.
15. Houriet, "Oz," pp. 92, 100-103.
16. Lamott, "Morningstar," p. 163.
17. Yaswen, "Sunrise Hill Community," p. 22.
18. Yaswen, "Sunrise Hill Community," p. 7.
19. Yaswen, "Sunrise Hill Community," pp. 7-8.
20. Yaswen, "Sunrise Hill Community," pp. 8-9.
21. Richardson, "Freefolk," p. 3.
22. Houriet, "Oz," p. 31.

## 8. They Also Serve: Communes with Missions

1. Philip Selznick, *TVA and the Grass Roots* (New York, 1966), p. 13.
2. Information on Koinonia is from personal reports and from William Hedgepeth and Dennis Stock, *The Alternative* (New York, 1970), pp. 175-181. Information on Reba Place comes from questionnaire returns and the community's own literature.
3. Statement pinned to a bulletin board in the Santa Monica, California, Synanon House. Information on Synanon comes from personal visits, interviews, and from Lewis Yablonsky, *Synanon* (Baltimore, 1967); Guy Endore, *Synanon* (Garden City, N.Y., 1968); Edward Sagarin, *Odd Man In* (Chicago, 1969).
4. Information on Cumbres comes from personal experience; I lived and worked with the group during the summer of 1969.
5. Sagarin, *Odd Man In*, p. 170.
6. Yablonsky, *Synanon*, pp. 88-89.
7. Information from Synanon literature.
8. Personal copy supplied by the author; used by permission.
9. Abraham Maslow, "Synanon and Eupsychia," *Journal of Humanistic Psychology*, 7 (Spring 1970), 28-35; Edgar Z. Friedenberg, "The Synanon Solution," *Nation*, 200 (March 8, 1965), pp. 256-261; Sagarin, *Odd Man In*, p. 144.

## 9. The Limits of Utopia

1. The concept of repersonalization was suggested by Suresh Srivastva. Because of their mutual emphasis on close relationships in small primary

groups, communes and encounter groups are closely related. In fact, historically utopias have used encounter and sensitivity techniques in mutual criticism, feedback sessions, and rituals.

2. Harvey Cox, *The Feast of Fools* (Cambridge, Mass., 1969), pp. 91-92.

3. William Hedgepeth and Dennis Stock, *The Alternative* (New York, 1970), p. 158.

4. Personal communication

5. Gordon Yaswen, "Sunrise Hill," mimeographed (Montague, Mass.).

6. Warren G. Bennis and Philip E. Slater, *The Temporary Society* (New York: Harper and Row, 1968).

7. Margaret Mead, "Towards More Vivid Utopias," *Science*, 126 (Nov. 8, 1957), 957-961; Wilbert E. Moore, "The Utility of Utopias," *American Sociological Review*, 31 (December 1966), 765-772.

8. George Kateb, *Utopia and Its Enemies* (New York, 1963), p. 12.

9. Joseph W. Eaton and Robert J. Weil, *Culture and Mental Disorders* (Glencoe, Ill., 1955) — one of the few psychiatric studies of communal life; Naphtali Golomb, personal communication.

10. Aldous Huxley, *Brave New World and Brave New World Revisited* (New York, 1965), p. 184.

11. Kateb, *Utopia*, p. 124; Naphtali Golomb, personal communication.

12. Kateb, *Utopia*, p. 118.

13. See Philip Rieff, *The Triumph of the Therapeutic* (New York, 1968), pp. 66-79.

14. Henrik Infield, *Cooperative Communities at Work* (New York, 1947), p. 23.

15. I am also compiling evidence that communal life has the potential for reducing the inequality between the sexes when coupled with a comprehensive set of economic and political institutions governed by the commune itself.

16. Menachem Rosner, "Communitarian Experiments, Self-Management Experience, and the Kibbutz," mimeo, 1970. Martin Buber, *Paths in Utopia* (Boston, 1958).

17. Quoted in Kateb, *Utopia and Its Enemies*, p. 12; Robert Boguslaw, *The New Utopians* (Englewood Cliffs, N. J., 1965).

18. Georg Simmel, "On the Significance of Numbers for Social Life," in *The Sociology of Georg Simmel*, ed. Kurt H. Wolff (New York, 1964), p. 88.

19. Paul Goodman, *Utopian Essays and Practical Proposals* (New York, 1964), p. 22.

20. Eaton and Weil, *Culture and Mental Disorders;* Carl Rogers, *Carl Rogers on Encounter Groups* (New York, 1970), p. 12; Edgar Z. Friedenberg, "The Synanon Solution," *Nation*, 200 (March 8, 1965), 256-261.

21. Deborah Kelly Weisberg, "A Cross-Cultural Study of Social Interaction," Senior honors thesis, Brandeis University, 1971; Abraham Maslow, *Eupsychian Management* (Homewood, Ill., 1965), p. 161; Philip E. Slater, *The Pursuit of Loneliness* (Boston, 1970).

22. Rogers, *Encounter Groups*, p. 13.

23. Erich Fromm, *The Sane Society* (New York, 1955), p. 320.

24. For research in progress on this topic, see Bennett M. Berger and Bruce Hackett, "Child-Rearing Practices of the Communal Family," Progress report to NIMH, 1970, mimeo.

## Appendix. Sample and Methodology Used for Study of Nineteenth Century Communes

1. See John Humphrey Noyes, *History of American Socialisms* (New York, 1961); Charles Nordhoff, *The Communistic Societies of the United States* (New York, 1965); William Alfred Hinds, *American Communities and Cooperative Colonies* (New York, 1961); Charles Gide, *Communist and Cooperative Colonies*, trans. Ernest F. Row (London, 1930).

2. Ivan A. Vallier, "Production Imperatives in Communal Systems," Ph.D. diss., Harvard University, 1959. He studied the kibbutz, Amana, and the Hutterites.

3. Neil J. Smelser, *Theory of Collective Behavior* (Glencoe, Ill., 1963), p. 313; Ralph H. Turner and Lewis M. Killian, *Collective Behavior* (Englewood Cliffs, N. J., 1957), p. 327.

4. Paul Meadows, "Movements of Social Withdrawal," *Sociology and Social Research*, 29 (September-October 1944-1945), 46-50.

5. Though a fairly extensive literature exists on nineteenth-century utopian communities, there are only a few comparative studies. These are generally descriptive, with the groups described separately and leading to a few summary conclusions. Notable contemporary, first-hand studies are A. J. Macdonald, "Materials for a History of Communities in the United States," Yale University Library, Manuscripts and Collections; Nordhoff, *Communistic Societies*; Noyes, *American Socialisms*; Hinds, *American Communities*. Few sociologists have examined the pre-1860 American communes, although Lockwood studied Oneida and Vallier included Amana in comparative perspective with the kibbutz. See Maren Lockwood, "The Oneida Community," Ph.D. diss., Harvard University, 1962; Vallier, "Production Imperatives in Communal Systems."

6. Arthur E. Bestor, Jr., *Backwoods Utopias* (Philadelphia, 1950), pp. 235-243. See also Ralph Albertson, "A Survey of Mutualistic Communities in America," *The Iowa Journal of History and Politics*, 34 (October 1936), 375-444; Alexander Kent, "Cooperative Communities in the United States," *Bulletin of the Department of Labor*, 35 (July 1901), 563-646; Kenneth William McKinley, "A Guide to the Communistic Communities of Ohio," *The Ohio State Archaeological and Historical Quarterly*, 46 (January 1937), 1-15; Ernest S. Wooster, *Communities of the Past and Present* (Newllano, La., 1924).

7. In addition to consolidating various locations of a single utopian experiment, I added one community that Bestor did not list, and I

dropped one of his cases (Celesta) because it consisted only of a man and his wife until after 1860.

8. Whitney R. Cross, *The Burned-over District* (New York, 1965), p. 331. Brook Farm, because it began as a Transcendentalist community, is not included among the twenty-two phalanxes, although it later became the leading phalanx.

9. Emile Durkheim, *The Rules of Sociological Method* (Glencoe, Ill., 1935), pp. 350–423.

# Index